Palestinian Arabic Voices

Authentic Listening and Reading
Practice in Levantine Colloquial Arabic

lingualism

ISBN: 978-1-962752-05-3

website: www.lingualism.com

email: contact@lingualism.com

Table of Contents

Introduction

Palestinian Arabic Voices is designed to help you improve your comprehension of Levantine Colloquial Arabic by using its audio component (available as free, downloadable MP3s from www.lingualism.com/audio) alongside the guided exercises in the book.

Six native speakers from around Palestine have each contributed six *audio essays* on various topics, which in total make up the 36 segments found in this book. The contributors spoke naturally and spontaneously without reading prepared texts. The audio essays were then transcribed in Arabic script with diacritics (tashkeel) and translated into English. Studying these texts is a unique opportunity to better understand the patterns, usage, and idiosyncrasies of Arabic as spoken by Palestinians today.

How can this book help me?

You will hear the speakers in Palestinian Arabic Voices occasionally make what you are sure are mistakes; you're likely right. Words may be mispronounced or misused; grammatical rules may not always be followed; sentences may be left unfinished if the speaker decides to rephrase what they are saying. This poses an extra challenge for listening. However, it is also very insightful to hear natural, spoken Arabic at various speeds by several native speakers. Unfortunately, this is something most coursebooks lack, in favor of carefully prepared, unnaturally slow, flawless speech. **It is hoped that Palestinian Arabic Voices fills that gap and provides some refreshingly natural, challenging opportunities for improving listening skills.**

Can I benefit from this book at my level of Arabic?

This book is best suited for intermediate and more advanced learners who have some knowledge of Levantine Arabic, or at least, Modern Standard Arabic. However, even lower-level students can reap some benefits from listening to and studying the segments. Just keep in mind that the goal is **not** to understand 100%. The first time you listen, depending on your level, you may understand, say, 1%, 10%, 50%, or 90% of what you hear in a segment. If, after going through the exercises and studying the text while relistening several times, you are able to increase the percentage you can understand, you've made progress and are successfully developing your skills and pushing your level up. If this mindset is adopted, the materials in Palestinian Arabic Voices can be useful to learners at a wide range of levels.

How to Use This Book

To get the most out of this book, you need to exercise a bit of **discipline**—discipline to resist reading the texts and their translations before you have thoroughly studied the listenings. This cannot be emphasized enough. Once you have read the texts and translations, the dynamics of what you can obtain from listening to the segments changes fundamentally. You should first listen to a segment *several* times while working your way through the exercises in the book. These have been designed to help you first understand the gist and gradually discover details as you relisten. Only once you have come to understand as much as you can through the exercises should you move on to study the text and translation that follow. This approach will result in maximum efficiency in improving your listening skills. A step-by-step guideline follows.

1. CHOOSE A SEGMENT TO STUDY: The segments can be studied in any order. The MP3s that accompany Palestinian Arabic Voices are available as free downloads at **www.lingualism.com/audio**, where you can also stream the audio.

2. TITLE AND KEYWORDS: *Before you listen the first time, be sure to read the title of the segment and study the keywords.* Going into a listening "blind"—without having any context, without even knowing the topic—makes listening comprehension in a foreign language extremely difficult. Just by knowing the general topic, we are able to improve the amount we can understand, as we are able to draw on knowledge from our past experiences, anticipate what might be said, recognize known words, and guess new words and phrases.

3. MAIN IDEA: *Now, determine the "Main Idea" from among the four choices.* If you are not fairly confident that you know the main idea, listen one more time to narrow down your choices by process of elimination. Once you are confident you have determined the main idea of the segment, check your answer. (Answers for the exercises are found at the end of each segment.) If you were incorrect, listen one more time with the main idea in mind.

4. TRUE OR FALSE: *Answer the "True or False" questions.* (Do not read ahead to the multiple-choice questions as some of these questions themselves may answer the true-or-false questions.) If you feel unsure of any of your answers, listen to the segment again before checking your answers. You will notice that a small number follows most of the answers in the answer key. These numbers correspond to the line number in the text and translation that reveals the answer. If you do not understand why you got an answer wrong, quickly look at the text and/or translation for that line number. (Here's where you have to use your self-discipline *not* to read beyond the specified line number!) Listen again and place a check next to each true-or-false question as you hear the answer.

5. MULTIPLE CHOICE: *Answer the "Multiple Choice" questions.* Follow the same guidelines as for the true-or-false questions. Note that both the true-or-false and multiple-choice questions are based on information found in the segment, according to the information provided by the speaker, regardless of the accuracy of the information. You can think of each question as being preceded by "According to _the speaker_,..." or "_The speaker_ mentions that...". Assume that the time of speaking is the present. That is, if a question asks, "Is she still in Gaza?" it means as of the time she recorded the segment.

6. **MATCHING: *Match the Arabic words and phrases to their English translations.*** You will learn by spending time playing with the words, so don't look up the answers too quickly. Try finding matches through educated guesses and by process of elimination. After you have matched the words and checked your answers, listen again while you check off the words as you hear them. The vocabulary in the matching exercises focuses mostly on high-frequency adverbs, connectors, and phrases. Such words are frequently heard in spoken language and are vital for connecting ideas to produce natural speech.

7. **TEXT AND TRANSLATION:** Now that you have worked your way through the exercises and have managed to pick up more of what has been said, you can feel free to move on to study the text and translation for the segment. This part is more *freestyle.* Depending on your level of Arabic and level of comfort with the text, you can approach this in several ways. For instance, you can cover the Arabic side and first read the translation; then, try to translate the English back into Arabic based on what you remember. Also, you can simply try to brainstorm some possible Arabic equivalents for the words or phrases in the English translation; then, check the Arabic side and see how it was actually said. Conversely, you can cover the English side first and relisten while you read along with the Arabic, perhaps pausing the audio to repeat each line aloud. In any case, the side-by-side arrangement of the Arabic text and its English translation allows you to cover one side and test yourself in various ways. You should be able to match up most words and phrases with their equivalents in English. You may want to highlight useful and interesting vocabulary and phrases you want to learn.

8. **VOCABULARY:** Vocabulary exercises follow the text and translation in the first half of the book. These exercises focus on content words—mostly nouns, verbs, and adjectives. The vocabulary that an intermediate learner already knows and that which they need to learn will vary greatly from person to person. Each exercise draws your attention to some interesting vocabulary items found in the text. Each item is followed by a reference to the line number where the answer can be found. You are also encouraged to continue to discover additional useful vocabulary—both words and phrases—which you can write in your own notebook.

9. **LISTEN AGAIN:** Try listening again later to the segments you have already studied. You will find that you can understand more and with more ease the following day. (Studies have shown that material learned is consolidated and organized in the brain during sleep.)

Visit www.lingualism.com/audio,
where you can find the free
accompanying audio to download or
stream (at variable playback rates).

The Texts and Translations

Lines

The text and translation for each segment have been divided into numbered "lines," which are not necessarily complete sentences or even clauses but are manageable chunks that can be studied.

Translations

Good style has, at times, been sacrificed in favor of direct translations so that Arabic words and phrases can easily be matched up to their English equivalents. You are encouraged to think of alternative ways lines could be translated into English.

Fillers

Fillers, which are used to signal that the speaker is thinking of what to say next, are a common and natural part of spoken language. To avoid cluttering the text, uh... (اااه...) and um... (ممم...) are not written. Words that function as fillers are always written but are often left untranslated, as they do not add substantial meaning to the sentence. يَعْني is the most common filler in Levantine Arabic and could translate as *that is, I mean,* or *you know.*

Another trait of spoken discourse is that the speaker may misspeak, then back up to correct himself or herself. Also, a speaker may decide to rephrase a sentence, or simply not finish it. These are all marked with ellipses (...) so that you can easily see that the *word* you didn't catch is, in fact, not a complete word at all or is an unfinished thought. These ellipses are meant to aid you in deciphering the listening. However, when you are reading for meaning, anything before an ellipsis can be ignored.

Introductions

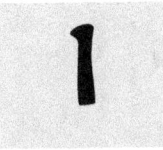

Najd's Introduction

Keywords

هنْدسة مدني civil engineering   تعْليق صوْتي voiceover   توْأم twin

Main Idea

a. Najd is a 27-year-old civil engineering graduate from Gaza with a large family, including a twin brother.
b. Najd is a 37-year-old journalist from Gaza who studied political science and works in media.
c. Najd is a widow and mother of two who lives in Ramallah and works as a voiceover artist.
d. Najd is an only child who recently graduated from medical school and lives with her aunt's family in Gaza.

True or False

1. Najd is currently working in the field of civil engineering.
2. Two of Najd's sisters got married and now live in Morocco.
3. Najd is the oldest sibling in her family.
4. Najd's parents were not planning on having more children after her older siblings.
5. Najd has left Gaza and is now in Egypt.

Multiple Choice

1. Why did Najd decide to get into the field of voiceover?

   a. People encouraged her because they liked her voice, and she found it a more diverse field than journalism.

   b. She had always dreamed of becoming a voiceover artist and used to mimic commercials on TV.

   c. Her twin brother recommended it to her, as he is also a successful voiceover artist.

   d. She was offered a job in the field before she finished her degree.

2. How many siblings does Najd have?

    a. Three brothers and two sisters   c. Four brothers and two sisters

    b. Five brothers and three sisters   d. Just a twin brother

3. What does Najd say about her current family situation?

    a. Some of her siblings have gotten married, but they still live in the same house.

    b. She lives alone in a different country.

    c. All her siblings still live with her in their family home.

    d. She lives with only her parents.

Matching

أقلّ	wasn't
إلى جانِب	in consideration
بِالتّالي	despite that
بِالْحِسْبان	so, therefore
بِالْمُناسبة	when
برْضو	consequently
بسّ	on this
على كُلّ حال	from inside
على هاي	in the same __
عمر	in any case
فا	(progressive marker)
في نفْس	from the same
لمّا	also, as well
ما كانِش	by the way
مع هيْك	besides
مِن داخِل	fewer
مِن نفْس	but

السّلامُ عليْكُم ، مرْحباً.	1	Peace be upon you, hello.
أنا نجْد عكّيلة ، أنا مِن فِلسْطين، مِن غزّة تحْديداً.	2	I'm Najd Akkeela, I'm from Palestine, from Gaza specifically.
نعم ، مِن غزّة.	3	Yes, from Gaza.
إحْنا حالِيّاً، يَعْني الكُلّ بيْعرف عن غزّة، في حالةِ حرْب.	4	We're currently, everyone knows about Gaza, in a state of war.
لكِن مع هيْك، أنا عم بعرّفْكُم عن نفْسي مِن داخِل غزّة.	5	But even so, I'm introducing myself to you from inside Gaza.
أنا عُمْري ٢٧ سنة.	6	I'm 27 years old.
خلّصِت هنْدسة مدني، اِتْخرّجِت مِن الجامْعة الإسْلامية، درسِت فيها خمْس سْنين والحمْدُ لله وخلّصِت.	7	I finished civil engineering, I graduated from the Islamic University, I studied there for five years, and thank God, I finished.
ودرسْت بعْدْها الـvoiceover. حبّيْت إنّو أدْخُل مجّال التّعْليق الصّوْتي لأنّو كْتير ناس سِمْعوني وسِمْعوا صوْتي، وحسّوا إنّو صوْتي بيْنفع لِلصّحافة والإعْلام.	8	And after that, I studied voiceover. I wanted to get into the field of voiceover because a lot of people heard me and heard my voice, and they felt that my voice was good for journalism and media.
بسّ أنا كُنْت حابّة إنّو أدْخُل شغْلة يَعْني مُتنوّعة أكْثر.	9	But I wanted to get into something more diverse.
فا لمّا سْمعِت عن مجال التّعْليق الصّوْتي، حسّيْت إنّو هدا المجال اللي أنا يَعْني عاجِبْني وحابّة إنّي فِعْلاً أكون فيه وحَ أبْدع فيه.	10	So, when I heard about the field of voiceover, I felt that this is the field that I like and really want to be in, and I'll excel in it.
والحمْدُ لله اتْوَفّقِت واشْتغلِت في التّعْليق الصّوْتي.	11	And thank God, I succeeded and worked in voiceover.
إحْنا يَعْني عيْلتْنا كْبيرة، اِسْماللّه عنّا خمْس إخْوة وْلاد وتلاث إخْوة بنات.	12	Our family is big, by God's will, we have five brothers and three sisters.
وبالمُناسبة، أنا خْلِقِت تَوْأم، يَعْني أنا إسْمي نجْد، وفلْقِةِ تَوْأمي إسْمو مُنْجِد.	13	And by the way, I was born a twin, my name is Najd, and my twin's name is Munjed.
فا إحْنا آخِر تْنيْن، آخِر نفريْن.	14	So, we're the last two, the last ones.
فا أهْلي يَعْني ما كانِش بالْحِسْبان إنّهُم يْجيبوني، بسّ الحمدُ لله اللي نصيب إنّي آجي على هاي الدُّنْيا.	15	So, my parents didn't plan to have me, but thank God it was meant for me to come into this world.

وِيَعْني عِنْدي: خالِد، عاهِد، مْحَمّد، أحْمد، ومُنْجِد طبْعاً، فلقةْ التّوْأم، وخُلُود، عُهود.	16	And I have Khaled, Ahed, Mohammad, Ahmad, and of course Munjed, my twin, and Khulood, and Uhood.
تمانْيَة، وبابا وماما طبْعاً، عشرة.	17	Eight, and my dad and mom, of course, ten.
فا إحْنا كُنّا عايْشين في البيْت عشر نْفار، بسّ طبْعاً أُخْتي... خَواتي التّنْتيْن لأنّهُم كْتير كْبار، يَعْني أكْبر مِنّي بِكْتير، اتْجَوّزوا.	18	So, we were ten people living in the house, but of course my sister... my two sisters, because they're much older, much older than me, got married.
وفي إلي أخّ في المغْرِب، بالتّالي صُرْنا أقلّ.	19	And I have a brother in Morocco, so we have become fewer.
يَعْني وإخْوتي اتْجَوّزوا، بسّ عايْشين معْنا في نفْس البيْت برْضو.	20	And my siblings got married, but they're still living with us in the same house too.
والحمْدُ لله على كُلّ حال يَعْني، وشُكْراً كْتير.	21	And thank God for everything, and thank you so much.

Vocabulary

1. knows[4] _____
2. I finished/graduated[7] _____
3. suits/works for[8] _____
4. I was born[13] _____
5. half/twin[13] _____

6. two people[14] _____
7. fate/destiny[15] _____
8. my sisters[18] _____
9. people[18] _____
10. we became[19] _____

_____

Answers

Main Idea: a **True-False:** 1. F[7-11] 2. F[19] 3. F[12-14] 4. T[15] 5. F **Multiple Choice:** 1. a[8-10] 2. b[12-16] 3. a[19-20]
Matching: بالْمُناسبة by the way / in consideration بالْحِسْبان / consequently بالتّالي / besides إلى جانِب / fewer أقلّ / عمر (progressive marker) / on this على هاي / in any case على كُلّ حال / but بسّ / also, as well برْضو / despite that مع هيْك / مِن / wasn't ما كانِش / when لمّا / in the same في نفْس / so, therefore فا / from the same مِن نفْس / from inside داخِل فلْقة **Vocabulary:** 1. بْيِعْرف 2. خلّصِت 3. بْيِنْفع 4. خِلِقِت 5. 6. نفريْن 7. نصيب 8. خَواتي 9. نْفار 10. صُرْنا

2 Suheil's Introduction

الفُنون القِتالية martial arts   لُغات languages   النّاصْرة Nazareth

Main Idea

a. Suheil is a 28-year-old teacher who lives in Jerusalem with his family.
b. Suheil is an 18-year-old artist from Hebron who spends most of his time painting and writing poetry.
c. Suheil is a university student living in Nazareth, working in the field of education.
d. Suheil is a 23-year-old who enjoys traveling and learning languages.

True or False

1. Suheil was born in Nazareth and has lived there for most of his life.
2. Suheil trained as a fitness coach and worked in that field for over five years.
3. Suheil spent several years studying in Germany before returning to Palestine.
4. Suheil enjoys training in martial arts like kickboxing and wrestling.
5. Suheil enjoys spending time both with his family and alone in nature.

Multiple Choice

1. Why did Suheil decide to stop studying in Germany?

    a. He didn't like the university.

    b. He couldn't make friends in Germany.

    c. He returned to Palestine because of a family emergency.

    d. He wanted to travel more instead of continuing his studies.

2. What did Suheil do after returning to Palestine from his travels in Europe?

    a. He returned to work as a fitness coach.

    b. He decided to resume his studies in Germany.

    c. He stopped traveling and settled in Palestine.

    d. He decided to go on an eight-month trip to India and Southeast Asia.

3. Which of the following languages does Suheil speak fluently?

    a. German   b. English   c. Spanish   d. *All of the above*

إسّا	as if
بالذّات	that's it/all
بِدّناش	now
خلص	several
زيّ كإنّو	not just
زيّ ما كان	from where
عَ	we don't want
عَ أساس	from the perspective of
عنّي	especially, specifically
في الآخِر	in the end
فيشِّ	if not for
كذا	there isn't
لحالو	like it was
لحالي	by myself
لَوْ لا	after
ما بعْد	by himself
مِش بسّ	to, on
مِن ناحْية	on the basis that
مِن وينْ	now
هسّا	about me

Text

أنا أُسْمي سُهيْل مِن مدينةْ النّاصْرة بشمال فلسْطين بأراضي الـ٤٨.	1	My name is Suhail, and I'm from Nazareth in northern Palestine, in the '48 territories.
أنا خلِقِت بمدينةْ النّاصْرة، إسّا عُمْري ٢٣ سِنِة.	2	I was born in Nazareth, and now I'm 23 years old.
تقْريباً كُلّ حَياتي عِشِت بمدينةْ النّاصْرة.	3	I've lived almost my whole life in Nazareth.

نقلْت ٣ مدارِس خِلال فترْةِ تعْليمي وتْخرّجِت بْعُمْري ١٨ سنة.	4	I switched schools three times during my education and graduated at the age of 18.
بعِد ما اتْخرّجِت، إجت فترْةِ الكوْروْنا واشْتغلِت كذا شغْلةِ.	5	After I graduated, the COVID period began, and I worked several jobs.
بعْدين قرّرِت إنّي أتْعلّم مُدرّب لـ... بصالةِ لياقة بدنية، فا عْمِلْت كورْس أكمّ مِن شهر، وبعْدين اشْتغلِت حَوالي سِنةِ ونُصّ بْهدا المجال.	6	Then I decided to study to become a fitness trainer, so I took a course for a few months and worked in that field for about a year and a half.
بعْدين قرّرِت بِدّي أطْلع أتْعلّم بِألْمانْيا،	7	After that, I decided I wanted to study in Germany.
فا طْلِعت على ألْمانْيا، اتْعلّمِت سِمِسْتِر واحد، عْمِلت ملان صْحاب مِن برّا، كانت جامْعة فيها ناس مِن كُلّ دُوَل العالم.	8	So I went to Germany, studied for one semester, and made a lot of friends from abroad—the university had people from all over the world.
بعْدين قرّرْت إنّو بِدّي أكمّل أسافِر وبِدّيش أكمّل أتْعلّم.	9	Then I decided I wanted to continue traveling and didn't want to keep studying.
فا حْمِلْت حالي وسافرت بـ... كان معي إقامة لأوروبّا، فا سافرِت كْتير بْأوروبّا، وعْمِلْت ملان صْحاب مِن هُناك.	10	So, I packed my things and started traveling. I had a residence permit for Europe, so I traveled a lot in Europe and made many friends there.
كمان رُحْت شهِر عَ المغْرِب.	11	I also spent a month in Morocco.
بعْدين صُرْت كْتير أحِبّ السّفر.	12	After that, I became very fond of traveling.
فا روّحِت عَ فلسْطين، ومِن هُناك طْلِعت مِشْوار تمن طُشْهُر مِن قبِل ما تِبْلِش الحرْب بِشْوَيّ.	13	I returned to Palestine and, from there, set out on an eight-month trip just before the war started.
وأنا بِالْهِنْد وبجنوب شرق آسْيا ألِفّ، فا عْمِلْت كْتير كْتير صْحاب وعِلاقات مع ملان ناس مِن كُلّ دُوَل العالم.	14	I was traveling in India and Southeast Asia, exploring. I made many, many friends and connections with people from all over the world.
غيرْ عن هيْك، أنا حدا كْتير بيحِبّ يِقْرا كُتُب، كْتير مِهْتمّ بِالتّاريخ، كْتير بفْتخِر بفلسْطينيتي وبالثّقافة والحضارة اللي عِنّا.	15	Aside from that, I'm someone who loves reading books, is very interested in history, and is very proud of my Palestinian identity, culture, and heritage.
وكْتير بحِبّ أقْعُد مع... أقضّي وقْت مع عيلْتي، وبتمرّن كيك بوكْسينْغ، وكمان مُصارعة، وكُلّ رياضات الفُنون القِتالية.	16	I also love spending time with my family, training in kickboxing and wrestling, and doing all kinds of martial arts.
وأنا كمان حدا كْتير بيحِبّ أقضّي وقِت بِالطّبيعة، وكمان أقضّي وقِت مع حالي لحالي.	17	I'm also someone who loves spending time in nature and also enjoys time alone.

وعِنْدي كْتير أصْدِقاء مِن بَرّا زيّ ما حكيْت، وكْتير بحِبّ العربي.	18 — I have many friends from abroad, as I mentioned, and I really love the Arabic language.
بحْكي كذا لُغة. بحْكي عربي، وبحْكي عِبْري كمان لأنّو إحْنا عايْشين حَوالْينا يَهود يَعْني، فا... كمان بحْكي إنْجْليزي طبْعاً مِن كُلّ السّفر اللي كُنْتو.	19 — I speak several languages. I speak Arabic, and I also speak Hebrew since we live near Jewish communities. I also speak English, of course, because of all the traveling I've done.
كمان بحْكي شْوَيّ إسْباني وشْوَيّ ألْماني، بِما إنّي كُنْت هُناك.	20 — I also speak a bit of Spanish and a bit of German, since I spent time there.
وكمان عِنْدي صديقة مُقرّبة جِدّاً مِن بلْجيكا، فا كمان أنا بحْكي شْوَيّ هولنْدي.	21 — I also have a very close friend from Belgium, so I speak a bit of Dutch as well.
فا كمان أنا كْتير معْني أتْعلّم لُغات، هاي كمان شغْلِة عنّي وهيْك.	22 — I'm also very interested in learning languages—that's another thing about me. That's it!

Vocabulary

1. I did/made[6] _____
2. begins[13] _____
3. I travel around[14] _____
4. I'm proud[15] _____
5. my family[16] _____

6. I said[18] _____
7. around us[19] _____
8. close (friend)[21] _____
9. thing/job[22] _____
10. interested[22] _____

Answers

Main Idea: d **True-False:** 1. T[1-3] 2. F[6] 3. F[7-9] 4. T[16] 5. T[16-17] **Multiple Choice:** 1. d[9] 2. d[13] 3. b[19] **Matching:** إسّا now / بالذّات especially, specifically / بِدْناش we don't want / خلص that's it/all / زيّ كإنّو as if / زيّ ما كان like it was / عنّي about me / في الآخِر in the end / فيش there isn't / عَ أساس on the basis that / عَ to, on / مِن ناحْيِة from the perspective of / مِن وين from where / هسّا now / لحالو by himself / لحالي by myself / لَوْ لا if not for / ما بعْد after / مِش بسّ not just / كذا several / بِفْتخِر 4. ألِّف 3. تْبلِّش 2. عْمِلْت .1 :Vocabulary بفْتخِر. 3. ألِّف / 4. معْني 10. / شغْلِة 9. / مُقرّبة 8. / حَوالْينا 7. / حكيْت 6. / عيلْتي 5.

3 Alaa's Introduction

Keywords

غَزّة Gaza   شُغُل work   أَطْفال children

Main Idea

- a. Alaa is a university student in Gaza studying computer science.
- b. Alaa is a 29-year-old nurse living in a village near Gaza City.
- c. Alaa is a 34-year-old mother of four from Gaza who works remotely.
- d. Alaa is a recently divorced mother of three living in Egypt and working as a chef.

True or False

1. Alaa completed her education in Gaza, attending government schools and university there.
2. Alaa works remotely because it's difficult to find local jobs in Gaza.
3. Alaa has two sons and two daughters.
4. Alaa has enough time to read for pleasure, and it remains one of her favorite hobbies.
5. Alaa's current focus is on working hard so she can rebuild her home after the war.

Multiple Choice

1. Why did Alaa leave Gaza for the first time in her life?

   a. To escape the war and protect her children   c. To travel and see new places

   b. To pursue higher education abroad   d. To attend a work conference

2. How does Alaa describe the job market for graduates in Gaza?

   a. Very difficult to find employment, especially in government or organizations

   b. Easy to find government jobs but nearly impossible to find employment in the private sector

   c. Easy to find employment in the private sector but not in government or organizations

   d. Full of opportunities only in certain sectors, such as technology and construction

3. What has Alaa's hobby of reading turned into?

   a. She continues to read for pleasure and enjoyment.

   b. She only reads work-related material to improve her skills.

   c. She reads mostly novels and fiction in her spare time.

   d. She stopped reading altogether.

Matching

إنّو	all of them/it
بِالْأخصّ	currently, now
بِدّي	well, good
برّا	because
بعْد هيْك	whether... or
حاليّاً	it's over/finished
خلص	very, a lot
زيّ	from scratch
سَواءْ... أوْ	after that
كْتير	I want
كُلّها	that (conjunction)
لأنّو	with
للْأسف	outside
مع	especially
مِن أوّل وجْديد	unfortunately
مِنيح	like

إسْمي آلاء، عُمري ٣٤ سنة. أنا مِن غزّة.	1	My name is Alaa; I'm 34 years old. I'm from Gaza.
انْوَلَدْت بغزّة وطول حَياتي عايْشة بْغزّة، ما طْلِعِت أبداً مِن غزّة.	2	I was born in Gaza and have lived my whole life in Gaza. I had never left Gaza.
أوّل مرّة طِلعِت بْحَياتي مِن غزّة خِلال الحرْب لأنّو كان وَضْع كْتير صعْب، فا اضطرّيْت إنّي أطْلع، وبِالأخصّ إنّو لَوْلا معي أطْفال صْغار.	3	The first time I left Gaza in my life was during the war because the situation was very difficult, so I had to leave, especially since I had young children with me.
كان يَعْني إنّو الخوْف... إنّو الواحد ما بيخاف على نفْسو كْتير، بيخاف على وْلادو أكْتر.	4	The fear was... it's not that you're very afraid for yourself, but you're more afraid for your children.
فا السّبَب إنّو أنا طْلِعِت إنّو هُوَّ الحرْب ووجود وْلاد بنات صْغار معي، فا هدا السّبَب اللي خلّاني أطْلع مِن غزّة.	5	So, the reason I left was the war and having young daughters with me. That's the reason that made me leave Gaza.
طْلِعِت بالحرْب، والحرْب كانت شغّالة، طْلِعِت مِن غزّة لأوّل مرّة بْحَياتي عَ مصِر.	6	I left during the war, while the war was ongoing. I left Gaza for the first time in my life for Egypt.
كانت تجْرُبة سيِّئة.	7	It was a bad experience.
بِالنِّسْبة لْدِراسْتي، أنا درسِت غالِباً يَعْني بْمدارِس حُكومة، زيّ أيّا بِنِت بْغزّة.	8	Regarding my education, I mostly studied in government schools, like any girl in Gaza.
درسِت بْمدارِسْها، وبعْد هيْك كمّلت طبْعاً جامْعة بْغزّة.	9	I studied in Gaza's schools, and after that, I, of course, went on to university in Gaza.
للشُّغُل... بِالنِّسْبة للشُّغُل، زيّي زيّ باقي كُلّ النّاس اللي بْغزّة، الخرّيجين، يمْكِن البطالة عِنّا عالية فا صعْب جدّاً تْلاقي وَظيفة سَواء حُكومية أوْ بْمُؤَسَّسة أوْ بالأوْنْرْوا.	10	As for work... regarding work, like all other people in Gaza, the graduates, unemployment here is very high, so it's very difficult to find a job, whether in government, an organization, or UNRWA.
يَعْني تُعدّ هدا إنْتَ محْظوظ كْتير.	11	It means that if you get one, you're very lucky.
طبْعاً، أنا ما حالفْني الحظّ، فا بديْت أدوِّر على شُغُل عن بُعْد لمُؤَسَّسات برّا أوْ لناس برّا.	12	Of course, I wasn't lucky, so I started looking for remote work with organizations abroad or with people abroad.
وبديْت أشْتغِل عن بُعْد.	13	I started working remotely.
لا يَعْني برّا، غالِبية غزّة غالِبْة الخرّيجين بْغزّة، الغالِبية العُظْمى ما بْتِتْوظّف بْوظائف حُكومية.	14	Yes, outside... most of Gaza, most of the graduates in Gaza, the vast majority don't work in government jobs.
بيكون شُغْلُهُم مُرْتبِط بْناس برّا، وبيشْتِغْلوا عن بُعْد. هيْك الغالِبية العُظْمى.	15	Their work is connected with people outside, and they work remotely. That's the vast majority.

مِتْزوّجة وعِنْدي أرْبع بنات، عِنْدي أخْوين وأُخْتين.	16	I'm married and have four daughters. I have two brothers and two sisters.
هِوايْتي كانت كْتير أحِبّ القْرايَة، ولِلأسف مع ضيق الوَقْت، وإنّو صار علي مسْؤوليّات تانْيَة، بدّي أشْتِغْل... مرّات بِتْواجهْني صُعوبات في الشُّغْل فا بضْطرّ إنّي أتْعلّم إشي جْديد عشان أطوّر حالي وأظلّني مْواكْبة.	17	My hobby used to be reading, but unfortunately, with the lack of time and having other responsibilities, including work... sometimes I face difficulties at work, so I'm forced to learn something new to develop myself and keep up.
لأنّو أنا بشْتِغْل بْسوق عالمي، فا بدّي أضلّني أنا مْواكْبة لأيْش بيصير في العالم كُلّو بطوّرو... كيف بِتْطوّر مجال شُغْلي.	18	Because I work in a global market, I need to stay up to date with what's happening in the world and how my field of work is evolving.
فا بقْدر... عشان أقْدر أظلّ مْواكْبة وماشْيَة بْشُغْلي اللي هُوَّ اللي برّا العالمي.	19	So that I can... so that I can stay up to date and continue in my work, which is with the global market abroad.
فا بطّل عِنْدي وَقْت للقْرايَة الصّراحة.	20	As a result, I honestly no longer have time to read
ما بْتذكّر يَعْني، يمْكِن إلي سْنين مُمْكِن تلت سْنين ما قريْت إشي يَعْني إشي أنا بحِبّو.	21	I can't quite remember... it's probably been three years since I last read something I truly enjoyed.
اللي بقْراه حالِيّاً هُوَّ عِبارة عن أشْياء عشان طوّر حالي، إلو عِلاقة بالشُّغُل أكْتر، مِش إشي أنا بحِبّو كهِوايَة.	22	What I'm reading now is only things related to work, to developing myself. It's more related to work than to something I enjoy as a hobby.
بحِبّ ألْعب رِياضة لأنّي كْتير بحِبّ يْكون إلي نِظام صِحّي.	23	I like to exercise because I really like to have a healthy lifestyle.
خُططي المُسْتقْبليّة كانت حالِيّاً انْتسفت.	24	My future plans are currently disrupted.
كان كْتير عِنْدي خُطط للمُسْتقْبل، سَواء بالنِّسْبة للبيْت للبنات للشُّغُل.	25	I used to have many plans for the future, whether regarding the house, my daughters, or my work.
حالِيّاً، كُلّها اتْغيّرت.	26	Right now, all of them have changed.
خُطّتي هِيَّ حالِيّاً الوَحيدة إنّو تْخلّص الحرْب، أرْجع على غزّة، أرْجع أبْني البيْت مِن أوّل وجْديد.	27	My only plan right now is for the war to end, for me to return to Gaza, and for me to rebuild the house from scratch.
فا قِلت لازِم أشْتِغْل مْنيح عشان لمّا تْخلّص الحرْب يْكون معي مصاري إنّي أقْدر أرْجع أبْني بيت.	28	So, I said I need to work hard so that when the war ends, I'll have money to be able to rebuild my house.
هاي هِيَّ خُطّة الحاليّة يَعْني فقط.	29	This is my only current plan.
أمّا الخُطط السّابِقة كُلّها يَعْني خلص راحت عَ الفاضي.	30	As for the previous plans, they're all gone—they've been completely wasted.

Vocabulary

1. I was born[2] _____
2. I was forced[3] _____
3. ongoing/running[6] _____
4. favored me[12] _____
5. I am forced to[17] _____

6. keeping up/updated[17] _____
7. were destroyed/derailed[24] _____
8. money[28] _____
9. well/good[28] _____
10. wasted/for nothing[30] _____

_____

Answers

4 Bader's Introduction

Keywords

مساحة surveying   وَظائِف jobs   بطالة unemployment

Main Idea

a. Bader is a 27-year-old living in a village near Ramallah, where he works in land surveying.
b. Bader is a 37-year-old businessman living in Bethlehem.
c. Bader is a young farmer residing in a small village near Jerusalem.
d. Bader is a recent university graduate working as a teacher in Hebron.

True or False

1. The population of Bader's village has grown to over twenty thousand residents.
2. Bader's village is about 27 kilometers away from Ramallah.
3. Bader works as an accountant in a local business office.
4. Bader studied at Birzeit University and majored in surveying.
5. Bader started his own business because of the limited job opportunities in Palestine.

Multiple Choice

1. Why was Bader's village originally called Khirbet Abu Falah?

   a. It was the site of an ancient battle.

   b. It was named after a famous leader from the village.

   c. It was a name chosen by the original settlers.

   d. It was once a small ruin with very few families living there.

2. What is the main reason Bader's journey to Ramallah takes much longer than expected?

   a. The roads are in poor condition.

   b. Public transportation is unreliable, and he does not have a car.

   c. The weather conditions often make travel difficult.

   d. There are many military checkpoints and traffic jams along the road.

3. What kind of work does Bader do in his office?

   a. Accounting and auditing for local businesses

   b. Surveying land and buildings, including dividing land and apartments

   c. Teaching business administration at a local school

   d. Managing construction projects across Palestine

Matching

إلو عِلاقة	as they say
بالرّغْمِ مِن	come and go
بالنِّسْبة لـ	in order to
بْتيجي وبِتْروح	good
بدّو	not much
تحْديداً	regarding, as for
طبْعاً	that is, I mean
عَ كُلّ حال	must, have to
عشان	by (passive)
فا بِالتّالي	related to
كمان	also
لازِم	together
لحتّى	until, so that
مِتِل ما بِحْكوها	anyway, in any case
مِش كْتير	wants
مع بعْض	of course
مِن قِبِل	despite
مِن... لـ	so consequently
مْنيحة	from... to
يَعْني	specifically

Text

مرْحَباً، إسْمي بَدِر مِن سُكّان قُرى، مدينةْ رام اللّه.	1	Hello, my name is Badr. I'm from a village near the city of Ramallah.
عُمْري ٢٧ سنة، ساكِن تحْديداً في قرْية إسْمْها قرْيةْ أبو فلاح، أوْ كما بيحْكولْها أوْ كما هيَّ معْروفة خِرْبةْ أبو فلاح.	2	I'm 27 years old and live specifically in a village called Abu Falah, or as it's also known, Khirbet Abu Falah.
سُمِّيَت خِرْبةْ أبو فلاح لأنّو يَعْني قرْية أبو فلاح كانت عِبارة عن قبل خِرْبةْ صغيرة، ساكِن فيها يَعْني ناس... عدد قليل مِن النّاس والعائِلات.	3	It's called Khirbet Abu Falah because, originally, Abu Falah was just a small hamlet where only a few people and families lived.
لكِن مع تقدُّم الزّمَن ومع تقدُّم الوَضِع والسُّكّان، صارت قرْية بيعيش فيها تقْريباً مِن خمْس تلاف لسبع تلاف نسمة.	4	But over time, with progress and an increasing population, it became a village with approximately 5,000 to 7,000 residents.
هاي القرْية بْتبْعُد عن مدينةْ رام اللّه تقْريباً ٢٧ كيلومتِر.	5	This village is about 27 kilometers from the city of Ramallah.
بْتحْتاج... يمْكِن الواحد يِحْتاج تقْريباً ثلْث ساعة بالسّيّارة على الطّريق الرّئيسي لحتّى يْروح مِن مدينةْ من قرْيةْ أبو فلاح لحتّى مدينةْ رام اللّه.	6	It usually takes about 20 minutes by car on the main road to get from Abu Falah to Ramallah.
هدا بالْوَضِع الطّبيعي، وبالوَضِع المفْروض يْكون الوَضِع الطّبيعي، لكِن إحْنا يَعْني بْفلسْطين دائماً في أوْضاع مِش طبيعية، وإحْنا دايْماً يَعْني تحْت احْتِلال.	7	That's under normal circumstances, in what's supposed to be the normal situation. But here in Palestine, we are always in abnormal situations since we are always under occupation.
فا بالتّالي الطّريق الواحد بْتوخد تقْريباً ساعة، ومرّات أكْثر، لحتّى الواحد يوصل رام اللّه.	8	Therefore, the same road can take about an hour, or even more, to reach Ramallah.
يَعْني مِن ثلْث ساعة لرُبع ساعة لساعة وأكْثر لحتّى نوصل مدينةْ رام اللّه بالسّيّارة،	9	It can take anywhere from 20 minutes to an hour or more by car to get to the city of Ramallah,
لأنّو في كْتير حَواجِز عسْكرية على الطّريق مِن قِبل الاحْتِلال، وكمان في أزمات بِتْكون يَعْني بْتيجي وبتْروح.	10	because there are many military checkpoints along the way set up by the occupation, and there are often traffic jams that come and go.
عَ كُلّ حال، أنا بشْتغِل في مكْتب مساحة.	11	In any case, I work in a surveying office.
أنا وأخوي شغّالين مع بعْض تقْريباً خمْس سْنين مع بعْض.	12	My brother and I have been working together for about five years.
هدا المكْتب بيشْتغِل مساحةْ أراضي، مساحةْ مباني، يَعْني إحْنا نعْمل فرز الأراضي، فرز شُقق وكذا،	13	This office works on land surveying, building surveying, dividing land plots, dividing apartments, and so on.

هاي الأُمور مَوْجودةٍ في البلد ومطْلوبة، ولكِن أنا بشْتِغِل في مجال يَعْني بْعيد عن مجال دِراسْتي.	14	These things are available and in demand here, but I'm working in a field far from my area of study.
أنا درسْت في جامعةٍ بيرْزيْت، تخصُّصي كان مُحاسبة وإدارةْ أعْمال.	15	I studied at Birzeit University, and my major was Accounting and Business Administration.
والشُّغُل اللي بشْتِغْلو إلو علاقة قْليلة بالمُحاسبة،	16	The job I work in has little to do with accounting,
لكِن أغْلبو عِبارة عن إدارةْ مكْتب وعِبارة عن شُغُل مَيْداني في المِساحة.	17	but most of it involves managing the office and fieldwork in surveying.
فا هاي الأُمور كُلْها بْتصير لأنّو الواحد كفلسْطيني، كخرّيج جْديد، بيضْطرّ إنّو يِشْتَغِل بِأيّ شُغْل،	18	All of this happens because, as a Palestinian and a new graduate, you are forced to work in any available job.
بِضْطرّ إنّو يِفْتح شُغُل خاص لحتّى يْقْدر يْأمّن وَظيفة، ولحتّى يِقْدر يِشْتَغِل أُمور تْكون مْنيحة.	19	You're forced to start your own business to secure a job and to find work that's decent.
لأنّو الوَظائف مِش كْتيرة، دايماً في بطالة، دايماً في... يَعْني في خِرّيجين كْثار بيتْخرّجوا مِن الجامْعات، لكِن عدد الوَظائف قْليل جِدّاً.	20	Jobs are scarce; there is always unemployment. There are always so many graduating from universities, but the number of jobs is very limited.
فا بِالتّالي الواحد بيعتْمِد عَ حالو أوْ مِتِل ما بِحْكوها، كُلّ واحد وشطارْتو.	21	So consequently, one depends on himself, or as they say, "Everyone depends on their own skills and abilities."

Vocabulary

1. they call it[2] _____
2. ruin/abandoned place[3] _____
3. checkpoints[10] _____
4. working[12] _____
5. division/sorting[13] _____

6. forced to[18] _____
7. secure[19] _____
8. graduates[20] _____
9. his skills/cleverness[21] _____
10. it takes (time)[8] _____

_____

Answers

Main Idea: a **True-False:** 1. F[4] 2. T[5] 3. F[11-17] 4. F[15] 5. T[18-21] **Multiple Choice:** 1. d[2-3] 2. d[8-10] 3. b[11-13]

Matching: بْتيجي وبِتْروح come and go / بِدّو wants / تحْديداً specifically / طبْعاً of course / عَ كُلّ حال anyway, in any case / عشان in order to / بِالنِّسْبة لـ regarding, as for / بالرّغْم مِن despite / إلو علاقة related to / مِتِل ما بِحْكوها as they say / لحتّى until, so that / لازِم must, have to / كمان also / فا بِالتّالي so consequently / يَعْني that / مْنيحة good / مِن... لـ from... to / لـ (passive) by / مِن قِبل / together مع بَعْض / بعْض not much / مِش كْتير / خِرّيجين is, I mean **Vocabulary:** 1. بيحْكولْها 2. خِرْبة 3. حَواجِز 4. شغّالين 5. فرز 6. بيضْطرّ 7. يْأمّن 8. بْتوخد 9. شطارْتو / 10. بْتوخد

5 Nihad's Introduction

Keywords

تُراث heritage	إعادةْ التّدْوير recycling
مُطرّزات embroidery	قاعِدِة شعْبية network of connections

Main Idea

a. Nihad is a single woman who works as a university professor and lives with her twin sister.
b. Nihad is a young graphic designer who recently completed her degree at Al-Arroub College.
c. Nihad is a volunteer and mother of twin boys, involved in cultural and women's empowerment activities.
d. Nihad is a retired teacher who spends her time writing about Palestinian culinary traditions.

True or False

1. Nihad eventually graduated with a degree in Arabic Language and Literature from Al-Quds Open University.
2. Nihad has worked consistently in jobs related to her degree.
3. Nihad teaches women how to recycle household waste and create products they can sell.
4. Nihad has always worked for financial reasons and has built a large social network through her paid jobs.
5. Nihad travels to different areas, including dangerous ones, to help women develop their skills and projects.

Multiple Choice

1. Why did Nihad stop studying at Al-Arroub College after her first year?

   a. The intifada made it difficult for her to continue studying.

   b. She wasn't interested in the subject.

   c. She moved abroad with her family.

   d. She decided to start working instead.

2. What is one example of Palestinian heritage that Nihad is working to preserve?

   a. Traditional farming methods

   b. Palestinian pottery

   c. The traditional Palestinian taboon oven

   d. Old Palestinian jewelry

3. What does Nihad emphasize about her experiences working with women in different areas?

   a. The financial rewards of her work and how this has helped her family enjoy a comfortable lifestyle

   b. The social network she has built and the importance of understanding our differences

   c. The difficult working conditions she faced because of the occupation

   d. The recognition she received from her community

Matching

أكْبر مِنّي بـ	not in, not with
بالْعكْس	outside
بِتْكون	older than me by
بِدّي	among
برّا	because of
بِسبب	I want
بعْدْها	on the contrary
للْيوْم	until today
ما إلْها عْلاقة بـ	after that
مِش بـ	than what
مِمّا	has no relation to
مِن ضِمْن	you become
نِهائِيّاً	absolutely
ويْن ما	wherever

إسْمي نِهاد وعُمْري ٤٤ سنةٍ.

مُتزوِّجة وأُمّ لِتَوْأم، مْحمّد ورُشْدي، ولدين.

زَوْجي إسْمو نْضال، أكْبر مِنّي بأرْبع سْنين.

في سنةْ الـ٢٠٠٠ كُنْت تَوْجيهي، رِحِت لأدْرُس في كلّية... كُلّيّةْ العَروب. رُحْت أدْرُس بَرْمجيّات وقَواعِد بَيانات.

درسْت أوّلْ سنةٍ، طبْعاً كانت الانْتِفاضة في سنةْ الـ٢٠٠٠، فا ما قْدِرِت إنّي أكمِّل بِسبب الأحْداث والغلْبة اللي كُنّا نُشْعر فيها يوْم يوْم.

تركِتْ يَعْني درسِت أوّلْ سنة وخلّصْتْها وتركِت.

في الـ٢٠٠٣ تزوّجِت، ٢٠٠٥ رجِعِت على جامعةْ القُدْس المفْتوحة ودخلِت تخصّص لُغة عربية وآدابِها.

اتْخرّجِت في الـ٢٠١٠، بسّ يَعْني ما اشْتغلِت على شْهادْتي نِهائِيّاً، مِش بْتخصُّصي.

يَعْني كُلّ الأشْغال مِن ٢٠١٠ لليوْم ما إلْها عْلاقة بْتخصُّصي نِهائِيّاً.

اتّجهِت لمَوْضوع دَوْرات ووَرْشات تدْريب للسّيِّدات في عنّا مركز تقافي في بلدْنا، أنا مِتْطوِّعة فيه،

فا كان عنّا مجْموعة نسْوية، كُلّ شهِر إلْهُم تدْريب.

كُنْت أنا أعْطيهُم دَوْرات في مجال إعادةْ التّدْوير مُخلّفاتْ البْيوت، مِن أقْمِشة، مِن بْلاستيْك، مِن مُخلّفاتْ المطْبخ، يَعْني شغْلات إنّهُم هُمّ يِسْتفيدوا مِنها تْصير عنْدْهُم مُنْتج ويِقْدروا إنّهُم يْسوّقوا لنفْسْهُم، يَعْني زيّ مصْدر دخِل إلْهُم.

بعْدْها، يَعْني كُلّ شهِر نعْطيهُم إشي طبْعاً هاي تطوُّع كانت، كُلّ شهِر نِتْعلّم إشي أنا وايّاهُم.

طبْعاً مع المُمارسة والتِّكْرار، بيصير عنْدك خِبْرة أكْتر مِمّا إنْتَ بِتْكون عنْدك الهِواية يَعْني.

1	My name is Nihad, and I am 44 years old.
2	I am married and a mother of twins, Mohammad and Rushdi, two boys.
3	My husband's name is Nidal; he is four years older than me.
4	In 2000, I was in my final year of high school and went to study at Al-Arroub College. I studied programming and databases.
5	I completed my first year, but unfortunately, because of the Intifada in 2000, I couldn't continue due to the events and hardships we faced daily.
6	So, I left—I completed the first year and then left.
7	In 2003, I got married. In 2005, I returned to Al-Quds Open University and majored in Arabic Language and Literature.
8	I graduated in 2010, but I never worked in my field of study at all.
9	All the jobs I've had since 2010 have had no relation to my field whatsoever.
10	I shifted to conducting training workshops for women at our local cultural center, where I am a volunteer.
11	We had a women's group, and every month, they had a training session.
12	I used to give them courses on recycling household waste, using fabrics, plastics, and kitchen scraps—things they could benefit from, turning them into products they could market and generate income from.
13	Every month, I'd teach them something new. This was voluntary work, and we'd learn together each month.
14	Of course, with practice and repetition, you gain more expertise than just having a hobby.

فا أنا عِنْدي هِوايةِ الخْياطة، إعادةِ التّدْوير، الشِّغْلات الْيَدَوية.	15	I have hobbies in sewing, recycling, and crafts.
كُلّ شهِر كان في إلْهُم تدْريب مُخْتلِف.	16	Each month, we had different training sessions.
مِن ضِمْن الأشْياء اللي هِيّ الاشْياء التُّراثية اللي كُنْت أعْطيهُم إيّاها المُطرّزات، فا كُنّا نْعلِّمْهُم المُطرّزات الفلسْطينية كيف بْتِنْعمل.	17	Among the things I taught were traditional crafts, particularly Palestinian embroidery. We would teach them how to create traditional Palestinian embroidered items.
حالِيّاً، بشْتْغِل في مَوْضوع كِتابِةْ التراث.	18	Currently, I am working in the field of documenting heritage.
يَعْني، في مثلاً عِنْدي حالِيّاً طابون فلسْطيني، الطّابون الأساسي اللي إمّي وجدّتي وسِتّي وكُلُّهُم كان عِنْدْهُم.	19	For instance, I currently have a Palestinian taboon oven, the traditional oven my mother, grandmother, and great-grandmother all had.
اللي نْحُطّ عليْه روْث الأغْنام الزِّبِد، فا أنا حالِيّاً عِنْدي واحد واكتبْت عنّو مقالات وصوّرْت ونشرْت مع وزارةِ الثّقافة، مع المُؤسّسات اللي عِنّا.	20	It's the kind where sheep manure is used for fuel. I've written articles about it, taken photos, and published them with the Ministry of Culture and local organizations.
اشْتغِلْت برّا الكوْم مع مُؤسّسات عالمية، اللي هِيّ هدفْها كان السِّتّات تِطْوير هِواياتْهِن، تِطْوير مشاريعْهِن.	21	I've also worked internationally with organizations focused on helping women develop their hobbies and projects.
فا أنا برّا الكوْم، اللي هِيّ دورة الخليل مناطِق.	22	Outside of Al-Kom, I conducted workshops in the Hebron region.
طبْعاً الخليل كْبيرة، مِنْها كْتير مناطِق في الخليل أغْلبْها كُلّها دخلْتْها.	23	Hebron is large, and I've covered many areas within Hebron.
ومدْفوع الأجِر كان وصار في قاعِدة شعْبية كْبيرة، الحمْدُ لله.	24	These were paid workshops, and they helped me build a large network, thank God.
يَعْني وينْ ما أروح فيه، إلي معارِف، في إلي صاحْبات.	25	Wherever I go now, I have connections and friends.
في هاي التّنوُّع، اللي إنْتَ بِتْحِسّو مِن بيئات مُخْتلِفة مِن تفْكير مُخْتلِف.	26	There's such diversity that you feel comes from different environments and ways of thinking.
مِن نماذج كْتير في الحَياة بِتْصادْفك فا إنْتَ بِتْكون يَعْني مُجبر إنّك تِتْعامل مع كُلّ النّاس.	27	You encounter various life experiences and must learn to deal with everyone.
بسّ برْضو، بيكون حِلو إنّو إنْتَ تِفْهم هاي النّاس كيف عايْشة، كيف أساليب حَياتْها، كيف تفْكيرها.	28	It's also beautiful to understand how people live, their lifestyles, and their ways of thinking.

حِلو يَعْني إنّو إنْتَ تِتْعامل مَعْهُم، وبالْعَكْس، يَعْني أنا ما كان عُمْري هدفي مادّي.	29	It's wonderful to work with them. I've never been motivated by money.
يَعْني كان كُلّ مرّة يِحْكوا معي إنّو "تعالي بِدّنا نوخْذِك عَ المِنْطِقة الفُلانية"، أحْياناً تْكُون خطر يَعْني، يْكُون فيها جيْش، يْكُون فيها مثلاً حَواجِز.	30	Every time someone would say, "Come, we need you in such and such area," even if it was dangerous, with military presence or checkpoints,
إشي احْكي: "لا، أنا بِدّي أروح"، مِش هدف مادّي نِهائيّاً، بهدف إنّو أنا أصِل لهادوْل السِّتات، إنّي أشوف شو احْتياجاتْهُم.	31	I'd say, "No, I want to go." My goal was never financial. My goal was to reach those women and see what their needs were.
وكُنّا نِتْساعد، كُنّا يَعْني نْعيش أيّام حِلْوة مع بَعْض.	32	We'd help each other and spend beautiful days together.
فا الحمْدُ لله، للْيوْم، يَعْني عِنْدي الحمْدُ لله قاعِدة شَعْبية بِتْجَنِّن، وأنا مبْسوطة كْتير مَعْهُم.	33	Thank God, until today, I have an amazing network of connections, and I am very happy with them.

Vocabulary

1. difficulties/hardship[5] _____
2. workshops[10] _____
3. women's/feminist[11] _____
4. waste/leftovers[12] _____
5. they market[12] _____

6. clay oven[19] _____
7. dung[20] _____
8. female friends[25] _____
9. forced[27] _____
10. needs[31] _____

---

6 Khaled's Introduction

Keywords

طُموح ambition	مُؤسّسات institutions
الشِّفاء healing	خِدْمات صحّية healthcare services

Main Idea

a. Khaled is a teacher who recently moved to the West Bank from Gaza.
b. Khaled is a 29-year-old doctor, born and raised in Gaza City.
c. Khaled is a young engineer living in Ramallah with his wife and two children.
d. Khaled is a 32-year-old business owner living in Khan Yunis.

True or False

1. Khaled completed his medical education at Al-Shifa Hospital in Gaza.
2. The first war Khaled personally experienced was in 2008, when he was in seventh grade.
3. Khaled has worked at both the Islamic University and Al-Shifa Hospital in Gaza.
4. Khaled described the war in October 2023 as the most brutal and destructive war Gaza has ever experienced.
5. Khaled believes Gaza will not recover from the most recent war.

Multiple Choice

1. What is Khaled's profession?

   a. Engineer   b. Teacher   c. Doctor   d. Lawyer

2. Which of the following sectors does Khaled describe as being severely impacted by the war?

   a. Educational institutions   c. Homes and infrastructure

   b. Health services   d. *All of the above*

3. What does Khaled say about the healthcare system in Gaza after the war?

   a. It is completely destroyed, with no medicine or services available.

   b. It is functioning normally.

   c. It has been partially restored.

   d. The situation has improved, but more support is needed.

إن شاء الله	until
بِالْكامِل	still
بْشكِل عامّ	the day when
بعْد كِدا	after that
حَ	just as it was
زيّ ما كانت	before that
عنّا	before
قبِل هيْك	at/with us
لِسّا	in general
لعنْد ما	God willing
لمُدِّةْ	for (duration)
ما فيش أيّ إشي	will (future marker)
مِن قِبل ما	there isn't anything
يوْم ما	completely

Text

مساء الخيْر! إسْمي خالِد مِن فلِسْطين، مِن قِطاع غزّة، وتحْديداً مِن مدينةْ غزّة.	1	Good evening! My name is Khaled. I'm from Palestine, the Gaza Strip, and specifically Gaza City.
انْوَلدْت فيها واتْربّيْت فيها، وعِشْت معْها بْذِكْرَياتْها لمُدِّةْ ٢٩ سنة.	2	I was born there, raised there, and lived with its memories for 29 years.
بمْشي في شَوارِعْها، بشُمّ هَواها، وبسْتجِم على بحرْها.	3	I walk its streets, breathe its air, and relax by its sea.
اتْنقّلِت في مدارِسْها مِن مدْرسة لِلتّانْية لِلتّالْتَة، لعنْد ما خلّصِت الثّانَوية العامّة اللي بْنْسمّيها عنّا التّوْجيهي.	4	I moved between its schools, from one to another to a third, until I completed high school, which we call Tawjihi here.

بعْد هيْك، الْتحقِت في أكْبر جامْعة في قِطاع غزّة، اللي هِيَّ الجامْعة الإسْلامية، واتْخرّجِت مِن كُلّيّة الطِّبّ بتقْدير عامّ جيِّد جدّاً كتقْدير لمجْهودي في هدي الكُلّيّة.

After that, I joined the largest university in the Gaza Strip, the Islamic University, and graduated from the Faculty of Medicine with a very good overall grade as a reflection of my effort in that college.

5

اِشْتغلت فيها مُعين لمُدّة سنة، درّسِت وتْعامِلِت مع كْتير طُلّاب وكْتير أطِبّاء، وعمِلتْلي هدي connections ومعارِف كْتير كْوَيِّسة.

I worked there as an assistant for one year, teaching and dealing with many students and doctors, which gave me many connections and very good relationships.

6

بعْد هيْك، اشْتغلِت في أكْبر مُسْتشْفى في قِطاع غزّة، اللي هِيَّ مُسْتشْفى الشّفاء، اللي بِتْوفِّر خِدْمات صحّية لكْتير مرضى وفي كْتير تخصُّصات، وفي كُلّ التّخصُّصات تقْريباً.

After that, I worked at the largest hospital in the Gaza Strip, which is Al-Shifa Hospital, providing healthcare services to many patients and in many specialties—almost all specialties.

7

اِشْتغلِت فيها لمُدّة ثلاث سنْوات تقْريباً.

I worked there for almost three years.

8

لأنّو، بدت الحرْب على قِطاع غزّة.

Then, the war on Gaza began.

9

قِطاع غزّة هُوَّ جُزْء صْغير مِن فلسْطين، مساحْتُه ٣٦٥ كيلومِترِ مُربّع، مُحاصر مِن ٢٠٠٦ للْيوْم، عانى مِن كْتير حُروب.

The Gaza Strip is a small part of Palestine, with an area of 365 square kilometers, under siege since 2006 until today, and has endured many wars.

10

أنا شخْصيّاً عايَشِت عدد مِش قليل مِنْها.

I personally have lived through quite a few of them.

11

بتْذكّر أوّل حرْب كانت حرْب الـ٢٠٠٨، كُنِت طِفِل لِسّا في صفّ سابِع.

I remember the first war, which was the 2008 war. I was still a child in seventh grade.

12

كُنِت عِنْدي امْتِحانات نِهائية، ويوْم ما روّحِت مِن الامْتِحان بدأِت الحرْب وصار القصِف.

I had final exams, and on the day I came home from an exam, the war began, and the shelling started.

13

والحرْب اللي بعْديها كانت حرْب سنةْ ٢٠١٢، بعِد كِدا ٢٠١٤، بعِد كِدا ٢٠٢٠ و ٢٠٢١.

The next war was the 2012 war, then 2014, then 2020, and 2021.

14

لكِن أصْعب حرْب وأقْسى حرْب وأطْول حرْب هِيَّ الحرْب الأخيرة، ٧ أُكْتوبِر ٢٠٢٣.

But the hardest, most brutal, and longest war was the most recent one, on October 7, 2023.

15

هدي الحرْب الجائْرة الهَوْجاء دمّرت قِطاع غزّة بالْكامِل، دمّرت البشر قبِل الحجر، دمّرت الأمّل، دمّرت الطُّموح، دمّرت الحَياة كُلّها بْشكِل عامّ.

This barbaric, raging war completely destroyed the Gaza Strip, destroying the people before the stones, destroying hope, destroying ambition, and destroying life as a whole.

16

كْتير مِن الأُسر فقدوا أحْبابْهُم، وكْتير مِن الأُسر انْمسحت مِن السّجِل المدني الفلسْطيني.

Many families lost their loved ones, and many families were erased from the Palestinian civil registry.

17

18	هدي الحرْب قضّت على مُعْظم مناح الحَياة، قضت على البُيوت، النّاس صارت تُسْكُن في خِيام.	This war has wiped out most aspects of life, destroying homes, leaving people living in tents.
19	قضت على المؤسّسات التّعْليمية، المدارس والجامْعات اللي التّعْليم اتْوَقّف فيها مِن حَوالي أكْتر مِن سنة.	It destroyed educational institutions—schools and universities—where education has been halted for over a year.
20	هدي الحرْب قضّت على المؤسّسات الصّحّية، على المُسْتشْفَيات، على العِيادات، على مراكِز الصّحّة الأوّلية.	This war destroyed healthcare institutions, hospitals, clinics, and primary healthcare centers.
21	ما فيش أدْوِية، ما فيش رعاية صحّية، ما فيش أيّ إشي.	There are no medicines, no healthcare services, and no anything.
22	هدي الحرْب حَوّلت بلدي، حبيبْتي، مَوْطِني، إلى خرابة.	This war turned my country, my beloved homeland, into ruins.
23	إن شاء الله ربّ العالمين حَ نِرْجع مِنْعمّرْها، وحتّى تِرْجع زيّ أوّل وأحْسن.	God willing, we will rebuild it and make it even better than before.
24	زيّ ما كانت تِنْتِفِض وتِرْجع بعِد كُلّ حرْب صارت قبِل هيْك، حَ نِرْجع.	Just as it rose again after every war that it endured before, we will rise again.
25	وحَ نمارِس هِواياتْنا حَ نِمْشي على بحرْها، ونْشِم هَواها النّظيف، ونِتْفرّج على بْيوتْها الحِلوة، وعلى شَوارعِها وأزِقّتْها وأسْواقْها.	We will resume our hobbies, walk by its sea, breathe its fresh air, admire its beautiful houses, its streets, its alleys, and its markets.

Vocabulary

1. was raised[2] _____
2. I relax[3] _____
3. I moved around[4] _____
4. teaching assistant[6] _____
5. brutal/oppressive[16] _____

6. was erased[17] _____
7. aspects[18] _____
8. was stopped[19] _____
9. ruins[22] _____
10. alleys[25] _____

_____

Answers

Main Idea: b **True-False:** 1. F5 2. T12-13 3. T6-7 4. T15-16 5. F23-25 **Multiple Choice:** 1. c5-7 2. d18-20 3. c21 **Matching:** إن شاء الله God willing / بالْكامِل completely / بْشكِل عامّ in general / بعْد كِدا after that / لعِنْد ما still / لِسّا before that / قبِل هيْك at/with us / عِنّا just as it was / زيّ ما كانت will (future marker) / حَ the day when يوْم ما before / مِن قبِل ما there isn't anything / ما فيش أيّ إشي for (duration) / لِمُدّة / until **Vocabulary:** 1. اتْربّيت 2. بسْتجِم 3. اتْنقّلِت 4. مُعين 5. الجائْرة 6. انْمسحت 7. مناح 8. اتْوَقّف 9. خرابة 10. أزِقّة

Daily Routines

7 Suheil's Daily Routine

Keywords

روتين يَوْمي daily routine   تَمْرين exercise   غُروب الشّمس sunset   مشاوير outings

Main Idea

a. Suheil balances work and family time while keeping an active and flexible lifestyle.
b. Suheil spends most of his day working long hours delivering food and doing other odd jobs.
c. Suheil spends his day mostly alone, hiking and reading books in nature.
d. Suheil's daily routine revolves around his cooking and drawing hobbies.

True or False

1. Suheil works as a full-time delivery driver with a set schedule.
2. Suheil enjoys spending time with his family in the evenings.
3. Suheil usually works on weekends delivering food and items.
4. On weekends, Suheil likes to stay home and spend time with his grandfather's family.
5. Suheil exercises every day for at least 30 minutes.

Multiple Choice

1. What does Suheil typically do in the afternoons?

    a. He delivers food and items for people.

    b. He exercises and reads a book.

    c. He spends time hiking in nature.

    d. He visits friends and family for lunch.

2. Which of the following skills is Suheil learning?

   a. Photography and dancing   c. Cooking and drawing

   b. Car repair and mechanics   d. *All of the above*

3. How does Suheil describe his time when he is traveling?

   a. He follows a similar routine to when he is at home.

   b. He spends his days resting and relaxing.

   c. He goes out every day to discover new things in the country he's visiting.

   d. He focuses on making social media content and earning money while traveling.

Matching

بِآخِر	like
بِدّي	whenever
تاعي	sometimes
حَوالي	I want
خُرّاف تاني	by myself
عَ	when
عم	(progressive marker)
لحالي	around
لمّا	and so on
مِتِل	my, mine
مرّات	different story
مِن بعْد	to, on
هيْك	at the end of
وهيْك	after
ويْنتا	like this

الرّوتين اليَوْمي تاعي هُوّ هيْك: أنا كُلّ يوْم بفيق حَوالي السّاعة سبْعة عَ الصُّبح، بفوت عَ الحمّام، بغسّل، بعْمل فطور، بقْرا شْوَيّ، وبنْزل بسلّم على دار سيدي.

1 My daily routine goes like this: every day I wake up around 7 a.m., go to the bathroom, wash up, make breakfast, read a bit, and then go down to visit my grandfather's house.

وبحْضر فيديوهات عَ اليوتْيوب، بتْعلّم شْوَيّ، برتّب أوضْتي والبيْت.

2 I watch YouTube videos, learn a little, tidy up my room and the house.

عَ الظّهْريات، بنْزل باكُل، وبالْعادِة بعْد الظُّهر بروح بشْتِغِل بعمليّات توْصيل إرْساليّات، أكِل، وأغْراض لناس مْعيّنة.

3 Around midday, I go down to eat, and usually after lunch, I work on delivery tasks—food or other items for specific people.

أنا شُغْلي ويْنتا بدّي بالْعادي بروّح بروح المغْرِب.

4 My work schedule is flexible, and I usually finish around sunset.

بالْعادي بحِبّ أروح... أطْلع أتْفرّج على غُروب الشّمِس، ومِن بعْد غُروب الشّمِس بروح... بحِبّ أقْعُد مع العيْلي، مِنْتِخرّف. مرّات بميّل عِنْد دار عمّاتي أوْ خالاتي.

5 I like to go out and watch the sunset, and after that, I head home. I enjoy sitting with my family and chatting. Sometimes, I stop by my aunts' or uncles' houses.

مرّات بيكون في عِنّا قعْدات باللّيْل بالْعيْلة مرّات مع صْحاب.

6 Sometimes, we have family gatherings in the evening or hang out with friends.

وبالله... بآخِر الأُسْبوع، بالْعادي بشْتِغِلْش، فا مرّات بطْلع مِشْوار مِن الصُّبح، مرّات لحالي مرّات مع العيْلي.

7 On weekends, I usually don't work, so sometimes I go on outings, either alone or with my family.

باخُد معي كْتاب بقْرا كْتير، بعْمل مسارات مشي بالطّبيعة مرّات.

8 I take a book with me and read a lot or go on hiking trails in nature sometimes.

بتْمرّن، تقْريباً كُلّ يوْم عِنْدي نُص ساعِة تمْرين مينيموم، وهيْك.

9 I exercise almost every day for at least half an hour.

وكمان كْتير بحِبّ أتْعلّم شغْلات جْديدِة، يَعْني ألْتقي بْناس جْديدِة، أخطّط للمشاوير، أحْكي مع صْحاب قُدما.

10 I also love learning new things, meeting new people, planning outings, and catching up with old friends.

وكمان بضلّ أدوّر على طُرُق اللي أعْمل فيها مصاري، مِن ناحْيَة فْريلانْسِيْنج أوْ مِن ناحْيَة إنّي ألاقي أشْغال جْديدِة.

11 I also continue looking for ways to make money, whether through freelancing or finding new jobs.

بْتعلّم كمان مهارات متنوّعة، مِتِل الرّسِم والطّبِخ و هيْك إشْياء.	12	I also learn a variety of skills, like drawing, cooking, and other things.
وهيْك، أكْتر إشي بحِبّ أقضّي وَقْت مع العيْلِة ومع صْحاب.	13	Overall, I love spending time with my family and friends the most.
ولمّا أنا مْسافِر، خُرّاف تاني بيكون، لأنّو كُلّ يوْم يَعْني بِدّي أروح أكْتشِف شغْلات جْديدِة بالْبلد اللي... عم بزورْها أنا، وهيْك.	14	When I'm traveling, it's a completely different story because every day I want to go explore new things in the country I'm visiting.

Vocabulary

1. I enter[1] _____
2. I wake up[1] _____
3. deliveries[3] _____
4. I drop by[5] _____
5. we chat[5] _____

6. I don't work[7] _____
7. by myself[7] _____
8. outing/trip[7] _____
9. I plan[10] _____
10. I keep/continue[11] _____

---

8 Alaa's Daily Routine

Keywords

روتين routine   حرْب war   رياضة exercise

Main Idea

- a. Alaa's schedule before the war and her love for the routine she maintained.
- b. Alaa's current routine as she and her family live as refugees in Egypt.
- c. Alaa compares her routine before the war to her current routine.
- d. Alaa focuses on her routine in the morning, the busiest time of her day.

True or False

1. Alaa used an alarm clock to wake up every morning at 5:50 a.m.
2. Alaa exercised every day for 30 minutes because she cared about her health.
3. Alaa describes herself as a homebody because of her responsibilities as a mother of four.
4. Alaa always made time for her hobbies and personal reading.
5. Alaa attended in-person courses during the day while her daughters were at school.

Multiple Choice

1. What did Alaa do after waking up her daughters and preparing them for school?

   a. She immediately started working on her laptop.
   b. She had coffee and exercised for 30 minutes.
   c. She went out to the gym.
   d. She went back to bed.

2. How did Alaa feel about her routine before the war?

   a. She felt it was boring and wished for more variety.
   b. She wanted to change her routine but didn't know how.
   c. She often complained about her busy schedule.
   d. She loved her routine and was thankful for it.

3. What does Alaa hope for before the year 2024 is over?

   a. To find a new job
   b. To travel with her family
   c. To return to her home and resume her routine
   d. To finish all her online courses

Matching

إلّا	I hope
بِالزِّبِط	before
بِتْمَنّى	after that
بدْري	during
بِدون	early
بُرغِم مِن	never (in my life)
بعْد ما	usually, most of the time
بعد هيْك	at the same time
بعدْها	after that
بْنفْس الوَقِت	without
خِلال	very, a lot
دايْماً	will/going to
رح	exactly
عُمْري ما	rarely, not much
غالِباً	despite
قبِل ما	maybe, possibly
كْتير	except; minus/before
مُمْكِن	after
يا ما	always

Text

مرْحبا، إسْمي آلاء، رح أتْكلّم عن روتيني اليَوْمي، طبْعاً قبِل الحرْب، قبِل سبْعة عشرة ألفيْن وتْلاتة وعِشْرين،	**1** Hello, my name is Alaa, and I'm going to talk about my daily routine, of course before the war, before October 7, 2023.
أنا مِن الأشْخاص اللي يَعْني إلي نِظام مُعَيّن ما بغْيّرو أبداً.	**2** I'm someone who sticks to a specific routine and never changes it.

يِمْكِن كـ... بَعْض النّاس يْقولوا كْتير مُمِلّ، بسّ أنا كان يَعْني يوْمي ماشي على نِظام مُحدّد ما بِتْغيّر فيه شي.	**3** Maybe some people would say it's very boring, but my days followed a fixed routine where nothing changed.
كُنْت أَصْحى الصُّبح بدْري. أنا مِن النّاس اللي بحِبّ أَصْحى بدْري كْتير.	**4** I used to wake up early in the morning because I truly enjoy starting my day early.
كُنْت اصْحى سِتّة... سِتّة إلا عشرة. كُنْت اصْحى بالزِّبط سِتّة إلّا عشرة. حتّى بدون مُنبِّه كُنْت أَصْحى.	**5** I used to wake up at six... ten to six, exactly at ten to six. Even without an alarm, I'd wake up.
أنا أُمّ، فا كُنْت طبْعاً أَصحّي بناتي للْمدْرسة. عِنْدي بِنتيْن في المدْرسة.	**6** I'm a mother, so, of course, I used to wake my daughters up for school. I have two daughters in school.
قبِل ما أصحّيهُم، كُنْت أَصلّي الفجِر، بعْدها أصحّيهُم.	**7** Before waking them up, I'd pray Fajr, then wake them up.
بعْد ما أصحّيهُم يَعْني، أعمِلْهُم... أجهِّزْلْهُم الفِطور قبِل المدْرسة، أساعِدْهُم باللِّبِس ملابِسْهُم قبِل ما يْروحوا عَ المدْرسة، ونْشوف إذا شِناط المدْرسة لازِمها إشي، وأجهِّز اللّانْش بوكْس. كْتير في كان تفاصيل.	**8** After waking them up, I'd prepare breakfast for them before school, help them get dressed, check if their school bags needed anything, and prepare their lunchboxes. There were many details involved.
بعْد هيْك، نِسْتنّى الباص، نْزلِّهُم يرْكبوا الباص.	**9** After that, we'd wait for the bus, and I'd send them off as they got on the bus.
كُنْت بعْدها أشْرب قهْوة وأعْمل رياضة.	**10** After that, I'd drink coffee and exercise.
كُنْت أعْمل رياضة لمُدّة ٣٠ دْقيقة، أنا شخْص كْتير بحِبّ أهْتمّ بْصِحّتي.	**11** I used to exercise for 30 minutes. I'm someone who really loves taking care of my health.
ومِش ما كُنْت أعْمل رياضة بِسبب إنّو الوَزِن أوْ شيْء هيْك، إنّو أنا كُنْت أعْمل رياضة لأنّي بحِبّ أهْتمّ بْصِحّتي.	**12** And it wasn't because of weight or anything like that—I exercised because I love taking care of my health.
وبعِدها، كُنْت بعْد الرِّياضة مُمْكِن آخُذ شاوَر، وبعْدها أبداً يَعْني أفْطر.	**13** After exercising, I might take a shower; then I'd have breakfast.
وبعِدها... عِنْدي بِنْت صْغيرة طبْعاً، لأنّو هدا السّبب اللي ما بيخلّيني أروح عَ الجّيم، لأنّي أنا مِضْطرّة أعْمل رياضة في البيْت.	**14** After that... I have a young daughter, of course, and that's the reason I don't go to the gym—I'm forced to exercise at home.
أنا تقْريباً كانت مُعْظم حَياتي في البيْت.	**15** Most of my life was at home.

يَعْني أنا شخص بَيْتوتي، أَوْ هُوَّ الظّروف المَوْجودة عِنْدي، وإنّو أنا أُمّ لأَرْبع أطْفال. هدا الإشي خلّاني إنّي ما أقْدر أطْلع كْتير بَرّا البيْت، أَوْ إنّي أَرْتْبِط بْإشي بَرّا البيْت فا كُنْت أعْمل رياضة مِن البيْت.

طبْعاً بعْدْها، بعد ما أفْطر، أَصحّي بِنْتي الصّغيرة، غالْباً أعْملْها فْطور، أهْتمّ فيها شْوَية، نُقْعُد نِلْعب مع بعْض.

خلال هدا الوَقْت، مثلاً مُمْكن أكون بِلْعب معْها، وبْنفْس الوَقِت بشْتِغِل على اللّابْتوب.

غالْباً كُنْت إذا ما بشْتِغِل على اللّابْتوب بْهدا الوَقْت، ألْعب معْها وأكون بحْضر دَوْرة تعْليمية أوْنْلايْن، طبْعاً إشي بيخُصّ مجال شُغْلي. كْتير كُنْت، بالرّغْم إنّو مِش مُتاح إلي إنّي أحْضر دَوْرات وِجاهية أَوْ بْشكِل وِجاهي، كُنْت دايْماً أدوّر عَ شِغْلات أوْنْلايْن بِتْناسِبْني.

يَعْني بعد هيْك، أضلّني قريب الظُّهُر على... تقْريباً على أذان الظُّهُر، أقوم عن اللّابْتوب شْوَيّة أجهِّز الغدا للبنات، يْروّحوا بعد هيْك مِن المدْرسة، قْريب تِنْتيْن ونُصّ، تلاتة بالزّبْط.

أنا كُلّ إشي كان يَعْني إنّو عَ السّاعة بالزّبْط ماشْية.

بعد هيْك، يْجهِّز الغدا، يِتْغدّوا، نِبْدأ أنا وإيّاهُم نفْس الإشي أكون فاتْحة اللّابْتوب، بشْتِغِل، بْنفْس الوَقِت بتبِّع معْهُم بْنُكْتُب واجبات المدْرسة بساعدْهُم، بعد هيْك طبْعاً نْضلُّنا شغّالين وبْنِدْرُس.

وكُلّ هدا الوَقْت، كُنْت أكون يَعْني فاتْحة اللّابْتوب، سَواء بحْضر إشي دَوْرة أَوْ بتْعلّم إشي جْديد.

أنا بحِبّ كْتير دايْماً أتْعلّم إشي جْديد، لأنّو زيّ ما اتْعلّمت إشي جْديد، بِتْوَقّف الدّنْيا يَعْني ما بقْدر أشْتِغِل.

16 I'm a homebody, or maybe it's the circumstances I live in, being a mother of four children. That made it impossible for me to go out much or commit to anything outside the home, so I exercised at home.

17 Of course, after breakfast, I'd wake my youngest daughter up, usually make her breakfast, take care of her for a while, and we'd sit and play together.

18 During that time, for example, I might be playing with her while also working on my laptop.

19 Usually, if I wasn't working on my laptop during that time, I'd be playing with her while attending an online course—of course, something related to my field of work. Despite not having access to in-person courses or training, I always looked for online options that suited me.

20 After that, I'd stay on the laptop until around Dhuhr prayer time; then, I'd prepare lunch for my daughters, who would come home from school around 2:30 or exactly at 3:00.

21 Everything in my day followed a strict schedule.

22 After that, I'd serve lunch, they'd eat, and then we'd start—me and them—the same thing. I'd have my laptop open,

23 working while helping them with their homework, supervising them, and studying together.

24 All this time, I'd still have the laptop open, either attending a course or learning something new.

25 I really love always learning something new because if I stop learning, it feels like the world stops, and I can't work.

بعد هيْك يجي وَقِت اللّيْل، عشا أعشّي البنات، أخلّيهُم أدخِّلهُم أنيّمْهُم، سَواء الصُّغار أوْ الكِبار، وترْجع على نفْس اللي هيّ أرْجع على اللّابْتوب.	**26** After that, evening would come—I'd give the girls dinner, put them to bed, whether the younger or the older ones, and then go back to my laptop.
بحِبّ أسْهر، بُرغِم مِن إنّي بصْحى بدْري.	**27** I love staying up late, despite waking up early.
يا ما كُنْت أنام كْتير، مُمْكِن أنام السّاعة ١١ باللّيْل، وبعدْها أرْجع على نفْس النِّظام والرّوتين.	**28** I wouldn't sleep much—maybe I'd go to bed at 11 p.m., and then I'd return to the same routine the next day.
عُمْري ما اتْذمّرْت مِن نِظام أوْ روتين حَياتي، نِظام وروتين حَياتي كان كْتير عاجِبْني.	**29** I never complained about my routine or my lifestyle. I really liked my routine and lifestyle.
كُنْت دايْماً أحْمِد ربّي على الرّوتين، ويمْكِن إنْتو... يمْكِن في كْتير ناس تِخْتِلف معي، بسّ أنا كُنْت كْتير بحِبّ روتيني.	**30** I always thanked God for my routine, and maybe many people would disagree with me, but I really loved my routine.
بتْمنّى بيوْم مِن الأيّام قبل ما تْخلّص هدي السّنة إن شاء الله ٢٠٢٤ ما بِتْخلّص الا والحرب مْخلّصة، وأنا راجْعة لروتيني ولبيْتي.	**31** I hope that someday, before the end of this year—God willing, before 2024 ends—the war will be over, and I'll return to my routine and my home.
كْتير اشْتقِت للرّوتين هدا، كْتير اشْتقِت أصحّي بناتي عَ المدْرسة. كْتير اشْتقْنا للبيْت.	**32** I miss that routine so much. I miss waking my daughters up for school. We miss home so much.

Vocabulary

1. routine/system[2] _____
2. forced to[14] _____
3. homebody[16] _____
4. in-person[19] _____
5. they return[20] _____

6. I follow along[23] _____
7. I complained[29] _____
8. I like it[29] _____
9. I hope[31] _____
10. I miss[32] _____

---

9 Bader's Daily Routine

Keywords

طبيعة nature   مجْموعة group   مهارة skill

Main Idea

a. Bader's strict daily routine and commitment to a fixed schedule
b. How Bader tries to break up the monotony of a normal routine
c. Bader's work in a garden and his love for planting flowers
d. Bader's love for hiking in nature, especially in the city of Hebron

True or False

1. Bader usually gets up early, around 5 o'clock in the morning.
2. Bader enjoys going on hiking trails to break his routine, particularly on weekends.
3. Bader and his sister often go on trails together for a change of scenery.
4. Bader can still go on trails and outings during the current situation in his region.
5. Bader has given up on trying to change his routine during the current war.

Multiple Choice

1. What kind of activities does Bader enjoy on weekends to break his routine?

   a. Going on trails and hikes
   b. Watching TV and relaxing
   c. Attending community meetings and social events
   d. Reading books and doing research

2. How does Bader describe the social aspect of his hiking experiences?

   a. He hikes alone to reflect on nature.

   b. He prefers not to socialize during hikes.

   c. He enjoys hiking with a group, where he makes friends and connections.

   d. He only goes hiking with his family members.

3. What other activities does Bader mention doing when he can't go hiking or on outings?

   a. He focuses on his studies and prepares for exams.

   b. He plays sports with friends.

   c. He enjoys painting and drawing.

   d. He spends time working in his garden and learning new skills on the computer.

بالْعادة	usually
بِتْصير	to, on
بِشْكِل عام	until, up to
تبعي	by means of
حالِيّاً	currently, now
حسب ما	becomes
عَ	in general
عِبارة عن	according to what
عن طريق	consists of
غيْر هيْك	when I am
لحدّ	besides that, other than that
لمّا أكون	but
ولكِن	my/mine

Text

بالنِّسْبة لِلرّوتين تبعي، بقْدر أحْكي إنّو روتين يَعْني مْنِحكي عادي، أوْ أنا بحاوِل إنّو ما أخلّيش يْكون هالرّوتين يْكون عادي.	1	Regarding my routine, I can say it's, let's say, normal—or I try not to let my routine be too normal.
لأنّو كيف يَعْني عادي؟ يَعْني إنّو روتيني لدرجة يَعْني الواحد بيصْحى مِن الصُّبح، بيجهِّز حالو للشُّغُل، بيروح مِن الشُّغُل على... يَعْني مِن البيْت على الشُّغُل، في الشُّغُل بُقْعُد فترة مُعيّنة، وبيرْجع عليْه.	2	Because how can it be normal? You know, a routine where someone wakes up in the morning, gets ready for work, goes from home to work, spends a specific amount of time at work, and then comes back home.
فا أنا يَعْني عادةً بحاوِل إنّو أكْسِر الرّوتين، بحاوِل إنّو أغيِّر الرّوتين اليَوْمي تبعي.	3	So, I usually try to break the routine; I try to change my daily routine.
فا مِن الأُمور اللي بحاوِل أغيِّرْها إنّو يَعْني أحاوِل أصْحى يَعْني طبْعاً بدْري.	4	One of the things I try to change is waking up early, of course.

بِشَكِلٍ عامّ، بَدْري عَ الفَجِر يَعْني بين السّاعة خَمْسة الصُّبُح، بحاوِل أَصْحى، بحاوِل إنّو يَعْني أَحسَّن مِن نَفْسي. طَبْعاً الواحِد بيصْحى لأنّو في... بيكون في صلاة وكذا، صلاة الفَجِر.

غير هيْك كمان بحاوِل إنّو في أيّام العُطَل الرَّسْمية، يَعْني عُطَل نهايةْ الأُسْبوع، زيّ أيّام جُمْعة وسِبْت، يَعْني بحاوِل دايْماً إنّو أُغيِّر مِن وَضْع... أُغيِّر قَعِدْتي بالبيْت.

فا شو بعْمَل؟ يَعْني كُنْت أنا دايْماً أحاوِل إنّو أسجِّل في زيّ مسارات بطْلَع مع مَجْموعة مسارات، طَبْعاً هايْكينْج، مسارات بطْلَع هان وهان مع مَجْموعة مُعيّنة نطْلَع على مسارات فلَسْطينية.

مْنوخُذ مسارات في أريحا، مسارات في مدينةْ الخَليل، مسارات في بيْت لَحِم. هاي المسارات بِتْكون في الطَّبيعة وفي الأماكِن التّاريخية.

يَعْني كمِثال، كُنّا في مسار في مدينةْ أريحا في وادي القِتّ، اللي هُوّ مسار جِدّاً طَويل.

هدا المسار عِبارة عن مسار جِدّاً جِدّاً طَويل، بيبلِّش مِن وادي القِتّ وبيمْتَد لحدّ البحر الميِّت.

بالعادة أنا وأُخْوَتي كمان نَفْس الإشي، مِنْحاوِل إنّو نْغيِّر يَعْني مِنْحاوِل نطْلَع مع بعض، مِنْغيِّر جَوّ.

فا بالتّالي كُنْت أنا دايْماً أحِبّ إنّو على الأيّام النّهايةْ الأُسْبوع إنّو أطْلَع في مسارات على... مع مَجْموعة.

وهاي المَجْموعة اللي كُنّا نطْلَع معْها كمان كُنّا نِعْمَل فيها صداقات وكذا وأصْحاب ويْصير فيها أصْحاب ومعارِف.

فا بالتّالي الأُمور بِتْصير جِدّاً أحْلى.

يَعْني الواحِد لمّا يْروح على مسار ويْقابِل مَجْموعةْ ناس جْديدة ويْشوف أصْحابو أيّام جُمْعة وكذا. طَبْعاً هاي الأصْحاب يَعْني ما بِتْشوفْها غير في المسارات، فا يَعْني بيكون دايْماً تَغْيير جَوّ.

---

5 Generally, I wake up at Fajr, around five in the morning. I try to wake up, and I try to improve myself.

6 Of course, one wakes up because of things like prayer, the Fajr prayer.

7 Besides that, I also try to make the most of official holidays, like weekends, such as Fridays and Saturdays. I always try to change my environment and avoid staying at home.

8 So, what do I do? I always try to sign up for hiking trips with a group, of course. These are hiking trails with a specific group, and we go on Palestinian trails.

9 We take trails in Jericho, trails in Hebron, and trails in Bethlehem. These trails are in nature and historical places.

10 For example, we went on a trail in Jericho in Wadi Qelt, which is a very long trail.

11 This trail is extremely long—it starts from Wadi Qelt and extends all the way to the Dead Sea.

12 My brothers and I usually do the same thing— we try to go out together and enjoy a change of scenery.

13 So, I've always loved going on trails during the weekends with a group.

14 Within this group we used to go with, we also built friendships and met new people.

15 As a result, things became much more enjoyable.

16 It's great when you go on a trail, meet a group of new people, and see your friends on Fridays and such.

17 Of course, these friends are ones you usually only see during the trails, so it's always a change of atmosphere.

18	ولكِن في الوَضِع الحالي بَعْد اللي صار حالِيّاً في الحرْب الحالية، يَعْني ما مْنِقْدر نْروح مسارات لأنّو جِدّاً الإشي مُعقّد، وما مْنِقْدر نْروح هاي الأمور.	However, in the current situation, after what happened with the current war, we can't go on trails because things are very complicated, and we can't do those activities.
19	فا يَعْني حالِيّاً دايْماً أنا بحاوِل، يَعْني حتّى لمّا أكون في البيْت، لأنّو ما بِقْدر أطْلع مسارات ولا أطْلع مثلاً طشّات، فا بحاوِل دايْماً إنّو يَعْني أغَيِّر جوّ عن طريق إنّو مثلاً أتْعلّم إشي جْديد عَ الكُمْبيوتر، أتْعلّم إشي جْديد، آخُذ شهادة جْديدة، أتْعلّم مهارة جْديدة.	So now, even though I'm at home and can't go on trails or outings, I always try to change the atmosphere by, for example, learning something new on the computer, taking a new course, getting a new certificate, or learning a new skill.
20	فا غير هيْك يَعْني ما في خيارات أُخْرى غير إنّو مثلاً كمان إنّو مِن الأشْياء اللي بحِبّ أعْملْها كمان إنّو اللي هُوَّ إنّو الحديقةْ المنْزِل الحاكورة بنسمّيها.	Beyond that, there aren't many other options. One of the things I enjoy doing is working on the garden at home, which we call the "hakoura."
21	أوْ الحاشورة حسب ما بيحْكوها أهْل القُرى اللي مِنْعيش في قُرى. بحاوِل إنّو هاي... إنّو نِزْرع... أزْرع ورِد، أزْرع كذا كذا، أزبِّط الأرض.	Or the "hashoura," as people in the villages call it. I try to plant flowers, plant other things, or fix up the land.
22	هاي الأمور جِدّاً يَعْني بِتْحاوِل الواحد إنّو يْخفِّف مِن المُعاناة اليَوْمية أوْ يَعْني نِحْكي مِن روتين اليَوْمي.	These things really help to ease the daily struggles or, let's say, break the daily routine.

Vocabulary

1. I stay/sit[2] _____
2. at dawn[6] _____
3. my sitting/staying[7] _____
4. trails/paths[8] _____
5. we take[9] _____

6. begins/starts[11] _____
7. we can/are able[18] _____
8. outings/trips[19] _____
9. reduce/ease[22] _____
10. home garden[20,21] _____

Answers

Main Idea: b **True-False:** 1. T[5] 2. T[8, 13] 3. T[12-13] 4. F[18] 5. F[19-20] **Multiple Choice:** 1. a[7-9] 2. c[14-17] 3. d[19-21]

Matching: currently, now / حالِيّاً / my/mine / تبعي / in general / بِشْكِل عام / becomes / بِتْصير / usually / بالعادة / besides غير هيْك / by means of / عن طريق / consists of / عبارة عن / to, on / عَ / according to what حسب ما / that, other than that / لحدّ / until, up to / لمّا أكون / when I am / ولكِن but **Vocabulary:** 1. بُقْعُد .2 عَ الفجِر / الحاكورة/الحاشورة .10 يْخفِّف .9 طشّات .8 مْنِقْدر .7 بيبلِّش .6 مْنوخُذ .5 مسارات .4 قعِدْتي .3

Childhood Memories

10 Najd's Childhood Memories

Keywords

ذِكْرَيات memories   البحر the beach   أهْل family

Main Idea

a. Najd describes her love for school and her academic achievements.
b. Najd shares various memories of playing with friends, her love for TV, and her family's travels.
c. Najd focuses on the challenges of growing up in Gaza and the impact of the war on her childhood.
d. Najd recalls her favorite subjects in school and how she excelled academically.

True or False

1. Najd describes her love for school and her academic achievements.
2. Najd shares various memories of playing with friends, her love for TV, and her family's travels.
3. Najd focuses on the challenges of growing up in Gaza and the impact of the war on her childhood.
4. Najd recalls her favorite subjects in school and how she excelled academically.

Multiple Choice

1. What was one of Najd's favorite childhood activities after school?

    a. Going to the library to study

    b. Recording her voice and making "radio" plays

    c. Reading books

    d. Watching TV and playing with neighborhood kids

2. What kinds of games did Najd play with her neighborhood friends?

    a. Soccer and basketball

    b. Cops and robbers, hopscotch, and "Nas w Nees"

    c. Video games and computer games

    d. Tennis and volleyball

3. Where did Najd spend some of the most enjoyable days of her childhood?

   a. At school

   c. At Sama Al-Arish, a compound in Egypt

   b. At the beach in Gaza

   d. At the zoo

Matching

أنا وإيّاها	I don't care about
الصّراحة	as if
تاني	when
زيّ ما	of course
طبْعاً	honestly
عنْجدّ	just like
عنْد ما	again
كإنّو	she and I
لغايةْ ما	really, truly
ما ليش دعْوَة	like what, as
مِثْلي متِل	until
مع بعِض	together
مع هيْك	despite that

مَرْحَبا، حابّة أَحْكيلْكُم عن ذِكْرَيات طُفولْتي.	1
	Hello, I'd like to tell you about my childhood memories.
في كْتير عِنْدي ذِكْرَيات حِلْوَة، الصَّراحة في طُفولْتي.	2
	I have many beautiful memories, honestly, from my childhood.
يَعْني كانت طُفولْتي جميلة وفيها طَبْعاً أَشْياء حِلْوَة وفيها أَشْياء مِش حِلْوَة أَكيد، مِتْلي مِتِل أيّ حدّ، بسّ فيها كمان أَشْياء حِلْوَة كْتير.	3
	My childhood was lovely, and of course, there were good things and bad things, like anyone else, but there were also many beautiful things.
يَعْني أنا كُنْت في مَدْرسة خاصّة، المَدْرسة كانت تْأَجِّز جُمْعة وسَبِت، وباقي الأَيّام الدِّراسة، تْكون فيها طَويلة مِن السّاعة تمانْيِة الصُّبح لِغايِةْ السّاعة تِنْتين.	4
	I was in a private school, and the school gave us Friday and Saturday off, and the other days were long school days from 8 a.m. to 2 p.m.
فا كُنْت كْتير أَقْعُد يَعْني فَتْرَة وَقِت في مَدْرِسْتي.	5
	So, I spent a lot of time at school.
كُنْت بسّ أَروّح مِن المَدْرسة، أَتْغَدّى، بعْد الغدا أَنْزِل عَ الشّارِع.	6
	When I'd come home from school, I'd eat lunch, and after lunch, I'd go out to the street.
ما ليش دَعْوَة في أيّا حاجة صارت في المَدْرسة، الواجْبات، أنا ما ليش دَعْوَة،	7
	I wouldn't care about anything that happened at school, or homework, I just didn't care.
أَنْزِل عَ الشّارِع، أَنْزِل أَضَلّ أَلْعَب مع وْلاد الجّيران وبنات الجّيران.	8
	I'd go out to the street and play with the neighborhood kids, both boys and girls.
نِلْعب حَجْلة، نِلْعب شُرْطة حرامي، وهُوَّ لُعْبِةْ مُطارَدة.	9
	We'd play hopscotch, cops and robbers, which is a chasing game.
كُنّك... و"ناس ونيس" أَوْ "ناس ونوس" حسب كُلّ حدا ما بعْرِف شو عمر بيسمّيها.	10
	And there's another game, "Nas w Nees" or "Nas w Noos," depending on what people call it.
كُنّا كْتير نِنْبِسِط.	11
	We had so much fun.
يَعْني كان في عِنّا إحْنا في البيْت، في عِنّا الطّابِق الأَرْضي، عِبارة عن حاصِل فاضي، فا كُنّا نْروح عليْه أنا ووْلاد الجّيران وبنات الجّيران وأخويا، عِنْدي أَخّ تَوْأَم، ونُقْعُد نِلْعب هْناك.	12
	At home, we had the ground floor, which was an empty storage space, so I'd go there with the neighborhood kids, both boys and girls, and my brother—I have a twin brother—and we'd play there.
"ناس ونيس" إنّو نِعْمِل كإنّو إحْنا قرايِب ونِزور بعض.	13
	"Nas w Nees" was like pretending we were relatives visiting each other.
كانت الأمانة يَعْني ذِكْرَيات جِدّاً رائِعة.	14
	Honestly, those were really wonderful memories.

وبعِد ما أخلِّص ألعب، يَعْني كانت يْأذِّن علَيْنا المغرِب، وأنا لِسّا بلعب، كُنْت أحِبّ اللُّعب كْتير الصّراحة.	15	After playing, when the evening prayer call came, I'd still be playing. I really loved playing, honestly.
بسّ مع هيْك كُنْت شاطْرة بمَدْرستي.	16	But even so, I was good at school.
بعْد ما كُنْت ألعب، كُنْت أطْلع فوق على الدّار وأشوف أَيْش عليّا واجبات مدرسية، أكْتُب الواجِب وبعِدْها أقْعُد عَ التِّلْفِزْيوْن.	17	After playing, I'd go upstairs at home, check what homework I had, do it, and then watch TV.
أنا كُنْت أحِبّ التِّلْفِزْيوْن جدّاً، كُنْت عاشقة لكُلّ أنْواع الرُّسوم أَيْش في رُسوم بْيجي عَ سْبيْستون، عَ MBC3، على آرْتيْنْز، آرْتيْنْز قناة قديمة.	18	I really loved TV. I was obsessed with all kinds of cartoons—whatever came on Spacetoon, MBC3, or ART Teenz. ART Teenz was an old channel.
على... بعد هيْك في صار نيكَلوْدْيوْن، أضلّ أحْضر لغايِةْ ما تْصير السّاعة ١٢ في اللّيْل وبعِدْها أنام، علشان طبْعاً تاني يوْم أرْجع تاني أروح عَ المدْرسة.	19	Later, Nickelodeon came along, and I'd watch until midnight, then go to sleep, of course, because the next day, I had to go back to school.
صراحة كُنْت أنام شْوَيّة في المدْرسة، وهاي مِن أكْتر الذّكْريات اللي مِتْذكِّراها، إنّو أنا كُنْت أنام كْتير شْوَيّ في المدْرسة،	20	Honestly, I'd sleep a bit at school, and that's one of the memories I remember most—I'd sleep a lot at school.
بسّ كُنْت شطّورة، يَعْني كُنْت مِن الأوائِل الحمْدُ لله.	21	But I was still a good student; I was one of the top students, thank God.
لكِن يَعْني اللُّعب كان ماخِد برْضو حيِّز كْبير في حَياتي.	22	But playing also took up a big part of my life.
وفي كمان مِن الذِّكْريات اللي أنا بتْذكِّرْها إنّو في إجازِةْ الصّيْف سافرْنا أنا وأهْلي عَ الأُرْدُن، وقعدْنا هناك يَعْني شهْرين، لأنّو أُخْتي كانت بدّها تتْجوّز.	23	Another memory I have is that during the summer vacation, my family and I traveled to Jordan and stayed there for two months because my sister was getting married.
فا قعدْنا هناك شهْرين، وعِنْد ما إجيْنا بدّنا نِرْجع، معْبر غزّة سكّر، وبالتّالي اتْحاصرْنا بالعْريش، اللي هيَّ منْطقة في مصر.	24	We stayed there for two months, and when we wanted to return, the Gaza crossing was closed, so we got stuck in Arish, which is a city in Egypt.
وهناك أنا عِشِت أحْلى ٢١ يوْم في حَياتي.	25	Those were the best 21 days of my life.
يَعْني اتْحاصرْنا ٢١ يوْم، المعْبر ظلّو مْسكّر ٢١ يوْم، فا أنا هِناك ضلّيْت ٢١ يوْم، بسّ يَعْني انْبسطِت جدّاً.	26	We were stuck for 21 days because the crossing stayed closed for 21 days, so I stayed there for 21 days, but honestly, I had a great time.
بابا، الله يِرْحمُه، أخذْنا على كُلّ مكان حِلو، كُنّا كُلّ أُسْبوع نُقْعُد في فُنْدُق شِكِل.	27	My dad, may he rest in peace, took us everywhere nice. Every week we'd stay in a different hotel.

كُلّ ٣-٤ تِيّام مرّات نُقْعُد في فُنْدُق تاني، رُحْنا عَ البحر، بحر العريش بيجنِّن، كْتير كان رائع.

Every three or four days, we'd switch to another hotel. We went to the beach—the Arish beach is amazing; it was really wonderful. **28**

رُحْنا على مطاعِم، رُحْنا على فنادِق كْتير ضَخْمة.

We went to restaurants and many big hotels. **29**

في مِنْطِقة هناك إسمْها سما العريش، هدا المكان يَعْني فيه عِبارة عن كومْباوْنْد. قعدْنا فيه هناك يِمْكِن خمس تِيّام، برْضو كانوا مِن أَحْلى أَيّام حَياتي.

There's a place there called "Sama Al-Arish." It's like a compound. We stayed there for maybe five days, and those were also some of the best days of my life. **30**

كُنّا نِصْحى الصُّبْح، نِنْزِل تحْت، عَ بوفيْه مفْتوح نِفْطر، كانت ذِكْرَيات عنْجدّ بِتْجنِّن.

We'd wake up in the morning, go downstairs to an open buffet, and have breakfast. Those were truly amazing memories. **31**

وكان فيّو مِنْطِقة للبِسْكِليْتات، نُقْعُد نْسوق البِسْكِليْتات نِتْجوّل في المكان.

There was also a biking area, and we'd ride bikes and explore the place. **32**

وفيه مناطِق سْباحة، حتّى بْتذكّر إنّو كان عِنْدهُم شرْط إنّو ممْنوع إلّا لازِم بْمايو، وأنا يَعْني ما كان عِنْدي مايو وكُنْت صْغيرة، فا ضلّيْتْني أسْتنّى لغايَة لمّا بِنِت مِن البنات اللي بيِسْبحوا وخلّصوا ورضيْت إنْها تعْطيني المايو تبعْها.

There were swimming areas too. I even remember they had a rule that swimsuits were mandatory. I didn't have a swimsuit, and I was little, so I waited until a girl who had been swimming finished and was willing to lend me hers. **33**

أخذِت المايو ونْزلْت سبحِت، وقعدْت أتْعلّم السِّباحة هناك، وطبْعاً ما عْرِفْتش الصَّراحة وغْرِقِت بسّ مِشي الحال يَعْني المُهِمّ إنّو أنا سبحِت يَعْني،

I took the swimsuit, went swimming, and started learning to swim there. Honestly, I didn't really learn, and I almost drowned, but it was fine—the important thing was that I swam. **34**

وعْمِلْنا هِناك كْتير أشْياء أكلْنا سمك، أكلْنا فْطير مُشلْتِت.

We did so many things there. We ate fish and meshaltet (layered pastry). **35**

كانت ذِكْرَيات عنْجدّ بِتْجنِّن في سما العريش.

The memories at Sama Al-Arish were truly amazing. **36**

بعْد ٢١ يوْم طبْعاً روّحْنا... روّحْنا تعْبانين جِدّاً، لأنّو في هديك الفترة ما في مِنْطِقة إلّا طْلِعْنا ورُحْنا وشُفْنا وجرّبْنا كُلّ حاجة، وكُلّ أَهْل مصِر هناك عِرْفوني.

After 21 days, we went back home... we went back completely exhausted because, during that time, we went to every place, saw everything, tried everything, and everyone in Egypt got to know me. **37**

كُلّهُم كانوا بيعْرِفوا "نجْد، نجْد، نجْد، نجْد"، الحمْدُ لله.

Everyone knew "Najd, Najd, Najd, Najd," thank God. **38**

والمُهِمّ بعْد ما روّحْنا يَعْني رْجِعْنا تاني طبْعاً للمُدْرسة ورْجعت تاني الحَياة المدْرسية.

Anyway, after we went back, I returned to school life, of course. **39**

كُنْت هِناك كُنْت في فترِةْ المدْرسة يَعْني لمّا يْكون في إجازة، إجازِةْ جُمْعة وسِبت، لأنّو أنا زيّ ما قُلْتِلْكوا مدْرسة خاصّة، فا كان عِنْدي يومَيْن إجازة.	40	During school time, when there was a weekend, Friday and Saturday, because as I said, I was in a private school, I had two days off.
أروح أبات عِنْد قريبة إلي إسمْها نور، كُنْت كْتير أنْبِسِط معْها.	41	I'd go stay over at a relative's house—her name was Noor. I had so much fun with her.
نِلْعب برْضو ألْعاب غريبة ألْعاب جْديدة. يَعْني الحمْدُ لله.	42	We'd play weird games, new games. Thank God.
بتْذكّر بمرّة أنا وإيّاها رُحْنا عَ البحر، برْضو عِنّا بحر في غزّة.	43	I remember once she and I went to the beach—we also have a beach in Gaza.
رُحْنا عَ البحر، وإشترِيْنا أنا وإيّاها نفْس الطقّية، وقعدْنا نِلْعب هْناك بالكْورة، وسبحْنا مع بعْض، وأكلْنا، جِبْنا شاوَرْما.	44	We went to the beach, bought matching caps, played ball there, swam together, and ate. We got shawarma.
أكلْنا شاوَرْما، وكانت عنْجدّ أيّام جِدّاً حِلْوة، وطُفولة كانت، الحمْدُ لله، جِدّاً جميلة.	45	We ate shawarma, and honestly, those were really beautiful days. My childhood, thank God, was truly wonderful.

Vocabulary

1. I don't care[7] _____
2. we have fun[11] _____
3. empty space[12] _____
4. clever/smart[21] _____
5. we got stranded[24] _____

6. amazing/awesome[28] _____
7. we walk around[32] _____
8. we went home[37] _____
9. I sleep over[41] _____
10. hat[44] _____

Answers

Main Idea: b **True-False:** 1. T[4] 2. T[16,21] 3. T[27] 4. F[34] 5. F[45] **Multiple Choice:** 1. d[6-9,18-19] 2. b[9-10] 3. c[30-36]

Matching: عنْجدّ / of course طبْعاً / like what, as زيّ ما / again تاني / honestly الصّراحة / she and I أنا وإيّاها / really, truly / just like مِثْلي مِتِل / I don't care about ما ليش دعْوَة / until لغايِة ما / as if كإنّو / when عِنْد ما / despite that مع هيْك **Vocabulary:** 1. ما ليش دعْوَة 2. نِنْبِسِط 3. حاصِل 4. شطّورة 5. اتْحاصرْنا 6. بيجنّن 7. نِتْجوّل 8. روّحْنا 9. أبات 10. طقّية / together مع بعْض

11 Bader's Childhood Memories

Keywords

كَنيسِة القِيامة Church of the Holy Sepulchre   القُدْس Jerusalem   حَواجِز checkpoints

Main Idea

a. Bader's favorite childhood activities include going to church with his family every week.
b. Bader's experience being detained at a military checkpoint when he was ten years old.
c. Bader's visit to Jerusalem and the impact of living under occupation during his childhood.
d. His memories of his family moving from a bustling neighborhood in Jerusalem to the village where he currently lives.

True or False

1. Bader lived in a village with many settlements during his childhood.
2. Bader describes his childhood, overall, as traumatic and stressful.
3. Bader has fond memories of visiting the Church of the Holy Sepulchre in Jerusalem with his family.
4. Bader describes the city of Jerusalem as a place full of history and memories.
5. Bader mentions that he wishes he could go back and relive his childhood.

Multiple Choice

1. How does Bader describe his childhood in general?

   a. As a calm period, despite the presence of the occupation

   b. As a time filled with constant wars and conflict

   c. As an uneventful time in a very peaceful village

   d. As a time when he traveled frequently

2. What does Bader mention about the situation in Jerusalem for Palestinians?

   a. It was a simple and peaceful place to visit.

   b. The presence of military checkpoints and soldiers made it a complicated and tense place.

   c. Palestinians were allowed to move freely without restrictions.

   d. There were no security issues or checkpoints in Jerusalem at the time.

3. What negative experience does Bader recall from his visit to Jerusalem?

    a. He got lost in the city.

    b. The soldiers stopped him for no reason.

    c. The presence of soldiers and military checkpoints made him feel restricted.

    d. He was unable to visit the church due to security issues.

Matching

بِالآخِر	from this
بِالزّبْط	from the time when
بِالْغلط	in the end
بِالنِّسْبة لإِلي	by mistake
برْضو	other/another
بْشكِل عامّ	possibly you
تاني	exactly
خلص	already
عَ كُلّ حال	not supposed to
على الأَقلّ	at least
على هيْك	like this, in this way
لِحدّ ما	anyway, in any case
مِش مفْروض	from the age of
مُمْكِن إِنّك	wherever
مِن عُمْر	until
مِن هاي	also, as well
مِن يوْمر ما	in general
ويْن ما	for me

بِالنِّسْبة لفترْة الطُّفولة بشوفْها، أَوْ يَعْني حسب ما بْتذكّرها، بْشكِل عامّ يَعْني على هيْك على بْشكِل عام مِن عُمْر الـ... خلّينا نِحْكي مِن يوْم ما وْعيت زيّ ما مْنِحْكيها لحدّ ما يَعْني فترْة المُراهقة.

1 Regarding my childhood, I see it—or as far as I can remember it, generally speaking—from the age of... let's say from the time I became aware, as we say, until my teenage years.

بقْدر أَحْكي إنّها هاي فترْة كانت جِدّاً حِلْوَة يَعْني بِالنِّسْبة لإلي كان يَعْني كان الوَضِع شوَيّ... ما في خلّينا نِحْكي حُروب كْتيرة.

2 I can say that this period was very beautiful for me. It was... the situation was somewhat... there weren't, let's say, a lot of wars.

مع إنّو في اِحْتلال دايْماً مَوْجود، لكِن كانت فترْة يَعْني فيها شوَيّة هيْك هُدوء، وأنا كمان بعيش في قرْية برْضو ما فيها كْتير مُسْتوْطنات.

3 Although there was always an occupation present, it was a period with some calm, and I also lived in a village that didn't have many settlements.

يَعْني هاد الـ... لمّا الواحد يْكون وهُوَّ صْغير خلص دايْماً بُرْبِط المَوْضوع في البلد نفْسو اللي عايِش فيها، لأنّو خلص بِالآخِر إحْنا يَعْني عايْشين تحت اِحْتلال قائِم.

4 When someone is young, they always connect things to the town itself where they live, because in the end, we are living under ongoing occupation.

عَ كُلّ حال، بْشكِل عام الفترْة الطُّفولة كانت جِدّاً حِلْوَة.

5 In any case, generally speaking, my childhood was very beautiful.

بتْذكّر إنّو مِن يَعْني ذكْرى مِن هاي الفترْة إنّو رِحْت على كنيسةِ القيامة مع أهْلي ومع إخْوِتي.

6 I remember one memory from that period when I went to the Church of the Holy Sepulchre with my family and my siblings.

كانت كنيسة في القُدْس، هاي مَوْجودة جِدّاً جميلة، كنيسة قديمة جِدّاً، وكان فيها تاريخ يَعْني عريق جِدّاً.

7 It was a church in Jerusalem, a very beautiful place, a very old church with a deeply rich history.

لمّا تُدْخُل فيها بتْحِسّ إنّو جدّ في فيها تاريخ، وفيها هيْك شُعور آخر.

8 When you enter it, you feel like it truly holds history, and it gives you a different kind of feeling.

بِالزّبْط يَعْني لمّا تُدْخُل على القُدْس، على مدينةِ القُدْس إنْتا بتْحِسّ حالك في مكان آخر، يَعْني بتْحِسّ حالك في مكان تاني بتْحِسّ حالك في مكان تاريخي، مكان كُلّو ذكْرَيات كُلّو ناس كانوا عايْشين فيه.

9 Exactly, when you enter Jerusalem, the city of Jerusalem, you feel like you're in a different place. You feel like you're in another world, in a historical place, a place filled with memories and the lives of people who once lived there.

عَ كُلّ حال، بسّ الإشي اللي بتْذكّرو إنّو كُلّو كان تجْرِبة حِلْوة هاي لمّا رحْت عَ كنيسة القيامة، لكن التّجْرِبة السّيّئة إنّو كانت كُلّها حَواجِز، كان كُلّها في جُنود معْهُم أسْلِحة.

10 In any case, what I remember is that the whole experience was wonderful when I went to the Church of the Holy Sepulchre. But the bad part of the experience was that it was full of checkpoints, and there were soldiers everywhere with weapons.

وكانوا بيطّلّعوا عليْك ويْن ما بِتْروح ويْن ما بْتيجي.

11 They would watch you wherever you went and wherever you came from.

ممْنوع تْروح مكان إنْتَ ما يَعْني إنْتَ ما مفْروض تْروح عليْه.

12 You weren't allowed to go to places you weren't supposed to.

إذا رحْت عَ مكان إنْتَ مِش مفْروض تْروح عليْه مثلاً، دخلْت حارة بالْغلط، حارة ثانْية بالْغلط، مُمْكِن إنْتَ يَعْني يعْتِقْلوك ويْودّوك عَ مكان ثاني، أوْ إنّو عَ الأقلّ يُقُعْدوا يِسْألوا فيك ويحْكولك ليْش رُحْت هُناك، وليْش رُحْت هُناك.

13 If you went to a place you weren't supposed to, for example, if you accidentally entered the wrong neighborhood, you could be detained and taken somewhere else, or at the very least, they would stop you, question you, and ask why you went there and why you were in that area.

يَعْني دايْماً الوَضِع في مدينةِ القُدْس مُخْتلِف، ودايْماً الوَضِع في مدينةِ القُدْس مُعقّد بالنِّسْبة للفلسْطينِيّين.

14 The situation in Jerusalem is always different, and the situation in Jerusalem is always complicated for Palestinians.

Vocabulary

1. we say it[1] _____
2. complete/total[4] _____
3. ancient/deep-rooted[7] _____
4. they look/watch[11] _____
5. by mistake[13] _____

6. neighborhood[13] _____
7. arrest you[13] _____
8. they sit/keep[13] _____
9. take you[13] _____
10. complicated[14] _____

_____

Answers

Main Idea: c **True-False:** 1. F[3] 2. F[5] 3. T[6-7] 4. T[9] 5. F[5] **Multiple Choice:** 1. a[2-3] 2. b[10-14] 3. c[10-13] **Matching:** بِشكِل عامّ / in general / بالآخِر in the end / بالزِّبْط exactly / بالْغلط by mistake / بالنِّسْبة لإلي for me / برْضو also, as well / على الأقلّ at least / عَ كُلّ حال anyway, in any case / خلص already / تاني other/another / in general / مِن عُمْر possibly you / مُمْكِن إنّك not supposed to / مِش مفْروض / لحدّ ما until / هيْك like this, in this way / ويْن ما wherever / from the time when مِن يوْم ما / from this مِن هاي / from the age of

Vocabulary: 1. مِنْحْكيها / 2. تامّ / 3. عريق / 4. بيطّلّعوا على / 5. بالْغلط / 6. حارة / 7. يِعْتِقْلوك / 8. يُقُعْدوا / 9. يُوَدّوك / 10. مُعقّد

12 Nihad's Childhood Memories

حطب firewood   شِعِر poetry   لمّة gathering

Main Idea

a. Nihad's memories of family gatherings and her village's close-knit community.
b. The challenges of growing up without electricity in a small village.
c. Nihad's education and her experiences at school in her village.
d. How modern life has improved communication in her village.

True or False

1. Nihad's family and neighbors would gather around a fire in the courtyard during cold, dry winter nights.
2. Nihad recalls that the courtyard gatherings often included people from other villages.
3. Nihad and her family used to stay up until midnight during their gatherings, even though electricity was cut off at 10:00 p.m.
4. Nihad mentions that she often sees all of her family and neighbors during the holidays.
5. Nihad says that times have changed, and she may not recognize some of her neighbors anymore.

Multiple Choice

1. How was electricity distributed in Nihad's village during her childhood?

   a. The electricity was on during the day and off at night.

   b. Every house had electricity all the time.

   c. Only the wealthiest families had electricity.

   d. Electricity was distributed in shifts to prevent overloading the generator.

2. Why does Nihad say it was difficult to get certain snacks like sunflower seeds during her childhood?

   a. Her family couldn't afford them.

   b. They weren't available in her village.

   c. Sunflower seeds didn't grow in her village.

   d. There were food shortages at that time.

3. What game did Nihad's family play during their gatherings that she still uses with her own children?

   a. A board game about Palestine   c. A trivia game about history

   b. A storytelling game   d. A poetry game where the last letter of a verse determines the next verse

Matching

إنّو	how many
بالدّوْر	like these days
حتّى	that (conjunction)
خلص	in those days
زيّ هاي الأيّام	finished, done
على هديك الأيّام	even
فا	in turn
كم	how rare
مِن بيْن	among
مِن... لـ	from... to
ويْن وويْن	so, therefore

Text

مِن ذِكْرَيات الطُّفولةِ، بتْذكّر كانت في أيّامِ أواخِر الثّمانينات أوّل التّسعين. يَعْني أنا كُنت ١٠ سْنين ٩ سْنين.	1	From my childhood memories, I remember the late 1980s and early 1990s. I was around 9 or 10 years old.
هيْك إشي طبْعاً إحْنا في بلدْنا، يَعْني الكوْم، صْغيرة يَعْني على هديك الأيّام، ما كان في عدد ناس وبْيوت وناس كْتير وهيْك يَعْني، كان لِسّا يمْكِن أبو ٥٠٠ نسمِة هيْك إشي يَعْني في كُلّ البلد.	2	Back then, in our village, which was small at the time, in Al-Kom, there weren't many people, houses, or families—maybe about 500 people in the whole village.
ما في دور كْتير، في عنّا مدْرسِة واحْدة كانت.	3	There weren't many houses, and we had only one school.
فا أنا بتْذكّر إنّو حتّى ما كان عنّا كهْربا قُطْرية.	4	I remember we didn't have a national electricity grid.

كان في مُخْتارْنا، مُخْتار البلد، كان جايب متور كْبير وشابِك كُلّ البْيوت شابِكْها للْكَهْربا يَعْني.

بَسّ يْوَزِّع مثلاً أوّل البلد، إلْهُم دوْر في اللّيل، يَعْني عَ السّاعة عشرة تِطْفي عَ الكُلّ.

طَبْعاً العشرة هاي... إحْنا يَعْني كإنّا سهْرانين كْتير، السّاعة عشرة صارت.

فا هاي السّاعة عشرة كانت مَوْعِد عَ الكُلّ: تِطْفي مثلاً أوّل البلد، يَعْطيهُم ساعْتيْن، يطْفي علَيْنا، يَعْطي عَ الوُسْط البلد، يطْفي علَيْهُم.

وطَبْعاً بالدّوْر عَ الآخِر البلد، إنّو عَ أساس ما يْصير ضغِط على المتور.

فا في هاي الفترات، إحْنا فترِةْ الشّتَويّة، وتْكون الجّوّ هيْك بارِد، ما في مطر، طَبْعاً أيّام المطر ما نِطْلع أكيد يَعْني،

بَسّ كُنّا أنا وإخْوْتي وعمْتي (عِنْدي عمّة أصْغَر واحْدِة في عمّاتي هيِّ) كُنّا نْجيب الحطب ونْجيب الكانون في الحوْش، هيْك نُقْعُد حَوالين النّار.

طَبْعاً الحوْش يَعْني هُوّ مساحة كْبيرة بيْن كُلّ بْيوت بيْتْنا، دارْنا ودار جدّتي ودار... ودور عْمامي.

نُقْعُد فيها، نُقْعُد في هاي المِنْطِقة، نْجيب الحطب ونْولِّع النّار، نْجيب تسالي، بِزِر المَوْجود.

طَبْعاً ما كان مُتَوَفِّر بِكثْرة زَيّ هاي الأيّام، يَعْني إذا بِدّنا نِشْتِري مِنْروح على مِنْطِقة ثانْية نْجيب هاي الأغْراض.

طَبْعاً السّهْرة إحْنا عنّا خلص، عشرة يَعْني نُصّ اللّيْل، لازِم الكُلّ يْقوم.

اتْبَلِّش يَعْني قبل أذان المغْرِب نْكون نْجَهِّزْلْها، نْصلّي المغْرِب ونْروح نُقْعُد معاهُم.

---

5 The village elder, our mukhtar, had brought a large generator and connected all the houses to it.

6 He would distribute electricity in turns. For example, the houses at the beginning of the village would have electricity for a few hours at night, and at 10 p.m., it would be turned off for everyone.

7 Back then, 10 p.m. felt like staying up very late for us.

8 At 10 p.m., the electricity for one part of the village would go off, and the next area would get electricity for two hours, then it would move on to the middle of the village, and so on, to avoid overloading the generator.

9 Eventually, the last part of the village would get its turn.

10 During the winter, when it was cold and not raining, we would go outside. Of course, on rainy days, we'd stay indoors.

11 But on other days, my siblings, my youngest aunt, and I would gather firewood and bring the brazier to the courtyard, where we'd sit around the fire.

12 The courtyard was a large, shared space between our house, my grandmother's house, and my uncles' houses.

13 We'd sit there, light a fire, and bring snacks—usually sunflower seeds, whatever was available.

14 Back then, such things weren't readily available like they are now. If we wanted to buy snacks, we had to go to another area to get them.

15 For us, staying up until 10 p.m. felt like staying up until midnight, and we'd all have to go to bed.

16 Before the evening prayer, we'd prepare everything, pray, and then go sit together.

أنا صحّ صْغيرِة بسّ كُنْت برْضو أشارِكْهُم يَعْني. | 17 | Even though I was young, I would still join in.

فا مِن بين هاي القعْدات لازِم إنّو الأكْبر مِنّا يِعْمِلوا زيّ مُسابِقة حزازير، ألْغاز وهيْك. | 18 | During these gatherings, the older ones among us would organize riddles and puzzles.

اللمّة نِحْكي قِصص، يِحْكوا إشي بخُصّ مثلاً في إثْراء معْرِفي إلْنا كُلّنا. | 19 | We'd share stories, and they'd tell us things to enrich our knowledge.

طبْعاً أنا أصْغر إشي بْإخْوِتي، الأكْبر مِنّي شْوَيّ يَعْني بيننا سنة سنتيْن، كُلّ واحِد والثّاني. | 20 | I was the youngest among my siblings, and the age difference between us was only a year or two at most.

بسّ إنّو صحّ صْغار، بسّ فهْمانين على عْمامي وعلى أبوي وأمّي، فهْمانين عليْهُم شو بيحْكوا، ومِنْشارِكْهُم، هُمّ بيشجّعونا يَعْني بْهاي القعْدات. | 21 | Even though we were young, we understood our uncles, aunts, and parents, participated in the discussions, and they encouraged us during these gatherings.

فا كان في أكْثر إشي مُسابِقة للْيوْم أنا بسْتخْدِمْها مع وْلادي، اللي هِيّ الشّعِر. | 22 | One of the activities that I still use with my kids today was a poetry competition.

إنّو إنْتَ تِحْكي بيْت شِعِر، وآخِر القافْية، آخِر حرْف في البيْت، لازِم اللي قُدّامك يَعْني إنْتَ بْحرف النّون لازِم واحِد مِن المَوْجودين يِحْكيلك بيْت شِعِر بيِبْدأ بْحرْف النّون. انْتهى بالْميم، لازِم الثّاني يْجيب بالْميم. | 23 | Someone would recite a line of poetry, and the last letter of the line would determine the first letter of the next person's line. For example, if the last letter was "n," the next person would start their line with "n." If it ended with "m," the next person would start with "m."

هاي الشّغْلات صحّ إنّها إلْها زمن، راحت. | 24 | These things, though they belong to the past, are gone now.

وكُلّ واحِد فينا اتْجوّز وأسّس عيْلة، وكُلّ واحِد في مكان. | 25 | Each of us got married, started families, and went our separate ways.

كُلّنا في نفس البلد يَعْني، أنا وإخْوِتي في نفس البلد وعْمامي في نفس البلد، بسّ وين ووين لمّا نِجْتمِع. | 26 | We all still live in the same village—my siblings and uncles—but it's rare for us to gather together.

يَعْني مُمْكِن بالْأعْياد حتّى مِش الكُلّ. | 27 | Maybe during holidays, but even then, not everyone comes.

ما بِتْشوف الكُلّ في العيد، يَعْني كُلّها كم دْقيقة وبيروحوا. | 28 | You hardly see everyone during Eid—it's just a few minutes together before they leave.

بسّ بيظلّ في حنين لهاي الأيّام. | 29 | But there's always nostalgia for those days.

فا هاي الأيّام، ما في، مُمْكِن يْمُرّ عنّي حدا ما أعِرْفو، وهُوّ يْكون جارْنا. | 30 | Nowadays, I might pass by someone I don't even recognize, and they could be my neighbor.

تْغَيّرت الأحْوال، كُلّ واحِد عايِش حَياتو وما بْيِعْرِف عن الثّاني إشي. | 31 | Times have changed. Everyone lives their own life and knows nothing about the other.

1. generator[5] _____
2. village elder/chief[5] _____
3. courtyard[11] _____
4. our house[12] _____
5. snacks[13] _____

6. gatherings[18] _____
7. riddles[18] _____
8. rhyme[23] _____
9. nostalgia[29] _____
10. passes by[30] _____

Answers

Main Idea: a **True-False:** 1. T[10-13] 2. F[11-13] 3. F[15] 4. F[26-28] 5. T[30] **Multiple Choice:** 1. c[6-9] 2. b[14] 3. d[22-23] **Matching:** إنّو that (conjunction) / بالدّوْر in turn / حتّى even / خلص finished, done / زيّ هاي الأيّام like these days / على هديك الأيّام in those days / فا so, therefore / كم how many / مِن بيْن among / لـ ...مِن from... to / ويْن وويْن how rare **Vocabulary:** 1. متور / 2. مُخْتار / 3. الحوْش / 4. دارْنا / 5. تسالي / 6. جعْدات / 7. حزازير / 8. القافْية / 9. حنين / 10. يمُرّ

Vacations

13 Suheil's Vacation

Keywords

تطوُّع volunteering   تقاليد traditions

Main Idea

a. Suheil tells us about their experiences traveling around Germany and how they shaped his career.
b. Suheil takes a life-changing trip to Spain, Morocco, and later India.
c. Suheil shares his dream itinerary for an upcoming trip around Asia.
d. Suheil tells us about a family trip to Thailand when he was a child.

True or False

1. Suheil's life-changing trip took place between semesters while he was studying in Germany.
2. Suheil's travels took him to Spain, Morocco, and then to several countries in South America.
3. Suheil became well-known for his travel experiences and now shares travel advice with others.
4. Suheil traveled with a large group of friends during his eight-month trip to India and Southeast Asia.
5. Suheil's trip made him realize his passion for traveling and inspired him to share his experiences online.

Multiple Choice

1. Which of the following activities did Suheil do during his travels?

   a. He volunteered in the desert with the Amazigh people in Morocco.

   b. He worked full-time as a tour guide.

   c. He spent his time alone, visiting tourist attractions.

   d. He focused on learning new languages.

2. How did Suheil manage to travel without spending a lot of money?

   a. He stayed in youth hostels or camped.

   b. He volunteered, stayed with local families, and hitchhiked.

   c. He worked as an air courier to get discounted flights.

   d. He received sponsorships for his travels.

3. What did Suheil discover about himself during his travels?

   a. He prefers to travel in groups rather than alone.

   b. He learned to rely on himself and be spontaneous during his trips.

   c. He enjoys planning everything in advance to avoid surprises.

   d. He decided to stop traveling after his first trip.

Matching

بِدّيش	since
بَرْضو	completely
بعِدْني	spontaneous
بما إنّو	from here
عَ الآخِر	from the perspective of
عفَوي	also, as well
عنْجدّ	still am
لحالي	in return for
ما كانْش	after that
مُقابِل	by myself
مِن بعْدْها	wasn't
مِن ناحْيَة	I don't want
مِن هون	that is, I mean
مِن وَقْتْها	from that time
يَعْني	really, truly

بِدّي أَحْكي عن العُطْلة تاعْتي اللي غيّرت حَياتي.	1 I want to talk about the trip that changed my life.
أنا بسّ كُنْت أتْعلّم بألْمانْيا، أخذِت قرار إنّو بِدّي أطْلع مِشْوار بين السِّمِسْتر والسِّمِسْتر، فا حجزِت تذْكرة طَيَران لإسْبانْيا والمغْرب.	2 When I was studying in Germany, I decided to take a trip between semesters, so I booked a flight ticket to Spain and Morocco.
ومِن وَقْتها قرّرِت إنّي بِدّي أكمّل أسافِر وبِدّيش أتْعلّم.	3 From that point, I decided I wanted to keep traveling and didn't want to continue studying.
فا أنا خِلال هدا المِشْوار كُنْت أنام بْهوسْتيلات، واتْعرّفِت على ملْان أصْدِقاء من كُلّ العالم، وعْمِلِت ملْان تجارِب، مِثْل التّطوُّع. اتْطوّعِت بالصَّحْرا مع الأمازيغ في المغْرب.	4 During that trip, I stayed in hostels, met many friends from all over the world, and had many experiences, like volunteering. I volunteered in the desert with the Amazigh people in Morocco.
كانت تجْرِبة كْتير حِلْوة.	5 It was a really beautiful experience.
وكمان اتْعلّمِت كيف أعْتمِد على حالي لأنّو كُنْت أسافِر لحالي، كيف أدبّر حالي بْلُغات بعْرِفْهاش.	6 I also learned how to rely on myself because I was traveling alone and had to manage with languages I didn't know.
كُلّو هدا، وعْمِلِت صْحاب جْداد طبْعاً، وطُرُق لأنّو الواحد يْسافِر بْتكاليف أقلّ.	7 All of this, plus making new friends, and finding ways to travel on a lower budget.
بما إنّو كُنْت بعْدني شبّ، فا كمّلِت أسافِر، وصُرْت أنام عِنْد عائِلات، وصاروا أصدِقائي يْعزْموني عِنْدهِن.	8 Since I was still young, I kept traveling and started staying with families, and my friends would invite me to their homes.
أروح، فا مِن المغْرب طْلِعِت على إيطالْيا وكمّلِت كمان مِشْوار كامِل بأوروبّا كُلّو، تطوّع، وإنّو أنام عِنْد ناس وأصْدِقاء.	9 I'd visit them, and from Morocco, I went to Italy and continued traveling all over Europe, volunteering and staying with people and friends.
ومِن بعْدْها، صُرْت حدا معْروف إنّو بيسافِر كْتير وهيْك، فا حمّلِت حالي.	10 After that, I became known as someone who travels a lot, so I packed my things.
ورُحِت كمان مِشْوار طَويل تمن أشْهُر على الهِنْد وجنوب شرْق آسْيا وغيْرو من الدُّوَل.	11 I also went on a long trip for eight months to India, Southeast Asia, and other countries.
ووقْتها برْضو نفْس الإشي، كُنْت أنعْزِم على أعْراس كمان.	12 During that time, the same thing happened—I even got invited to weddings.
صُرْت كْتير أسافِر بِطريقة اللي أكون بالشّعِب، يَعْني مِش آخُد فُنْدُق وأظلّ بالأوتيل يَعْني لحالي، بسّ أزور المحلّات السِّياحِية.	13 I started traveling in a way that immersed me in the local culture. I didn't just stay in hotels or by myself, only visiting tourist spots.

لا صِرْت أنام بالْقُرى ويْن النّاس بيعيشوا، يَعْني صِرْت ألاقي تطْبيقات اللي النّاس تِعْزِمْني عِنْدها.	**14** No, I started staying in villages where people live, using apps to find people who would host me.
مِن ناحْيَة إنّي أوْ إنّي أتْطوّع عِنْدها بمزرعة أوْ إنّو أساعِدْهِن بْشُغُل بيْت أوْ هيْك أشْياء، ومُقابِل إنّو يَعطوني أكِل ومحلّ أنام يَعْني فا...	**15** Sometimes, I'd volunteer on farms or help people with housework in exchange for food and a place to sleep.
هاي كْتير فوّتتْني على القُرى والحَياة اليَوْمية تاعِت النّاس، لأنّي كُنْت أنا عايِش كَواحِد مِن الشّعْب، يَعْني عمليّاً.	**16** This got me into villages and into the daily lives of people because I was living as one of them, practically speaking.
فا جرّبِت إنّي أعيش مع كْتير شُعوب، واتْعرّفِت على كْتير عادات وتقاليد، وعْمِلِت كْتير أصْدِقاء.	**17** I experienced living with many different cultures, learned about many customs and traditions, and made many friends.
ومِشْوار الهِنْد كمان فُتِت على محلّات اللي حسّيت حالي رْجِعِت كْتير بالزّمن لوَرا.	**18** In India, I also visited places that felt like stepping back in time.
كمان الْتقيت بْصبية اللي كْتير بحِبّها أنا، عمِلْنا مِشْوار كْتير حِلو مع بعْض، وكان كْتير حِلو عن جدّ.	**19** I also met a girl I really loved. We traveled together and had a very beautiful experience.
فا هاي كان كْتير إشي حِلو صار معي خِلال السّفر، وكمّلْنا بْجنوب شرْق آسْيا: تايلانْد، لاوْس، كَمْبوْدْيا، وفيِتْنام.	**20** That was something amazing that happened to me during my travels, and we continued through Southeast Asia: Thailand, Laos, Cambodia, and Vietnam.
كان مِشْوار كْتير كْتير حِلو.	**21** It was an absolutely wonderful trip.
كُنّا نِسْتأجِر مطورات ونِطْلع عليْهِن أيّامات بالجْبال، وكمان أنْواع أكِل جرّبِت كْتير.	**22** We'd rent scooters and spend days riding in the mountains, and I tried many kinds of food.
فا كان كْتير عنْجدّ كْتير مُفيد إلي كمان إنّي أعْتِمد على حالي.	**23** It was really very beneficial for me to learn to rely on myself.
ما كُنْتِش أتْمأّت يَعْني ويْن بدّي أنام اللّيْلة. كان كُلّ إشي عفَوي جدّاً جدّاً جدّاً.	**24** I didn't complain about where I would sleep at night—everything was very spontaneous.
يَعْني ألْتقي بْشخْص بالشّارِع، يْقولْلي: "تيجي تْنام عِنْدي اليوْم"، أقولْلو "يلّا".	**25** I'd meet someone on the street, and they'd say, "Why don't you stay at my place tonight?" I'd say, "Sure."
كمان أسُبوعين، يِبْعتْني عِنْد إبِن عمّو بْبلد تانْية، يْلفْلفْني بالْبلد، يْعرّفْني على الحارة عِنْدو، يْذوّقْني أكلاتْهِن الشّعْبِية، وهيْك.	**26** Then, two weeks later, they'd send me to their cousin in another town, where they'd show me around, introduce me to their neighborhood, and let me try their traditional foods.
فا مِن هون عنْجدّ، يَعْني، صُرْت كْتير أحِبّ السّفر.	**27** From that, I truly started to love traveling.

كمان كُنْت أعْمل هايكينْج، آخُد تريمْبات مع ناس، فا مِن هون كمان ما كانْش كْتير يُكلّفْني.	28	I also did hitchhiking, taking rides with people, so it didn't cost me much.
وهيْك واليوْم يَعْني حتّى مدينةْ النّاصْرة وفلسْطين ملان ناس صارت تِعْرِفْني إنّي بسافِر وملان ناس بْتوخِد مِنّي نصائح وهيْك.	29	Now, even in Nazareth and Palestine, so many people know me as a traveler, and many ask me for advice.
كمان عْمِلِت فيدْيوهات عن السّفر عَ التّيكْتوك واليوتْيوب وإنْستاغْرام فا كْتير بحِبّ السّفر،	30	I've also made travel videos on TikTok, YouTube, and Instagram, and I really love traveling.
ويَعْني هاي السّفْرة اللي بعْد التّعْليم غيّرت حَياتي عَ الآخِر.	31	This trip after studying completely changed my life.

Vocabulary

1. I don't want[3] _____
2. I don't know it[6] _____
3. they invite me[8] _____
4. I went back[18] _____
5. motorbikes[22] _____

6. spontaneous[24] _____
7. lets me taste[26] _____
8. shows me around[26] _____
9. takes[29] _____
10. completely[31] _____

Answers

Main Idea: b **True-False:** 1. T[2] 2. F[20] 3. T[29-30] 4. F[6, 24] 5. T[27, 29-30] **Multiple Choice:** 1. a[4] 2. b[7-8, 14-15, 28]

3. b[6, 23-24] **Matching:** بدّيش I don't want / برْضو also, as well / بعِدْني still am / بِما إنّو since / عَ الآخِر

completely / عفْوي spontaneous / عنْجدّ really, truly / لحالي by myself / ما كانْش wasn't / مُقابِل in return

for / من بعْدْها after that / من ناحْيَة from the perspective of / من هون from here / من وَقْتْها from that time

/ يَعْني that is, I mean **Vocabulary:** 1. بدّيش / 2. بعْرِفْهاش / 3. يْعِزْموني / 4. رْجِعِت / 5. مطورات / 6. عفْوي /

7. يْذوّقْني / 8. يْلفْلِفْني / 9. بْتوخِد / 10. عَ الآخِر

Keywords

القُدْس Jerusalem   البحر the sea

Main Idea

a. Nihad's emotional and spiritual experiences visiting holy sites in Jerusalem.
b. The beauty of the cities of Akka, Haifa, and Jaffa.
c. A funny story about the first time Nihad and her family visited Jerusalem.
d. The differences between various historical sites in Palestine.

True or False

1. Nihad visited Akka, Haifa, and Jaffa for the first time in 1999 before the second intifada began.
2. Nihad mentions that the Dome of the Rock and the Al-Aqsa Mosque are part of the same structure.
3. Nihad describes her second visit to Al-Aqsa in 2018 as feeling just like her first visit.
4. Nihad says it is currently easy to visit Al-Aqsa Mosque and its courtyards.
5. Nihad expresses a deep longing to visit Al-Aqsa again, even just to stand in its outer courtyards.

Multiple Choice

1. What did Nihad do when she entered the courtyards of Al-Aqsa Mosque?

    a. She started taking photos with her family.

    b. She experienced a deep sense of spirituality and reverence.

    c. She called her mother to tell her where she was.

    d. She was overwhelmed and fainted.

2. When did Nihad return to Al-Aqsa after her first visit in 1999?

    a. She never returned after her first visit.

    b. She returned the following year in 2000.

    c. She visited again in 2018 during Ramadan.

    d. She returned in 2022 with her whole family.

3. How does Nihad describe her connection to Al-Aqsa and the Dome of the Rock?

   a. As a simple feeling of curiosity

   b. As an experience she doesn't fully remember

   c. As an event she prefers not to think about

   d. As something beyond words, connected to the soul

Matching

بالأجْواء	if it were
بالنِّسْبة إلي	once again
حتّى لَوْ	because
شو ما	something like that
عشان	in the atmosphere
كإنّك	until today
كمان مرّة	no matter what
لأنّو	for a long time
لحالْها	or
للْيوْم	by itself
لَوْ كان	as if you
ما إلو	for me
مِش عارِف	in order to
مِن زمان	don't know
هيْك إشي	even if
ولّا	doesn't have

<table>
<tr>
<td>مِن أَجْمَل الأَماكِن اللي رُحْت إلْها، رُحْت على الدّاخِل الفلسطيني: عكّا، وحَيْفا، ويافا. رُحْنا عَ القُدْس كمان.</td>
<td>1</td>
<td>One of the most beautiful places I've visited is the Palestinian interior: Akka, Haifa, and Jaffa. We also went to Jerusalem.</td>
</tr>
<tr>
<td>الشُّعور لمّا تْشوف البحر لأوّل مرّة بْحَياتك وتْكون يَعْني إنْتَ لِسّا في مرْحلِة إنّو إنْتَ ١٧-١٨ سنِة، هيْك إشي يَعْني.</td>
<td>2</td>
<td>The feeling of seeing the sea for the first time in your life, especially when you're around 17 or 18 years old, is unforgettable.</td>
</tr>
<tr>
<td>أنا في الـ٩٩-ألفيْن رُحِت، لِسّا ما كانت مْبلْشِة الانْتِفاضة الثّانْية.</td>
<td>3</td>
<td>I visited in 1999–2000, just before the Second Intifada started.</td>
</tr>
<tr>
<td>فا كان الشُّعور إنّو هيْك، إنْتَ بِدّك تْفوت لعُمْق البحر، بِدّك تْحِسّ بالأَجْواء، بِدّك تْعيش لميّنا الصّدف عن الشّط. وكان يَعْني شُعور بيجنِّن.</td>
<td>4</td>
<td>The feeling was incredible. You just want to dive into the depth of the sea, feel the atmosphere, and live the moment. We collected seashells on the shore—it was an amazing experience.</td>
</tr>
<tr>
<td>أنا وإخْوِتي وأُمّي وأبوي، بعْدها حكالْنا أبوي إنّو بِدْنا نْروح على الأَقْصى.</td>
<td>5</td>
<td>My parents, my siblings, and I stood there, and then my father said we should go to Al-Aqsa Mosque.</td>
</tr>
<tr>
<td>طبْعاً لمّا تْفوت إنْتَ ساحات الأَقْصى، سُبْحان الله، شُعور لا يوصف.</td>
<td>6</td>
<td>When you enter the courtyards of Al-Aqsa, subhanAllah, it's an indescribable feeling.</td>
</tr>
<tr>
<td>شُعور كإنّك إنْتَ فايِت على هيْك هالِة مِن الرّوحانية، هالِة مِن الخُشوع.</td>
<td>7</td>
<td>It's like stepping into a spiritual aura, a space of reverence.</td>
</tr>
<tr>
<td>مِش عارِف إنْتَ تْدمّع وَلّا تِضْحك وَلّا تُسْجُد وَلّا تِنْبِسِط.</td>
<td>8</td>
<td>You don't know whether to cry, laugh, bow in prayer, or just feel joy.</td>
</tr>
<tr>
<td>وَلّا... يَعْني قُبّةْ الصّخْرة لحالْها، تمازُج الأَلْوان اللي فيها، هَيْبِتْها، جمالْها، لمْعِةْ القُبّة.</td>
<td>9</td>
<td>And then there's the Dome of the Rock—the blend of colors, its majesty, its beauty, the shine of the dome.</td>
</tr>
<tr>
<td>طبْعاً القُبّة مُخْتلفِة تماماً عن المسْجِد.</td>
<td>10</td>
<td>Of course, the dome is completely separate from the mosque.</td>
</tr>
<tr>
<td>المسْجِد لحال مسْجِد الأَقْصى لحال والقُبّة لحال، قُبّةْ الصّخْرة.</td>
<td>11</td>
<td>Al-Aqsa Mosque is one thing, and the Dome of the Rock is another.</td>
</tr>
<tr>
<td>فا يَعْني وْقِفِت هيْك عَ البَوّابة، بِدّك تِطْلع الدّرجات عشان تْشوف قُبّةْ الصّخْرة نفْسْها.</td>
<td>12</td>
<td>I stood at the entrance, wanting to climb the steps to see the Dome of the Rock itself.</td>
</tr>
<tr>
<td>هيْك مِش عارِف، مِخْتارة، مبْسوطة، يَعْني مِشْواري.</td>
<td>13</td>
<td>I felt overwhelmed—excited and happy—just unsure how to process the experience.</td>
</tr>
<tr>
<td>الأَوّلاني حِلو في عكّا ويافا وهيْك، بسّ شُعور مُخْتلِف تماماً.</td>
<td>14</td>
<td>My first trip to Akka and Jaffa was beautiful, but this was a completely different feeling.</td>
</tr>
</table>

إنّو إنْتَ نِفْسك تْروح تُحْضُنْها.	15	You feel like you want to embrace it.
فا كان شُعور إنّو يا اللّه، ليْه مِن زمان أنا ما إجيت؟ ليْه ما كانوش ياخْذونا؟ وسُبْحان اللّه، كان الإشي رهيب جِدّاً، وإلْها هيْبِتْها، إلْها مكانة.	16	I kept thinking, why haven't I come here before? Why didn't they bring us earlier? SubhanAllah, it was an incredible experience—it holds so much majesty and significance.
لليوْم نِفْسي أرْجع أزورها.	17	To this day, I long to visit again.
أنا زُرْتْها كمان مرّة في الـ٢٠١٨، في كانت رمضان، ورُحِت مع دار أخوي، مع مرْت أخوي ووْلادْهُم.	18	I visited again in 2018 during Ramadan with my brother's family—his wife and kids.
كان يَعْني، إنّو هيْك كُلّ مرّة بِتْروحْها كأنْها أوّل مرّة.	19	Every time you go, it feels like the first time.
شُعور بيجنِّن، شُعور للْيوْم شو ما أحْكي عنّو، لأنّو هُوّ مُتّصِل بالرّوح فا ما بْتِقْدر توْصِفو.	20	The feeling is indescribable—it's connected to your soul, and words can't capture it.
لوْ كان شُعور مثلاً بِيشْبه الأكل، بْتِحْكي طعْمو كذا، بسّ هُوّ هيْك شُعور ما إلو وَصِف، ما إلو أيّ تشْبيه.	21	If it were like food, you could describe its taste, but this feeling has no description or comparison.
فا إن شاء اللّه إنّو نِرْجع نْصلّي بِالأقْصى كمان مرّة، نْزور.	22	InshaAllah, we'll return to pray at Al-Aqsa again and visit.
يَعْني حتّى لوْ نْكون في السّاحات الخارِجية، هاي حِلِم بالنِّسْبة إلي إنّي أرْجع أشوفو.	23	Even being in the outer courtyards would be a dream for me—to see it again.
الأيّام هاي مُسْتحيلِة تماماً.	24	These days, it feels completely impossible.

Vocabulary

1. you enter[4] _____
2. he told us[5] _____
3. aura/atmosphere[7] _____
4. blending[9] _____
5. grandeur/majesty[9] _____

6. confused[13] _____
7. amazing/awesome[16] _____
8. I wish/long[17] _____
9. comparison[21] _____
10. impossible[24] _____

_____

Answers

Main Idea: a **True-False:** 1. T[2-3] 2. F[10-11] 3. T[19] 4. F[24] 5. T[22-23] **Multiple Choice:** 1. b[6-8] 2. c[18] 3. d[20-21]

Matching: عشان / no matter what شو ما / even if حتّى لوْ / for me بالنِّسْبة إلي / in the atmosphere بالأجْواء / لوْ / until today للْيوْم / by itself لحالْها / because لأنّو / once again كمان مرّة / as if you كإنّك / in order to / something هيْك إشي / for a long time مِن زمان / don't know مِش عارِف / doesn't have ما إلو / if it were لوْ كان / like that وَلّا or **Vocabulary:** 1. تْفوت 2. حكالْنا 3. هالة 4. تمازُج 5. هَيْبِة 6. مِحْتارة 7. رهيب 8. نِفْسي / 9. تشْبيه 10. مُسْتحيلِة

15 Khaled's Vacation

Keywords

مشاوي barbecue   البحر الأبْيَض المتُوسِّط The Mediterranean Sea

Main Idea

a. Khaled describes a trip to Alexandria, Egypt with his family when he was young.
b. Khaled talks about his dream vacation rather than one he's already been on.
c. Khaled recounts a memorable day spent with friends enjoying food, games, and relaxation.
d. Khaled shares his love for card games and how they are a big part of his outings with friends.

True or False

1. Khaled and his friends always have grilled food for breakfast when they go to the sea.
2. Khaled prefers to swim after lunch rather than before.
3. Khaled describes the dessert after lunch as kunafa made Nablus-style over charcoal.
4. Khaled prefers sitting and talking with friends rather than playing games or swimming after their afternoon nap.
5. After dinner, everyone leaves the chalet and goes home.

Multiple Choice

1. What kind of food do Khaled and his friends typically prepare for lunch during their outings?

    a. Sandwiches   b. Grilled food   c. Pizza   d. *None of the above*

2. What is one of the activities Khaled and his friends do in the afternoon after their nap?

    a. Swimming   c. Playing football or volleyball

    b. Fishing   d. *All of the above*

3. What do Khaled and his friends do at the end of the day?

    a. They clean up and leave right away.

    b. They set the date for their next outing.

    c. They have a barbecue by the sea.

    d. They play more football and volleyball.

إن كانت	from above
بِالْعادة	before... by
بِالْغالِب	after
بِتْظلّها	remains, stays
بعد ما	like that
بعْديها	usually
بْنِظلّنا	we keep on
زيّ كِدا	until when
سَواء كان	wherever
قبِل... بـ	if it was
لازِم	must, have to
لعنْد ما	mostly
مِن بينْ	from among
مِن فوْق	wherever we came
وينْ ما	whether it was
وينْ ما إجينا	after it
وينْ ما رُحْنا	wherever we went

الآن، بدّي أتْكلّم عن آخِر رِحْلة مِنْسمّيها "طشّة"
طْلِعْناها مع بعْض أنا وصْحابي.

آخِر واحْدة كانت مِن تقْريباً سنة، قبل الحرْب بْشهِر
تقْريباً.

بالْعادة إحْنا بِنْروح على البحر، لأنّو المُتنفّس
الوحيد لسُكّان قِطاع غزّة هُوَّ البحر الأبْيض
المُتوسِّط.

بيكون مْجهّز قريب منُّه مجْموعة مِن الشّالِيْهات،
هيَّ الأماكِن اللي بِتْكون فيها بِرْكِة سْباحة وغُرْف
بسيطة مِسْتأجرة يوْم كامِل، بْيِبْدأ من صباح هدا
اليوْم لصباح اليوْم اللي بعْدُه.

كان بْيِبْدأ اليوْم بْفقْرِة الْفطور.

الْفطور بالْعادة المشْهور عنّا هُوَّ الفول والفلافِل
والحُمّص والبصل والمُقبّلات التّانْية مِتِل الفِجِل
والجرْجير، ولازِم معْها كُبّايِة الشّاي.

بعْد هيْك، بْنِنْزِل نِسْبح بْساعْتيْن تلاتة، وهدي
السّباحة بِتْخلّي بعْض الألْعاب بالْكورة مثلاً أوْ
الغطِس أوْ غيْرُها.

بعْد هيْك، بْنِطْلع مِنترّيّح شْوَيّة ونِبْدأ نْحضّر للْغدا.

الغدا بالْغالِب بيكون مشاوي.

بِنْقسِّم حالْنا مجْموعات وفِرق، مجْموعة بِتْجهِّز
الكانون، اللي هُوَّ عِبارة عن إشي معْدني مُسْتطيل
الشّكِل، مِنِشْوي عليْه.

مجْموعة بِتْجهِّز الأشْياء اللي حَ نِشْويها، إن كانت
فْراخ مثلاً، شيش طاووق أوْ صْدور فْراخ أوْ جناحين
فْراخ، أوْ غيْرُها أوْ اللّحْمة.

بِنْجهِّز العرايِس، اللي هيَّ سانْدويشات كُفْتة أوْ
الكباب، اللي هيَّ أصابيع اللّحْمة المشْوية.

بعْد هيْك، تيجي مجْموعة اللي بِتْشغِّل الكانون
وبِتوقِّف للشْوْي.

---

1 Now, I want to talk about the last trip—or as we call it, "Tashsheh"—that I went on with my friends.

2 The last one was about a year ago, approximately a month before the war.

3 Usually, we go to the sea because the only escape for the residents of the Gaza Strip is the Mediterranean Sea.

4 Nearby, there are areas prepared with a group of chalets—these are places that have swimming pools and simple rooms rented for a full day, starting from the morning of that day until the morning of the next day.

5 The day would start with breakfast.

6 Breakfast usually consists of our famous dishes: fūl (fava beans), falafel, hummus, onions, and other appetizers like radishes and arugula, and, of course, a cup of tea.

7 After that, we'd go swimming for two to three hours. This swimming includes some games like ball games or diving or others.

8 After that, we'd come out, rest a bit, and start preparing for lunch.

9 Lunch is usually barbecued food.

10 We divide ourselves into groups and teams: one group prepares the "kanoun," which is a rectangular metal grill we use for barbecuing.

11 Another group prepares the items to be grilled, whether it's chicken, shish tawook, chicken breasts, chicken wings, or other things like meat.

12 We prepare "arayes," which are sandwiches filled with kofta or kebabs, which are grilled meat fingers.

13 After that, another group lights the grill and starts the barbecuing.

وبْتِسْتَنّى الاكِل لعِنْد ما يِسْتِوي ويتْطلّعو بعْد ما يِسْتِوي وأهمّ مجْموعة اللي هيّ مجْموعة تجْهيز السّفْرة، اللي بْيِفْردوا الشّراشِف، وبيحُطّوا الصّحون والكُبّايات والمُقبّلات وغيرْها.

14

They wait for the food to be ready, and once it's cooked, the most important group—the group that sets the table—spreads the tablecloths, arranges the plates, cups, and appetizers, and other things.

بعِد ما يِسْتِوي الأكِل ويِنْحط عَ السّفْرة، نبْدأ ناكُل ونِشْرب، مع الأكِل العصير، سَواء كان عصير جاهِز أوْ عصير فرْشٍ.

15

Once the food is ready and placed on the table, we start eating and drinking juice, whether it's store-bought or fresh juice.

بعِد مرْحلِةْ الغدا، بنِبْدأ نجهّز لمرْحلِةْ الحِلْويّات، اللي بالْغالِب بِتْكون كُنافة نابُلْسية على الفحْم.

16

After the lunch phase, we start preparing for dessert, which is usually kunafa Nabulsiya cooked over charcoal.

بِتْكون الكُنافة مِن فوْق، وتحْتيها جِبْنة عكّاوي.

17

The kunafa is layered with a top crust and Akkawi cheese underneath.

بعِد هيْك، بْناكُل الكُنافة مع فِنْجان القهْوَة السّادة.

18

After that, we eat the kunafa with a cup of black coffee.

بعْديها، بْتيجي مرْحلِةْ القيْلولة.

19

Then comes the nap phase.

بْناخُذ قيْلولة بسيطة.

20

We take a short nap.

بعِد هيْك بْنِصْحى، بنِبْدأ نعْمل بعض الفعاليّات زيّ ألْعاب الشّدّة والشّطرنْج أوْ غيرْها.

21

After that, we wake up and start doing some activities like card games or chess or other games.

المجْموعة ما بِتْحُبّ الألْعاب بْترْجع تِسْبح.

22

The group that doesn't like games goes back to swimming.

وأنا مِن بينْ المجْموعة التّالْتة اللي بِتْحُبّ تِحْكي وتِتْحدّث بْتِحْكي قصصْها وحَوادِيثْها ومُغامراتْها ومشاكِلْها.

23

I'm part of the third group that likes to sit and talk, sharing stories, adventures, and problems.

بِنْحاوِل نْشوف حُلول لمشاكِل بعِض.

24

We try to find solutions to each other's problems.

وبْنِظلّنا نعْمل زيّ كِدا لعِنْد ما يِجي فقْرةْ المسا، بِنْجيب الكوْرة ومِنْصير نِلْعب كُرِةْ قدم أوْ كُرِةْ طائِرة حسب الإشي المُتَوَفّر في الشّاليه.

25

We continue like this until the evening comes. We grab a ball and start playing either soccer or volleyball, depending on what's available at the chalet.

بعْد هيْك، بيكون الواحد رِجِع يْجوع بِنْجهّز للْعشا وبْنِتْعشّى مع بعِض.

26

After that, hunger returns, and we start preparing dinner and eat together.

وبعِد هيْك، في ناس بِتْروح تْروِّح على بْيوتْها، وفي ناس بِتْبات الفِكْرة في الشّاليه.

27

After that, some people go home, and some stay overnight at the chalet.

اللي هُوَّ بيكون خُروج وهُروب مِن الضّغْط اللي بيكون في مكان العمل.

28

This is considered a getaway and escape from the stress of work.

بْنُقْعُد مع بعِض بْنِتعرّف على بعِض أكْتر، ونِصْنع فيه ذِكْرَيات حِلْوَة، وهدي الذِّكْرَيات بِتْظلّها معْنا العُمُر كُلّو بِتْظلّها معْنا وِيْن ما رُحْنا وِيْن ما إجينا.	29	We sit together, get to know each other better, and create beautiful memories—memories that stay with us for a lifetime, wherever we go, wherever we are.
وبِنْحدِّد مَوْعِد الطّلْعة القادِمة في نِهايةْ هدا اليوْمر.	30	And at the end of this day, we set the date for the next outing.

Vocabulary

1. trip/outing[1] _____
2. chalets[4] _____
3. grill[10] _____
4. meat sandwiches[12] _____
5. dining spread/table[14] _____

6. tablecloths[14] _____
7. appetizers[14] _____
8. afternoon nap[19] _____
9. chess[21] _____
10. goes home[27] _____

Answers

Main Idea: c **True-False:** 1. F[6] 2. F[7-8] 3. T[16-18] 4. T[23] 5. F[27] **Multiple Choice:** 1. b[10-12] 2. d[21-25] 3. b[30]

Matching: إن كانت if it was / بالْعادة usually / بالْغالِب mostly / بِتْظلّها remains, stays / بعِد ما after / بعْديها after it / بْنِظلّنا we keep on / زيّ كِدا like that / سَواء كان whether it was / بـ... قبِل before... by / لازِم must, have to / لعِنْد ما until when / مِن بِين from among / مِن فوْق from above / وِيْن ما wherever / وِيْن ما إجينا wherever we came / وِيْن ما رُحْنا wherever we went **Vocabulary:** 1. طشّة / 2. شاليْهات / 3. كانون / 4. عرايِس / 5. السُّفْرة / 6. شراشِف / 7. مُقبِّلات / 8. القَيْلولة / 9. شِّطرنْج / 10. تْروّح

Hobbies

16 Najd's Hobby

Keywords

هِوايَة hobby   رَسْم drawing

Main Idea

a. Najd's love for various talents like drawing, karate, and swimming.
b. Najd's struggles in school and how she overcame them through drawing and music.
c. Najd's achievements as a professional karate athlete and artist.
d. Najd's passion for voiceover work and how it relates to her artistic talents.

True or False

1. Najd wanted to pursue karate as a child because she was inspired by cartoons on Spacetoon.
2. Najd had formal training in drawing from a young age.
3. Najd had to stop practicing karate after reaching the green belt due to COVID-19.
4. The only hobby Najd could easily practice in Gaza without limitations was swimming.
5. Najd stopped drawing because she didn't enjoy it anymore.

Multiple Choice

1. What was one of the main obstacles Najd faced in pursuing her hobbies?

   a. Lack of interest

   b. The blockade in Gaza made it difficult to practice certain hobbies

   c. Her studies took up too much time

   d. She had too many hobbies and couldn't focus on one

2. Which hobby did Najd eventually improve after almost finishing school?

   a. Karate and other martial arts   c. Music, especially playing the piano

   b. Drawing, particularly portraiture   d. Table tennis

3. What talent did Najd mention wanting to develop but had limited access to resources for in Gaza?

   a. Music   b. Singing   c. Drawing   d. Swimming

بْإنّو	I don't have
بالنِّسْبة إلي	at least
بالنِّهايَة	that (because)
بِسبب	because of
تاعْتي	in the future
حتّى لَوْ	oh Lord
عَ الأقلّ	like what
عَ طول	without
لقُدّام	since I was
للأسَف	mine/my
لهيْك	in the end
ما عِنْديش	unfortunately
مِتِل ما	therefore, so
مِن الأوّل	because of how much
مِن غيْر	immediately
مِن كُتْر ما	for me
مِن وأنا	even if
يا ربّ	from the beginning

Text

أنا يَعْني عِنْدي أكْتر مِن مَوْهِبة، الصّراحة، وأنا مِن النّوْع اللي بيحِبّ يَعْني كْتير أشْياء.	1	I have more than one talent, honestly, and I'm the type of person who likes a lot of things.
ما عِنْديش بسّ إنّو حاجْتيْن وأركِّز عليْهُم، لأ، بحِبّ إنّي أدْخُل في أكْتر مِن شغْلة.	2	I'm not the kind who only has one or two things to focus on—I like getting involved in many different things.
بسّ أكْتر حاجتيْن أنا كُنْت كْتير حابّة إنّو أطوّرْهُم هُوّ حُبّي للرسِم وحُبّي للفُنون القِتالية.	3	But the two things I was most passionate about developing were my love for drawing and my love for martial arts.

أنا يَعْني مِن وأنا صْغيرة كان نِفْسي أدْخُل في الكاراتيه، بالذّات الكاراتيه، لأنّو كُنْت أتْفرّج عَ الرُّسوم المتَحرّكة على سْبيسْتون. كانوا دايماً يجيبوا عن الكاراتيه ورْسومات عن الكاراتيه، فا كُنْت كْتير حابّة إنّو أدْخُل الكاراتيه.

Since I was young, I always wanted to do karate, especially karate, because I used to watch cartoons on Spacetoon. They always showed karate and drawings about karate, so I really wanted to do karate.

4

وحتّى لَوْ إنّي كُنْت في غير غزّة المُحاصرة، كان يِمْكِن دخلْت الأوْلُمْبياد في الكاراتيه مِن كُتْر ما بحِبُّه.

Even if I weren't living in besieged Gaza, I might have made it to the Olympics in karate because of how much I love it.

5

لكِن لِلأسف ما اتْحقّقت أُمْنيتي مِن وأنا طِفْلة إنّي أدْخُل كاراتيه، لهيْك ركّزْت أكْتر على مَوْهِبْتي التّانْية اللي هيَّ الرّسِم.

But unfortunately, my childhood dream of doing karate didn't come true, so I focused more on my other talent, which is drawing.

6

أنا كُنْت إنّو أيّ حاجة أشوفْها بقْدر أرْسُمْها، سَواء على شنْطة على دفْتر، أيّ رِسْمة أشوفْها وتعْجِبْني، خلص، أنا هادي الرّسْمة حابّاها أرْسُمْها.

I used to be able to draw anything I saw—on a bag, a notebook—anything I liked, I'd want to draw it.

7

وهدا الإشي كان عِنْدي مَوْهِبة يَعْني أنا ما عُمْريش في حَياتي اتْدرّبِت على الرّسِم، لا.

This was a talent I had—I had never trained in drawing in my life.

8

أوّل إشي أشوفُه عَ طول أرْسِمُه.

The first thing I saw, I'd immediately draw it.

9

وحبّيت برْضو إنّي أنا أطوّر مِن مَوْهِبِة الرّسِم تاعْتي.

And I wanted to develop my drawing talent too.

10

بسّ لِلأسف برْضو، لأنّو أنا مِن غزّة، كان الإشي صعْب.

But unfortunately, since I'm from Gaza, it was difficult.

11

ويَعْني مَوْهِبِة الرّسِم بِدّها وَقِت، وأنا كُنْت أكْتر بركِّز على دِراسْتي، لأنّو الواحد طبْعاً لازِم يْركِّز على دِراسْتُه في أوّل حَياتُه.

Drawing requires time, and I was more focused on my studies because, of course, you need to focus on your education early in life.

12

ولما كْبِرِت، بدّيت إنّي أرْجع تاني أطوّر مَواهْبي.

When I grew up, I started returning to develop my talents again.

13

كُنْت حابّة طبْعاً كمان مِن مَواهْبي اللي أنا كُنْت حابّاها الموسيقى، كُنْت كْتير حابّة إنّي أتْعلّم على أيّ آلة، بسّ برْضو هاي الدّورات عنّا جدّاً قليلة.

One of the talents I loved was music. I really wanted to learn an instrument, but courses here are very limited.

14

وكُنْت حابّة كمان إنّو أتْعلّم تِنس الطّاوْلة، جدّاً بعْشق تِنس الطّاوْلة.

I also wanted to learn table tennis—I absolutely adore table tennis.

15

وكانوا إخوتي دايماً يِلْعبوا تِنس طاوْلة مع بعْض. كان في عِنّا تحِت مكان فيّو طاوْلةِ تِنِس، وكانوا هُمّا دايماً يِلْعبوا وهيْك.

16 My brothers would always play table tennis together. We had a table downstairs, and they'd always play there.

بسّ برْضو هُمّ يَعْني إنّهُم شباب بيقْدروا يِلْعبوا كْتير، لكِن أنا لأنّو بِنت ما بقْدر إنّي أنْزِل وألْعب وهيْك.

17 But since I'm a girl, I couldn't just go down and play like they did.

بسّ كُنْت كْتير حابّة إنّو أنا أطوّر حالي حتّى في تِنِس الطّاوْلة، وبرْضو أدْخُل فيها أولُمْبياد.

18 Still, I really wanted to improve at table tennis and even participate in the Olympics.

بحِبّ السّباحة جِدّاً جِدّاً جِدّاً، أنا بعْشق السّباحة.

19 I absolutely, absolutely love swimming. I adore swimming.

عِنْدي مَواهِب كْتير الحمْدُ لله، بسّ للأسف بطبيعةِ المدينة اللي أنا عايْشة فيها والحِصار، الإشي هادا كان صعْب إنّك إنْتَ تَمارِس أيّا هِوايَة.

20 I have many talents, thank God, but because of the nature of the city I live in and the siege, it was hard to practice any hobbies.

الهِوايَة الوَحيدة اللي كان أنا قادِرة إنّي أنا أمارِسْها مِن غيْر أيّا مشاكِل هِيَّ الرّسِم.

21 The only hobby I could practice without issues was drawing.

فا لمّا كْبِرت وخلّصِت تقْريباً يَعْني مِن المدْرسة، قرّرِت إنّي أنا أطوّر حالي بالرّسِم.

22 So, when I finished school, I decided to improve my drawing skills.

الحمْدُ لله، اتْعلّمِت البوْرْتْرِيه، لأنّو ما كان كافي بالنِّسْبة إلي إنّي أنا بسّ أشوف أيّا إشي وألْقُطو.

23 Thank God, I learned portrait drawing because just drawing whatever I saw wasn't enough for me.

كُنْت حابّة إنّي أرْسُم وُجوه النّاس وملامِحْها.

24 I wanted to draw people's faces and features.

اتْعلّمِت البوْرْتْرِيه، اللي هُوَ رسِم الوُجوه، وأوّل رسْمة لإلي، ما حد صدّق إنّو هاي أوّل رسْمة لإلي، لأنّو بالنِّهايَة هدي مَوْهِبة كانت عِنْدي مِن الأوّل.

25 I learned portrait drawing, which is drawing faces, and my first portrait—no one believed it was my first because, in the end, it's a talent I had from the start.

وقعدِت فتْرة أرْسُم، لكِن بِسبب شُغْلي في التّعْليق الصّوْتي وشُغْلي في الهِنْدسة المدنية كمان، اضطرّيْت إنّو أبْعد عن الرّسِم، لأنّو الرّسِم بْياخُد وَقِت.

26 I spent a while drawing, but because of my work in voiceover and civil engineering, I had to step away from drawing because it takes time.

بالنِّهايَة، والكاراتيْه برْضو أنا طوّرِت حالي فيها.

27 In the end, I also improved in karate.

دخلِت كاراتيْه بسّ خلّصِت الجّامعة، اتْخرّجِت مِن الجّامعة بديْت آخُذ دَوْرات في الكاراتيْه.

28 I joined karate after finishing university. After graduating, I started taking karate courses.

ووَصِلِت للحِزام الأخضَر، وللأسَف ما كمّلِت بِسبب الكورونا، لأنّو صار الحجِر الصّحّي، ومِتِل ما بتعْرفوا وَقّف كُلّ إشي وَقْتها.	**29** I reached the green belt, but unfortunately, I couldn't continue because of COVID. When the lockdown happened, everything stopped.
وقعدِت في البِيت سِتّ شْهور، تقْريباً سِتّ شْهور حجِر صِحّي، يَعْني ما في أيّا مجال لْتْمارِس أيّا هِوايَة خارجية.	**30** I stayed home for about six months, roughly six months of lockdown, with no way to practice any outdoor hobbies.
لكِن إنْبسطِت، وكُنْت كْتير مبْسوطة يَعْني، بْإنّو ع الأقَلّ وْصِلِت للحِزام الأخضَر وصار عِنْدي فِكْرة كْتير كْبيرة عن كاراتيه.	**31** But I was happy, really happy, that at least I reached the green belt and gained a lot of knowledge about karate.
وإن شاء الله يا ربّ، هيْك لقُدّام، نِرْجع تاني ونْكمّل، نْمارِس هِواياتْنا، وغَزّة تْصير أحْسن مِن الأوّل، ونْطوّر كُلّ حاجة.	**32** God willing, moving forward, we'll return, continue, and practice our hobbies, and Gaza will become better than before, and we'll develop everything.
شُكراً كْتير إلك.	**33** Thank you so much.

Vocabulary

1. I trained[8] _____
2. I'm passionate about[15] _____
3. they can/are able[17] _____
4. portrait[23] _____
5. features[24] _____

6. takes[26] _____
7. quarantine[29] _____
8. becomes[32] _____
9. we develop[32] _____
10. we continue[32] _____

_____

17 Alaa's Hobby

Keywords

القِراءة reading   روايات novels   الهُدوء calm

Main Idea

a. How Alaa became a professional translator through her love of books.
b. How Alaa's reading interests shifted from Egyptian novels to history books and Agatha Christie.
c. Alaa's experiences reading about UFOs and mysterious phenomena.
d. How reading opened a window to the outside world, enriching her knowledge and imagination.

True or False

1. Alaa began reading for pleasure when she was around 10 years old.
2. Alaa's favorite novels to read as a child were small Lebanese pocket novels.
3. Alaa typically only reads Arabic books, focusing on topics related to the Arab world.
4. Alaa became most interested in reading about mysteries and phenomena like the Bermuda Triangle when she was an adult.
5. Reading played a significant role in enriching Alaa's vocabulary and improving her ability to express herself.

Multiple Choice

1. What is true about the Egyptian pocket novels that Alaa would read?

   a. They were the only type of books readily available in Gaza.

   b. They were given to her by her school.

   c. She found them difficult to understand because of the dialectal differences.

   d. They helped her learn about Egyptian culture, customs, and language.

2. How did reading help Alaa during the 2007-2008 war?

   a. It gave her information on how to survive in conflict zones.

   b. It provided her with an escape from the news and the harsh reality of war.

   c. It allowed her to write her own war stories.

   d. It inspired her to become a journalist.

3. How has reading contributed to Alaa's work life?

   a. It helped her develop her writing skills, and she has since published several novels.

   b. It taught her how to manage a business.

   c. It made her an expert in marketing.

   d. It enriched her vocabulary and provided a background for her work in translation.

Matching

بِالنِّسْبة لـ	regarding, as for
بِدّي	when
برْضو	so, therefore
حتّى	even
حَوالي	although
شو ما	of course
طبْعاً	through
عشان	whatever
غيْر إنّو	also, as well
فا	in order to
كمان	around me
لمِّن	I want
مِش	also, as well
مع إنّو	not
مِن خِلال	besides that, moreover

هِوايْتي المُفَضّلة القِراءة.	1 My favorite hobby is reading.
بدِيْت قِراءة مِن بَدْري كْتير، يِمْكِن كان عُمْري ٢٠٠١، أوْ يِمْكِن حتّى قَبِل كان عُمْري ١٠ سْنين.	2 I started reading very early—maybe in 2001, or maybe even earlier, when I was 10 years old.
بدِيْت قِراءة بْروايات صْغيرة، أوْ مِش رِوايات، كُنّا نْسَمّيها رِوايات الجيْب.	3 I started by reading small novels—or not even novels; we used to call them pocket novels.
يَعْني لأنّو صْغيرة كْتير هيْك، وبْتِنْحط في الجيْبة.	4 Meaning, they were very small, and you could put them in your pocket.
كانت رِوايات مِصْرية، كان السّوق كُلّو ومكاتِب غزّة مْلْيانة مِنْها.	5 They were Egyptian novels, and the market and bookstores in Gaza were full of them.
وْرقْها أصْفر وحجِمْها صْغير، مُمْكِن تْحُطّها صْغيرة كْتير.	6 Their paper was yellow, and they were small in size—you could easily fit them in your pocket.
كانت عِبارة عن رُسومات وفيها كِتابة قليلة.	7 They had drawings and very little writing.
يَعْني بدِت... أنا مِن خِلالْها بدِيْت أَعْرِف الشّعْب المِصْري، كيف بِيفكّر، شو بْيِحْكي، أيْش مشاكْلو، أكْلِهُم، عاداتْهُم، تقافِتْهُم، حتّى طريقِتْهُم بالحْكي لأنّو كانت مكْتوبة باللُّغة العامية.	8 Through them, I started to learn about Egyptian society—how they think, what they talk about, their problems, their food, their customs, their culture—even the way they speak, because they were written in colloquial language.
بعِد هيْك، بدِيْت أغيّر أوْ بدِيْت مع الواحد إنّو أنا بكْبر فا بدِيْت أغيّر اتّجاهاتي،	9 After that, I started to change, or as I grew up, I started to change my preferences.
وبطّلت هدي الرِّوايات، بسّ إنّو هيّ يَعْني بطّل أنا بسّ بِدّي أَعْرِف عن العالم العربي، أوْ إنّو العالم اللي برّا غزّة، هدا كيف بيعايِش أوْ كيف بيفكّر.	10 I stopped reading those novels. It wasn't just that I wanted to learn about the Arab world or the world outside Gaza—how they live or think.
لأنّو العالم اللي برّا غزّة عالم مُخْتلِف نِهائيّاً عن العالم الـ... عالم غزّة.	11 Because the world outside Gaza is entirely different from Gaza itself.
يَعْني عالم غزّة... أنا ما أَعْتقِد في عالم بْيِشْبِهو.	12 The world of Gaza... I don't think there's any place like it.
فا بيضلّ عِنّا فُضول، لأنّو غزّة مُغْلقة وغالباً حِصار، ما فيها مطار ما فيها مينا.	13 So, we always have curiosity because Gaza is closed off and mostly under siege. There's no airport, no seaport.
إنّك تْسافِر.... إذا بِدّك تْسافِر، تْسافِر عن طريق مصِر، وصعْب جدّاً الطّريق لْمصِر إنّك تْسافِر بعْدْها عَ المطار وتْسافِر للْعالم. كان الإشي صعْب.	14 If you want to travel... if you want to travel, you have to go through Egypt, and it's very difficult to get to Egypt and then to the airport to travel to the world. It was hard.

فا أنا كان عِنْدي دايماً فُضول أعْرف كيف العالم هدا اللي برّا، كيف النّاس عايشة، أيْش عاداتْهُم، أيْش...	15	So, I was always curious to know about this world outside—how people live, what their customs are, what...
كانت القراءة، والكُتُب... الكتاب أوّ الرِّواية، حتّى لَوْ إنّو الرِّواية كانت تِنْقِلّي صورة كيف هدول النّاس.	16	Reading and books... books or novels, even if they were novels, gave me an image of how those people lived.
انْتقلت بطّلت بسّ قراءة الكُتُب العربية إنّو هيّ بْتِشْفي يعْني... أوْ بْتعْطيني الإشي اللي أنا بدّي إيّاه انْتقلت بعد هيْك لأقْرا الرِّوايات زيّ روايات أجاثا كْريسْتي.	17	I shifted—I didn't just read Arabic books anymore because they couldn't fully satisfy... or give me what I wanted. I moved on to reading novels like Agatha Christie's.
تقْريباً، قرأت يمْكِن كُلّ روايات أجاثا كْريسْتي،	18	I probably read all of Agatha Christie's novels.
كُنْت ما أقوم عن الرِّواية، إلّا وانا قرأت يعْني مُخلّصاها.	19	I wouldn't put the novel down until I finished it.
شو ما يْصير في البيْت؟ شو ما يْصير حَوالِيّ؟ أنا لازِم أخلّصْها، بِدّي أعْرِف شو بِدّو يصير.	20	Whatever was happening in the house, whatever was happening around me, I had to finish it. I needed to know what would happen.
فا الرِّواية كانت بالنِّسْبة إلي، والكُتُب كانت نافِذة إنّو... لهدا العالم اللي برّا غزّة.	21	So, novels, for me, and books were a window into that world outside Gaza.
كيف هدا العالم كان عِنْدي دايماً فُضول إنّي أعْرِف هدا العالم.	22	I was always curious to know about that world.
القراءة نمّت عِنْدي المُفْردات، يمْكِن صِرْت أحْسن كْتير بالتّعْبير بِسبب القراءة.	23	Reading developed my vocabulary—I think I became much better at expressing myself because of reading.
أقْدر أعبّر عن حالي، عن شو بيدور بْراسي.	24	I could express myself and what was on my mind.
يمْكِن القراءة أكْتر حاجة لعْبت دوْر أوْ لِعْبت معي بْحَياتي.	25	I think reading was the most significant thing that played a role in my life.
بعْد هيْك يعْني بديْت مِن زمان في القراءة، لِعْبت معي دوْر إنّ أنا صِرْت أعْرف عن العالم الخارجي.	26	From early on, reading played a role in helping me learn about the outside world.
بطّل بسّ العالم الخارجي، صِرْت أدوِّر على كُتُب بِدّي اقرا أعْرِف عن مثلاً عن شغلات اللي هيّ يمْكِن غامِضة، يعْني الاشياء مثلاً المُتعلّقة بمُثلّث برمُودا، أوْ أشْياء بْتِتعلّق بإنّو وينْها السُّفن بْتِخْتفي.	27	It wasn't just the outside world anymore—I started looking for books about things that might be mysterious, like the Bermuda Triangle or things related to why ships disappear.

قِصص هادي يَعْني أنا كانت مُسَيْطِرة عليَّ، وبِدِّي كْتير يَعْني أَعْرِفْها.	**28** These kinds of stories controlled my thoughts, and I was very eager to learn about them.
أيْش الأطْباق الطّائِرة؟ القِراءة كْتير بِتْنَمّي الخَيال.	**29** What are flying saucers? Reading greatly stimulates the imagination.
مِن خِلال هدي الكُتُب أنا الكُتُب اللي قرأتها كانت بْتِحْكي عن الأطْباق الطّائِرة، وكُنْت دايماً أدوِّر على الأشْياء حتّى الكُتُب اللي فيها غُموض يْكون في حَوادِث واقِعية صارت وبِتْوَثِّق أشْياء هيْك، فا كُنْت أدوِّر عَ هدا النّوْع مِن الكُتُب.	**30** Through these books, I read about flying saucers. I always looked for things—even books with mysteries or real-life incidents that documented such things. I always searched for that type of book.
بعْديها، مع التّطوُّر أوْ مع أنا كيف كْبِرت، صِرْت أقْرا أشْياء تانْية أشْياء إلْها عِلاقة بالتّاريخ.	**31** Later, as I grew older, I began reading other things, things related to history.
صِرْت أحِسّ إنّو الحاضِر بعيد نفْسو، أوْ الحاضِر بعيد الماضي.	**32** I started feeling that the present repeats itself, or that the present repeats the past.
إنّو أنا بقرأ كُتُب في التّاريخ، بعْرِف إيْش كان يْصير.	**33** When I read history books, I learned what used to happen.
حبّيْت كْتير أقْرا كُتُب عن تاريخ فلسْطين، ومين الشّعوب اللي عاشوا فيها.	**34** I loved reading books about Palestinian history and the peoples who lived there.
وأنا كْتير كُنْت... إجت فتْرة كُنْت كْتير مُغْرمة في هدا المَوْضوع.	**35** I became very passionate about this topic for a while.
القِراءة زوّدتْني بْمعْلومات وبْحقائِق، خلّتْني عِنْدي مُفْردات قادْرة	**36** Reading enriched me with information and facts. It gave me vocabulary and skills.
ألاحِظ على الفرِق بيْني وبيْن اللي كانوا يَعْني كانوا أصْدِقائي، ومعي مِن جيلي.	**37** I noticed the difference between myself and my friends, those who were my age and in my class.
كُنْت أعْرف معْلومات هُمّ لأنّهُم كانوا يْقضُوا وقتِهُم بْأشْياء تانْية.	**38** I knew things they didn't because they spent their time on other things.
فا صارت عِنْدي معْلومات كْتيرة مُخْتلِفة عن النّاس اللي بْجيلي أوْ اللي بْنفْس سِنّي ومعي بِصْفوف بالمَدْرسة.	**39** So, I had a lot of different knowledge compared to people my age or those in my class at school.
القِراءة أنا بالنِّسْبة إلي ليْش القِراءة؟ لأنّها بْتعْطيني إحْساس بالرّاحة، بْتعْطيني إحْساس بالهُدوء.	**40** For me, why reading? Because it gives me a sense of comfort and calm.
غيْر إنّو أنا كُنْت أحِسّ إنّو أنا مُنْفصِلة عن العالم، أنا لِمِّن أقْرأ كْتاب، بركِّز فيه بْدَرجة رهيبة.	**41** Besides, I felt disconnected from the world when I was reading a book—I'd focus on it intensely.

بحِسّ بِأَحْداثو كْتير، ما بقْدِرْش أَنْفِصِل عنّو.	42	I'd feel deeply immersed in its events; I couldn't detach myself from it.
يَعْني أنا مُمْكِن أقْرا الكِّتاب، يْنمّي خَيالي، وبْنفْس الوَقِت يَعْني أضلّني مِتأثّرة بِاللي قرأتو مُمْكِن يوْمينْ أوْ تلاتة.	43	I could read a book, and it would stimulate my imagination, and at the same time, I'd remain affected by what I read for two or three days.
وغيْر إنّو أنا بِالنِّسْبة إلي الوَضِع صعْب اللي كان بْغزّة، يِمكِن كُنْت أحِبّ أهْرُب من قُصّةْ الأخْبار والحُروب والقصص اللي بتْصير.	44	Also, given the difficult situation in Gaza, I often wanted to escape the news, the wars, and everything happening.
بتْذكّر بِالحرْبْ الـ٢٠٠٧ - ٢٠٠٨، أنا كُنْت حاطّة راسي، ما بِدّي أسْمع أخْبار، كُنْت حاطّة راسي بِالكِّتاب بِدّي أنْفِصِل بْأيّ شكِل عن العالم وعن الحرْب اللي أنا فيها.	45	I remember during the 2007–2008 war, I refused to listen to the news. I buried myself in a book, wanting to disconnect in any way from the world and the war I was in.
فا القِراءة كْتير أهمّ إحْساس إنّك بتْحِسّ بِالقِراءة بِالرّاحة بِالهُدوء بِالْانْفِصال عن العالم الصّعْب اللي إنْتَ بتْعيش فيه.	46	Reading provides the most important feeling—it gives you comfort, calm, and an escape from the harsh world you're living in.
كمان، القِراءة لِعْبت معي دوْر في مَوْضوع إنّو أنا مثلاً. بعْد هيْك، اشْتغلِت في اللي هُوَّ الترّجْمة. وفا أنا عِنْدي خلْفية عن الإشي اللي بترجْمو، عِنْدي خلْفية عن ثقافةْ هدا الشّعْب عن عاداتْهُم، عن كيف بيفكّروا.	47	Reading also played a role in my work. Later, I worked in translation. Reading gave me a background about the cultures of the people I was translating for—their customs and how they think.
عِنْدي خلْفية برْضو إنّو، أنا قرأتْ كْتير فا صارعِنْدي القُدْرة على إنّي أساعِد في كِتابةْ كُتُب أطْفال.	48	I also had a background because I had read so much, so I was able to help with writing children's books.
بِالنِّسْبة إلي، القِراءة نقلتْ لي ثقافةْ وعادات البُلْدان التّانْية، اللي كان أنا صعْب كشخّص عايِش بْغزّة أوْصِلّها.	49	For me, reading brought me the culture and customs of other countries that were hard for someone living in Gaza to reach.
فا القِراءة كانت وَسيلة يَعْني رائِعة وهِوايَة. ما أعْتقد في هِوايَة تانْيَة بتْعْطيك نفْس الإحْساس اللي أعْطتْني إياه القِراءة.	50	So reading was an amazing tool and a hobby. I don't think there's another hobby that can give you the same feeling reading gave me.

1. I stopped/quit[10] _____
2. curiosity[13] _____
3. port/harbor[13] _____
4. going on/happening[24] _____
5. dominating/captivating[28] _____
6. passionate about[35] _____
7. of my generation[39] _____
8. I focus[41] _____
9. intense/terrible[41] _____
10. I escape[44] _____

_____

18 Khaled's Hobby

Keywords

المشي walking   الغُروب sunset   المغْرِب Maghrib prayer

Main Idea

a. Khaled's daily routine of walking, which helps him release negative energy, stay fit, and find peace.
b. Khaled's love for fishing by the sea and how it helps him relax.
c. How photography has intensified Khaled's love for his homeland and its people.
d. Khaled's exploration of different sports and fitness routines in Gaza.

True or False

1. Khaled spends most of his walking time in parks and urban areas.
2. Khaled sometimes jogs or runs during his walks to stay physically fit.
3. Khaled enjoys watching the sunset during his walks by the sea.
4. Khaled's favorite part of his walk is listening to fishermen talk about their daily catch.
5. Khaled often brings friends with him on his walks by the sea.

Multiple Choice

1. Which of the following activities does Khaled **not** mention during his evening walks?

   a. Jogging or running
   b. Listening to podcasts
   c. Swimming in the sea
   d. Buying sunflower seeds and cold water

2. What is the significance of the mosque by Corniche Street for Khaled?

   a. It's where he meets friends before continuing his walk.

   b. It's where he goes to listen to religious lectures after his walk.

   c. It is his destination to end his walk each day.

   d. It provides him with a peaceful place to pray Maghrib while hearing the call to prayer and the sound of waves.

3. What makes Corniche Street enjoyable for walking, according to Khaled?

   a. Its kiosks selling drinks and snacks
   b. The beautiful views of the sea
   c. The wide sidewalk and seating areas
   d. *All of the above*

أَثْناء	and like this
إلى جانِب إنّو	gradually
بِالتّالي	above
بْطولو	my/mine
بعِد هيْك	meaning that
تبعي	in this state
جُوّا	especially
خُصوصاً	let me
خلّيني	along it
شْوَيّة شْوَيّة	together
على هالْحال	let's not forget
فوْق	besides that it...
ما نِنْساش	after that
مع بعِض	from it
معْناه	during
مِنّو	inside
وهيك	consequently

صباح الخير! خلّيني أتْكلّم عن هِواياتي.	1	Good morning! Let me talk about my hobbies.
أنا عِنْدي كْتير هِوايات، لكِن أحبّها لقلْبي المشي.	2	I have many hobbies, but the one dearest to my heart is walking.
المشي، إلى جانِب إنّو مُفيد صحيّاً وبينشِّط الدّوْرة الدّمَوية وبيساعِد على التّركيز وبيحسّن الذّاكِرة، بيقوّي القلْب، برْضو كمان بيفضّي الطّاقة السّلْبية عِنْد الإنْسان، وبيخلّي يُكمّل يَوْمو بطاقة إيجابية.	3	Walking, in addition to being healthy, improving blood circulation, helping with focus, enhancing memory, and strengthening the heart, also helps release negative energy in a person and lets them continue their day with positive energy.
كُنْت مِتعوّد أخصّص جُزْء كْبير مِن يَوْمي، حَوالي ساعة ونُصّ، ساعْتين، ساعْتين وشْوَية، للمشي.	4	I used to dedicate a large part of my day, around an hour and a half, two hours, or even a bit more, to walking.
وخُصوصاً مُعْظم هدا الوَقت بقْضي في المشي على البحر.	5	Most of that time, I would spend walking by the sea.
بحر غزّة كْتير حِلو، الهَوا كْتير لطيف، والموْج... وصوْت الموْج بيساعِد الإنْسان على التّأمُّل وعلى التّركيز.	6	Gaza's sea is very beautiful. The air is very pleasant, and the sound of the waves helps a person meditate and focus.
ومِنّو يُفضْفِض بِتْحِسّ البحر بيحْكي معك، وبِتْحْكي معو، وبِتْحِسّو صار جُزْء مِنّك، بِتْشْكيلُه هُمومك،	7	And it lets you vent—you feel like the sea is talking to you, and you talk to it. You feel it becomes part of you; you pour your worries out to it.
وبِالتّالي هيْك كان يْساعِدْني إنّي أفرّغ الطّاقة السّلْبية اللي عِنْدي.	8	And so, it would help me release the negative energy I had.
بعْض الأوْقات ما كُنْتِش بسّ أمْشي، كُنْت أهرْوِل ومرّات أجْري.	9	Sometimes, I wouldn't just walk; I would jog or even run.
جُزْء مِن الرّياضة يَعْني هُوّ اللِّياقة البدنية.	10	It's part of exercise, meaning physical fitness.
وأضلّي على هالْحال لعِنْد ما تُغْرُب الشّمِس.	11	I'd keep at it until the sun started to set.
وَقْت الغُروب كان كْتير حِلو، وإنْتَ بِتْراقب الشّمس تْلاقيها بِتْنزِل شْوَيّة شْوَيّة لعِنْد ما تُغْتَص جُوّا البحر.	12	Sunset was very beautiful. As you watch the sun, you see it slowly sink until it disappears into the sea.
ما نِنْساش إنّو كان في بعْض الصّيّادين بيطْلعوا بْهالوَقِت، بيكونوا جايْيِن اللي صادوه، الأسْماك الغزّاوية أوْ الفِلسْطينية المميّزة، مِنْها اللّوكُوس، والدّينيس، وسُلْطان إبْراهيم، وغيرْها مِن أنْواع كْتير.	13	Let's not forget that at that time, some fishermen would return, bringing what they'd caught—those unique Gazan or Palestinian fish, like grouper, sea bream, Sultan Ibrahim, and many other kinds.

هُوَّ اللي بيشجِّع على المشي على شارِع البحر إنّو في شارِع بِنسمّيه شارِع الكوْرْنيش.	14 What makes walking along the seafront appealing is a road we call Corniche Street.
هدا الشّارِع يَعني جْديد وكان مرْصوف كوْيِّس، والرّصيف فيه عريض، بْتِمْشي فيه براحْتَك.	15 This road is new, well-paved, and has a wide sidewalk where you can walk comfortably.
بْطولو إنْتَ ماشي في مناطِق مُخصّصة هيَّ للأْكْشاك اللي بيبيع الميّا، اللي بيبيع البِسْكوت، اللي بيبيع العصير البارِد اللي بيبرِّد عليْك أثْناء المشي، يْبيع المشْروبات السّاخِنة.	16 Along it, there are designated areas with kiosks selling water, biscuits, cold drinks to refresh you during your walk, and hot drinks.
بعْض القعدات البسيطة.	17 Some simple seating areas, too.
أنا كُنْت بحِبّ أختار الميّة البارْدة، أشْتري شْوَيّة بِزِر، أحُطّ السّمّاعات في وْداني، وأمْشي وأتأمّل البحر وأتأمّل الغُروب وأنا أسْمع البودْكاسْت تاعي.	18 I used to love picking cold water, buying some seeds, putting my headphones on, and walking while reflecting on the sea and the sunset, all while listening to my podcast.
بعْد ما يْخلِّص الغُروب، معناه إجا وَقْت صلاةْ المغْرِب، كان عِنّا جامِع كْتير حِلو، مُصمّم ومبْني على الكوْرْنيش مُباشرةً.	19 After the sunset, it meant it was time for Maghrib prayer. There was a very beautiful mosque designed and built directly on the Corniche.
بْتوقف فيه، بْتِشوف البحر بْتِسْمع صوْت البحر مع صوْت الأدان.	20 You'd stop there, see the sea, and hear the sound of the sea alongside the call to prayer.
هدا بْيِعْمل جوّ كْتير كْتيرحِلوْ في خُشوع وفي طمأنينة وسكينة، بيساعِد على التّركّيز في الصّلاة.	21 This created a very beautiful atmosphere of serenity, tranquility, and peace, helping you focus in prayer.
بعْد الصّلاة، كُنْت أتْقابل مع صْحابي مرّات، ونِتْحدّث ونِمْشي شْوَيّة صْغيرة مع بعْض، وبعِد هيْك أكمِّل الطّريق للبيْت مشي، بسّ بيْتي كان قريب وهدا كان مِن حُسُن حظّي.	22 After prayer, I would sometimes meet up with my friends, chat, and walk a little with them, then continue my way home on foot— fortunately, my house was close.
وهيْك بكون بقْضي المسا تبعي على البحر، اللي بتْمنّى أرْجع لُه وأمْشي فيه، وأتأمّل الصّيادين، وأتأمّل موْج البحر، وأكمِّل أحْكي معو وأتْحدّث معو، وأصلّي المغْرِب على البحر، وأرْجع للرّوتين تاعي.	23 That's how I'd spend my evening by the sea, wishing I could go back to it, walk along it, observe the fishermen, reflect on the waves, continue talking to the sea, pray Maghrib by the sea, and return to my routine.
لكِن الحمْدُ لله ربّ العالمين.	24 But praise be to God, Lord of all worlds.

Vocabulary

1. used to[4] _____
2. jog[9] _____
3. waterfront[14] _____
4. kiosks[16] _____
5. sunflower seeds[18] _____
6. mine/my[18] _____
7. my ears[18] _____
8. reverence[21] _____
9. tranquility[21] _____
10. I spend (time)[23] _____

19 Najd: Culture

Keywords

| الفِلْفِل الأَخْضَر green chili | طبيخ اللّبن cooked yogurt | تَطْريز embroidery |

Main Idea

a. The history of Palestinian clothing and embroidery.
b. The importance of spices in Gazan cuisine and how they differ from other Palestinian regions.
c. A detailed exploration of popular Palestinian and Gazan dishes, including how they are made and enjoyed.
d. Najd's experience as a chef in Gaza and how she learned to make traditional dishes.

True or False

1. Green chili peppers are a common side dish with almost every meal in Gaza.
2. Najd prefers Palestinian maqluba with chicken.
3. Qudrah is a dish that is traditionally made in clay pots for the best flavor.
4. Tabikh laban is made with chicken, yogurt, and onions.
5. Najd mentions that maqluba can be made with various vegetables, depending on personal preference.

Multiple Choice

1. What is one of Najd's favorite dishes that is less known outside of Gaza?

   a. Kibbeh   b. Maqluba   c. Qudrah   d. Tabikh laban

2. What is special about the way maqluba is prepared?

   a. The vegetables are grilled before cooking.

   b. The vegetables are fried before cooking, and the rice is cooked with the flavor of the fried vegetables.

   c. It's only made with meat, not vegetables.

   d. The rice is cooked separately from the vegetables.

3. Which of the following is part of the cultural heritage of Palestine that Najd mentions?

a. The maqluba made only with chicken

b. The use of fish in most dishes

c. The falahi dress with Palestinian embroidery

d. *None of the above*

Matching

إلْها	like
بِتْشتهِر بـ	consists of
بْتمنّى	in general
بْشكِل عام	somewhat
تحْديداً	must therefore
جمْب	I hope
عِبارة عن	among the most
غيْر	famous for
فِش مجال	next to, beside
مِتِل	has
مِن أكْتر	that is, I mean
مِن تْحْت إيْديْنا	by our hands
نوْعاً ما	no way (around it)
بِيْقى لازِم	other than
يَعْني	specifically

مَرْحَباً، بِدّي اليوْم أَحْكيلْكُم عن الثَّقافة الفِلَسْطينية، الثَّقافة الغزّاوية تحْديداً.

مِن أكْتَر الحاجات اللي أهِل غزّة مشْهورين فيها طبْعاً هُوَّ الأكِل.

الأكِل يَعْني العِشِق لكُلّ إنْسان.

الثَّقافة الغزّاوية مشْهورة بأنّها بتْحِب الأكِل الحرّاء أوْ البحْراء، يَعْني عنّا أيّا مِن غزّة بِيْقى لازِم يكون بيحِبّ الفِلْفِل الأخْضَر، هدا إشي أساسي جمْب الأكِل.

وطبْعاً، مِن الأكّلات اللي جِدّاً مشْهورة بالثَّقافة الفِلَسْطينية هيَّ الإدْرى أوْ القِدْرة الفِلَسْطينية.

ويُفضّل إنّها تِنْعمل باللّحْمة وفي فُخّار.

بنْحِبّ نعْمل الإدْرى في الفُخّارة لأنّها يَعْني إلْها طعَم خُرافي في الفُخّارة، ولكِن لَوْ بِدّها تِنْعمل عَ النّار برْضو عادي بطنْجرة عَ النّار، تمام. وطبْعاً كمان المقْلوبة الفِلَسْطينية.

المقْلوبة مشْهورة طبْعاً في كُلّ المُدْن الفِلَسْطينية.

المقْلوبة مِن الأكّلات المُفضّلة لكُلّ الفِلَسْطينيين تقْريباً، تِتْكوّن مِن بطاطا، بيتِنْجان، زهْرة أَوْ كُرْنُب، بصل كْتير يَعْني، وبنْدورة، وبتِنْعمل بالْجاج وبِاللّحْمة برْضو، بسّ أنا برْضو، كنْجِد، بفضّلْها بِاللّحْمة.

المقْلوبة الفِلَسْطينية فِكّرِتْها إِإنّو رُزّ بْيِسْتوي مع هادي الخُضار المقْلية.

تُنْقلّى الخُضْرة بتِقْلي البيتِنْجان، بتِقْلي البنْدورة، بتِقْلي البطاطا، والبصل، كُلُّهُم بْتِقْليهُمْ، والرُّزّ يَعْني، بيكون هيْك بسّ شْوَيّ تِسْتوى نَتْفة صْغيرة.

بعْديها بتْحُطُّهُم كُلُّهُم مع بعْض وبتِسْتويهُم كُلُّهُم مع بعْض، فا الرّزّ بْياخُد نكْهة خليط الخُضار، بيكون إلْها طعِم جِدّاً رائع.

1 Hello, today I want to tell you about Palestinian culture, specifically Gazan culture.

2 One of the most famous things about the people of Gaza is, of course, their food.

3 Food is, after all, a passion for everyone.

4 Gazan culture is known for loving spicy food. Anyone from Gaza has to love green chili—it's a staple alongside every dish.

5 One of the most famous dishes in Palestinian culture is idra (or qidra).

6 It's best made with meat and in a clay pot.

7 We like to make idra in a clay pot because it has an amazing flavor that way, but it can also be cooked on a regular stove in a pot—it's fine either way. And of course, there's also Palestinian maqluba.

8 Maqluba is famous in all Palestinian cities.

9 Maqluba is a favorite dish for almost all Palestinians. It's made with potatoes, eggplants, cauliflower or cabbage, a lot of onions, tomatoes, and it can be cooked with chicken or meat, but I personally prefer it with meat.

10 The idea of Palestinian maqluba is that the rice cooks together with the fried vegetables.

11 You fry the eggplant, fry the tomatoes, fry the potatoes, and the onions—all of them are fried—and the rice is cooked just a little beforehand.

12 Then you put everything together and cook them all together, so the rice absorbs the flavor of the vegetable mixture, and it tastes amazing.

وحلاوةِ المقلوبة إنّو بْتِقدر تعمِلْها بأيّ خُضْرة إنْتَ بتْحِبّها.	13	The great thing about maqluba is that you can make it with any vegetables you like.
يَعْني في ناس بتْحِبّها بالبِتِنْجان بسّ، ما بتْحِبّ الكُرنُب مثلاً، في ناس بتْحِبّها بالْكُرنُب، بالقرع بأشياء تانْية مُختلفة.	14	Some people prefer it with just eggplants and don't like cabbage, for example. Some prefer it with cabbage or squash, or other different vegetables.
كُلّ واحد هُوّ حُرّ طبْعاً أيْش الخُضْرة اللي يِختارْها.	15	Everyone is, of course, free to choose whichever vegetables they like.
وفي مِن الأكْلات اللي أنا بحِبّها جِدّاً واللي قليل اللي بيعْرفوها، يمكِن بسّ أهِل غزّة في فلسْطين، طبيخ اللّبن.	16	One of the dishes I love very much, and that not many people know about—maybe just people from Gaza in Palestine—is cooked yogurt.
طبيخ اللّبن يَعْني هدا الأكْلة المُفضّلة تاعتي.	17	Cooked yogurt is my absolute favorite dish.
طبيخ اللّبن عِبارة عن لبن مطْبوخ، وبرْضو بْينْعمِل باللّحْمة، ما بْينْعمِل بالْجاج، بْينْعمِل باللّحْمة والبصل.	18	It's basically cooked yogurt, and it's also made with meat—not chicken—but with meat and onions.
بصل ولحْمة ولبن، وبْينْطبخوا ويتْقلّبوا مع بعض.	19	Onions, meat, and yogurt are cooked together.
مِن أزْكى الأكْلات اللي مُمْكِن تاكلْها، بالذّات إذا كُنت بتْحِبّ اللّبن والأشْياء الحامْضة نوْعاً ما.	20	It's one of the most delicious dishes you can eat, especially if you love yogurt and slightly tangy flavors.
وطبْعاً زيّ ما قُلْنا الفِلْفِل جمب اللّبن، يَعْني إنْتَ عم تاكُل اللّبن، بيْقى لازِم تاكل فِلْفِل أخْضر، فِش مجال.	21	And of course, like I said, chili goes alongside yogurt—you have to eat green chili with it; there's no other way.
وكمان أيْش؟ في يَعْني... في كمان أكْلات تانْية كْتير أكيد إحْنا بنْحِبّها، مِتل قلّاية البندوْرة أوْ طبيخ البندوْرة.	22	What else? There are other dishes we love, like fried tomatoes or tomato stew.
بنْدوْرة بنْهرْسْها وبنُطْبُخْها.	23	You crush the tomatoes and cook them.
طبيخ البندوْرة مُمْكِن يكون بِشْتركوا فيه أهِل الشّام كُلّهُم بْشكِل عام، مِش بسّ فلِسْطين، طبيخ البندوْرة الكُبّة أوْ الكِبّة.	24	Tomato stew might be common among all Levantine people, not just in Palestine. There's also tomato stew with kubbeh.
هاي الأكْلة سورية، بسّ كمان بْفِلِسْطين بنْعمِلْها.	25	That's a Syrian dish, but we also make it in Palestine.
أكْتر الأكْلات اللي مشهورة إنّها مِن فِلسْطين هيَّ المقْلوبة والقِدْرة (أوْ المقْلوبة والإدْرى.)	26	The most famous dishes that are considered Palestinian are maqluba and qidra (or maqluba and idra).

27	وطَبْعاً يَعْني، ثقافةِ فلِسْطين بالأَكِل بالذّات غنية جِدّاً جِدّاً، وفيها كْتير تنَوُّع وفايْدة طبْعاً.		And of course, Palestinian food culture is very rich, with so much variety and, of course, nutritional value.
28	وفلِسْطين طبْعاً تشْتهِر بْأشْياء كْتير غير الخُضار، غيْرِ الأَكِل، غيْرِ الحِمْضيّات.		Palestine is famous not just for its vegetables, food, or citrus fruits.
29	تشْتهِر بِالثّوب الفلّاحي بِالتّطْريز الفلّاحي الثّوب الفِلسْطيني.		It's also famous for the traditional embroidered Palestinian thobe (dress).
30	فلِسْطين حِلْوَة كْتير، وغزّة كمان حِلْوَة كْتير.		Palestine is beautiful, and Gaza is also very beautiful.
31	وأنا يَعْني بتْمنّى مِن كُلّ حدا إنّو يِقْدر يِجي على غزّة يْزورْها وياكُل مِن تْحْت إيْدينا أكْلاتْها.		I hope everyone gets the chance to visit Gaza, see it, and taste its food made by our hands.
32	وشُكْراً كْتير.		Thank you so much.

Answers

Main Idea: c **True-False:** 1. T[4] 2. F[9] 3. T[6-7] 4. F[18] 5. T[13-15] **Multiple Choice:** 1. d[16-17] 2. b[11-12] 3. c[29]

Matching: جمْب / specifically / تحْديداً / in general / بْشكِل عام / I hope / بتْمنّى / famous for / بتْشتهِر بـ / has / إلْها / next to, beside / عبارة عن / consists of / غيْر / other than / فِش مجال no way (around it) / مِتِل / like / مِن أكْتر / that / يَعْني / must therefore / يِبْقى لازِم / somewhat / نوْعاً ما / by our hands / مِن تْحْت إيْدينا / among the most / الحجر الصّحّي / is, I mean **Vocabulary:** 1. اتْدرّبِت .2 / بْياخُد .7 / ملامِح .6 / البوْزْترْيه .5 / بيقْدروا .4 / بعْشق .3 / تْصير .9 / نْطوّر .10 / نْكمّل .8

20 Suheil: Culture

Keywords

العادات والتّقاليد customs and traditions   أعْراس weddings   النّاصْرِة Nazareth

الدّبْكة dabkeh (A traditional Palestinian dance)

Main Idea

   a. The differences between Christian, Muslim, and Jewish wedding traditions in the Nazareth.
   b. The different types of food served at Palestinian weddings.
   c. An overview of Palestinian wedding traditions.
   d. Suheil's personal experience attending weddings in Palestine.

True or False

   1. Nazareth is about fifty percent Christian and fifty percent Muslim.
   2. In Christian weddings, the engagement usually lasts for about a year before the wedding.
   3. Suheil mentions that Dabke is only performed at Christian weddings in the Nazareth area.
   4. Suheil mentions that it's common for Christian weddings in the 1948-Territories to include traditional Palestinian clothing like keffiyehs and thobes.
   5. Suheil enjoys weddings and says that they typically have large numbers of guests, often between 500 and 2,000 people.

Multiple Choice

   1. Which of the following is part of the Christian wedding traditions described by Suheil?

       a. The groom wears a traditional thobe during the wedding.

       b. The couple gets married by the sea.

       c. The groom's family comes to the bride's house for a "Bride's Exit" ceremony.

       d. The wedding takes place after a two-week engagement period.

   2. What is the "Ta'aleel" that Suheil mentions in Christian weddings?

       a. A traditional dish served at weddings.

       b. A type of music played during the wedding.

       c. A pre-wedding week of parties for the bride and groom with family and friends.

       d. A special wedding prayer.

3. Which of the following is a common feature of both Christian and Muslim weddings in Palestine, according to Suheil?

   a. A large amount of food, especially meat.

   b. Only close family members are invited to the wedding.

   c. The wedding lasts for several days.

   d. The wedding is always held at a family member's home.

Matching

بِالأوّل	so that's how
بِالْعادِة	from... to
بْنَفْس	from when
تاني يوْم	even
حتّى	sometimes
عبيْن ما	as if
فا هيْك	authentic
قُحّ	at first
كإنّو	from that time
مرّات	in the same
مِن بعْد	next day
مِن لمّا	after
مِن وَقْتْها	until
مِن... لـ	usually

واحِدِة مِن أَحْلى العاداتِ والتَّقاليد عِنّا هون في فلَسْطين هيّ الأعْراس والزَّواج.

1 One of the most beautiful traditions we have here in Palestine is weddings and marriage.

فا أنا هون بِدّي أَحْكي عن الزَّواج بمِنْطِقِةْ النّاصِرِة.

2 So here, I want to talk about weddings in the Nazareth area.

طَبْعاً مِن كُلّ مِنْطِقة لمِنْطِقة بْفلَسْطين شْوَيّ صْغيرة بْتِخْتِلِف العادات، ولكِن في مِنْطِقةِ النّاصِرة كمان بْتِخْتِلْف بين مسيحية وإسلام.

3 Of course, from one area to another in Palestine, traditions differ slightly, and even in Nazareth, they differ between Christians and Muslims.

النّاصْرة فيها حَوالي خمْسين بالمِيّة مسيحية خمْسين بالمِيّة إسْلام.

4 Nazareth is about 50% Christian and 50% Muslim.

عِنْد المسيحية بالْعادِة يَعْني بوخِد العُرْس أكْمَر مِن سِنة تا يْسير من لمّا يْلْتِقوا بْبعْض.

5 Among Christians, usually, weddings take a few years from the time the couple meets.

فا عبيْن ما الواحد الشّب العادي بيدوِّر على عروس، بيروح بيسْأل، وبالْعادة لمّا يْلاقي واحْدِة، بيتعرّف عليها وبْيِتِّفْقوا، بيجي بُطْلُب إيدْها مِن أبوها.

6 So, when a young man is looking for a bride, he asks around, and usually, when he finds someone, they get to know each other and agree, and then he asks for her hand from her father.

وبعْدين في مَوْسِم العُرْس بِعْملوا خُطْبِة بالأوّل، وبعْد بْسِنِة تقْريباً بِعْملوا العُرْس.

7 Then, during the wedding season, they have an engagement first, and about a year later, they hold the wedding.

بيحجْزوا قاعة، وبيجيبوا مُغنّي وكُلّ شي.

8 They book a hall, hire a singer, and arrange everything.

وعلى ليلةِ الكْليل، بيكون في قبل الكْليل أُسْبوع كامِل تعاليل مِنْسمّيها، اللي هيّ بالْبيْت بْتكون اللي العروس لحال مع عيْلِتْها وأصْحابْها والعريس لحال مع عيْلْتو وأصْحابو، كإنّو آخِر إُسْبوع بالْعزّابية.

9 On the night of the wedding, there's usually a week before it with celebrations we call "ta'aleel." The bride stays with her family and friends, and the groom with his family and friends, like a final week of being single.

وبيكون في ليلِة للْعروس، اللي بالْعادِة بيعْزموا أهل العريس وبيكون في ليْلِة اللي هيّ زْيانِة للْعريس.

10 There's a night for the bride where they usually invite the groom's family, and another night called "zayaneh" for the groom.

اللي بيحلْقولو وكمان بيلبّسوه طرابيش وحطّات وبيحِمْلوه وبيزقْفوا كمان ليلة كْتير حِلْوة هاي كمان بيعزْموا أهل العروس العيْلة المقرّبة يَعْني،

11 During "zayaneh," they shave his head, dress him in traditional clothing like tarboushes (fezzes) and kufiyas, carry him, and clap—it's a very fun night. They also invite the bride's close family.

وبيكون في بِالْعادة بعْد الكْليل... قبِل الكْليل بيكون في طلْعِة عروس فا بيجو أهْل العريس على بيْت العروس.	12	Before the wedding ceremony, there's a "bride's exit" where the groom's family comes to the bride's house.
بتكون هيَّ لابْسِة الفُسْتان الابْيَض مْزبْطي حالها ويكون البيْت مْزيّن بالْورد.	13	She's dressed in a white gown, all prepared, and the house is decorated with flowers.
بيجي أكْبر شخْص بْعيْلِة الزّلِمي بيجي بُطْلُب إيد العروس مِن أكْبر شخْص بْعيلِة العروس.	14	The eldest person in the groom's family formally asks for the bride's hand from the eldest person in the bride's family.
فا بُطْلُب إيدْها ومِن وَقْتْها بيروحوا عَ الكْنيسة بيكون العريس مع أخوه أوْ إبِن عمُّه، الشّبين بيسمّوه، وبيكونوا عم بيسْتنّوا بالكْنيسة.	15	After this, they go to the church, where the groom waits with his brother or cousin, who's called the "shabeen" (best man).
بيروحوا وبيكون بيسْتنّى العروس، بيكون باعتِلْها سيّارة حِلْوة، ليموزين، بْتوخِدْها للكْنيسة.	16	A fancy car, usually a limousine, is sent to bring the bride to the church.
ومِن وَقْتها بيتزوّجوا، وبعْد ما يِتْزوّجوا بيكون في أوْ ريسبْشِن أوْ سهْرة بعْد الكْليل.	17	After they get married, there's either a reception or an evening party after the ceremony.
وبعدْها بْنفْس اللّيلة أوْ تاني يوْم، بِالْعادة بيطْلعوا شهِر عسل عشان يِنْبِسطوا مع بعض وهيْك بأوّل شهِر مِن حَياتْهِن مع بعض. فا هيْك.	18	On the same night or the next day, they usually go on a honeymoon to enjoy their first month together. That's how it is.
عِنْد الإسْلام، في عادات شْويّ مِخْتِلْفة.	19	Among Muslims, the traditions are a little different.
عِنْدْهِن ليلِة حِنّة، بيعْملوا أكْتر دِحية، حِدّة هاي الشِّغْلات.	20	They have a "henna night," which includes dabkeh and other celebrations.
فا الغناني كمان بِتْكون غيْر.	21	The songs are also different.
أنا عيْلْتي مسيحية، فا أغْلب العِراس اللي حْضرِتْها هيَّ عْراس مسيحية، ولكِن حْضرْت كمان شْويّ عْراس إسْلامية.	22	My family is Christian, so most of the weddings I've attended are Christian ones, but I've also attended some Muslim weddings.
مرّات حتّى بِالعْراس المسيحية كمان، مْنِلْبِس اللِّباس التّقْليدي الفلسْطيني، مع حطّات وطرابيش، وجلّابية. أهْل الضِّفة وغزّة بيفكِّر أكْتر بيعْملوها هاي.	23	Sometimes, even in Christian weddings, we wear traditional Palestinian clothing with kufiyas, tarboushes, and galabiyas. People in the West Bank and Gaza do this more.
بالـ٤٨، بالشّمال، شْويّ أقلّ.	24	In the '48 areas, in the north, it's less common.
ولكِن العِراس عنّا أجواءْها كْتير حِلْوة.	25	However, our weddings have a very joyful atmosphere.

الدّبْكِة دايْماً مِنْفوّتْها بْآخِرِ السّهْرة، يَعْني بْكُلّ سهْرة أوْ تعْليلةٍ، دايْماً بالْآخِرِ مِنْفوّت دبْكة، ضَروري يَعْني.	26	Dabkeh is always part of the end of the evening. In every party or celebration, dabkeh is always included—it's essential.
وبيكون في كْتير أكِل، كْتير لحْمة.	27	There's always lots of food and lots of meat.
إحْنا العرب بْشكِل عامّ، كُلّ العرب، كْتير مِنْحِبّ اللّحْمة إحْنا.	28	We Arabs in general, all Arabs, love meat.
فا بيكون في كْتير أكِل، وكتير لحْمة، وكتير حِلو.	29	So, there's a lot of food, a lot of meat, and lots of sweets.
وطبْعاً كُلّ الغناني، غناني عربية تقْليدية، عن الحُبّ والزّواج وهيْك، وعن البْلاد والأرض والوَطن كمان.	30	And of course, the songs are traditional Arabic songs about love, marriage, and also about the land and the homeland.
فا أنا كْتير بحِبّ العْراس، عنْجدّ كْتير كتير.	31	I really love weddings—truly, a lot.
والمعازيم بيكونوا كْتار.	32	The guests are many.
يَعْني بيكون في بالتّعاليل بيكونوا حَوالي مية واحد اللي بالبْيْت، وبالسّهْرات بيكون في حَوالي خمِسْميّة.	33	For the pre-wedding celebrations, there are usually about 100 people at the house, and for the main evening parties, there are around 500.
وفي سهْرات بِتْوَصِّل لحَوالي ألْف وألْفيْن، وإذا كان حدا معْروف يَعْني، مُمْكِن تْوَصِّل أكْتر. فا هيْك.	34	Some weddings even reach 1,000 or 2,000 guests, and if it's someone well-known, it can be even more. That's how it is.
إن شا اللّه بِتْجرِّب عُرْس فلسْطيني قُحّ.	35	God willing, you'll get to experience a purely Palestinian wedding someday.

Answers

Main Idea: c **True-False:** 1. T[4] 2. T[7] 3. F[26] 4. F[24] 5. T[33-34] **Multiple Choice:** 1. c[12] 2. c[9] 3. a[27] **Matching:** بالأوّل

so فا هيْك / until عبيْن ما even / حتّى / next day / تاني يوْم in the same / بْنَفْس / usually بالْعادة / at first

from مِن وَقْتْها / from when مِن لمّا / after مِن بعْد / sometimes مرّات / as if كإنّو / authentic قُحّ / that's how

that time / مِن ...لـ from... to

21　Alaa: Culture

تَطْريز embroidery　تُراث heritage　تُوْب/ثَوْب thobe (a traditional dress)

Main Idea

a. The cultural significance of Palestinian embroidery and efforts to preserve it as part of Palestinian heritage.
b. The techniques used in Palestinian embroidery and how they have evolved over time.
c. Alaa's personal experiences learning embroidery as a child in Gaza.
d. The differences between Palestinian embroidery and other types of embroidery around the world.

True or False

1. Palestinian embroidery dates back more than 3,000 years, originating with the Canaanites.
2. The design and colors of Palestinian embroidery have remained the same throughout history.
3. The design and color of the Palestinian dress depend on the age of the person wearing it and the village it represents.
4. UNESCO recognized Palestinian embroidery as an intangible cultural heritage in 2012.
5. Alaa believes that the responsibility for preserving Palestinian embroidery lies primarily with schools and educational institutions.

Multiple Choice

1. Why does Alaa mention the Israeli Defense Minister's wife in the context of Palestinian embroidery?

    a. To show that Israeli officials often admire Palestinian fashion

    b. To illustrate the collaboration between Palestinian and Israeli designers

    c. To talk about a famous Israeli embroidery exhibition

    d. To explain how the occupation has attempted to claim Palestinian dress as their own

2. What event does Alaa describe as a "cultural victory" for the Palestinian cause?

    a. The recognition of Palestinian dress by UNESCO

    b. The opening of the first Palestinian embroidery museum

    c. The popularity of Palestinian embroidery styles used around the world

    d. The publication of a book about Palestinian embroidery

3. Why does Alaa emphasize the role of Palestinian women in preserving embroidery?

   a. Women are the ones who create and export the embroidery to other countries.

   b. Women in Palestine are the only ones allowed to wear the embroidered dress.

   c. Women, especially mothers and grandmothers, pass down the tradition and teach it to future generations.

   d. *None of the above*

Matching

بِحَيْث	such that, in a way that
حسب	for a long time
حَوالي	still
على إنّو	as much as possible
على كاهِل	in terms of
غيْر	according to, depending on
في ما يتعلّق بِـ	must, obligated to
قْدِر الإمْكان	approximately, about
ما زال	since the days of
ما كفّاهُم	upon (responsibility)
مثلاً	from (the time) when
مِن أيّام	other than, not
مِن حدّ ما	regarding, concerning
مِن حَيْث	for example
مِن زمان	not enough for them
واجِب عليْها	on the basis that

كُلّ بلد إلْها تُراثْها الخاصّ، وإلْها ثَوْبْها الخاصّ.	1 Every country has its own heritage and its own traditional dress.
التّطْريز الفلسْطيني اللي كانوا يِسْتخدموه أجْدادنا على الثَّوب، وكانوا يِلْبسوه الكِبار بالعُمُر.	2 Palestinian embroidery, which our ancestors used on the traditional dress, was worn by the elders.
حتّى الآن، الأُمَّهات الفلسْطينيّات وأنا واحْدة مِن النّاس، اللي كُنْت صْغيرة، مِن حدّ ما بدأت... يَعْني في عُمْر السِّت سبْعة سِتّ سنَوات سبع سنَوات، بدأت أتْعلّم كيف التّطْريز الفلسْطيني.	3 Even now, Palestinian mothers—and I'm one of them—when I was young, starting at the age of six or seven, began learning how to do Palestinian embroidery.
كُلّ أُم واجِب عليْها في فِلسْطين إنّها تْعلِّم بِنْتها كيف بيتِمّ التّطْريز الفلسْطيني.	4 It is every mother's duty in Palestine to teach her daughter how Palestinian embroidery is done.
هدا جُزْء مِن واجِبْها عشان تِقْدر تْحافِظ على هدا الإرث وعلى هدا التّاريخ.	5 This is part of her duty to preserve this heritage and this history.
التّطْريز الفلسْطيني بدا مِن زمان، مِن حَوالي أكْتر مِن ٣٠٠٠ سنة، مِن أيّام الكنْعانيّين. هُمّ أوّل مِن بدوا بالتّطْريز.	6 Palestinian embroidery began a long time ago, over 3,000 years ago, during the time of the Canaanites. They were the first to start embroidery.
كان التّطْريز بْيِخْتلِف، وما زال بْيِخْتلِف حسب القرْية المَوْجودة... المَوْجود فيها الثَّوب.	7 Embroidery used to differ, and it still differs, depending on the village where the dress comes from.
كُلّ توْب بْيِرْمُز لقرْية مُعيّنة، وبْنفس الوَقْت كُلّ توْب بْفلسْطين بْيِخْتلِف لوْنو، وبْيِخْتلْفوا الرُّسومات اللي مْطرّزة على التّوْب حسب إذا كان رح تِلْبسو صبية، أَوْ رح تِلْبسو طفْلة صْغيرة، أَوْ كانت رح تِلْبسو سَيِّدة كْبيرة بالعُمُر.	8 Each dress represents a specific village, and at the same time, every Palestinian dress differs in its color and the designs embroidered on it, depending on whether it's worn by a young woman, a little girl, or an elderly lady.
مُحاولات كانت الاِحْتلال مِن زمان إنّهُم يِسْرقوا هدا الإشي.	9 For a long time, the occupation has tried to steal this heritage.
حتّى التُّراث الفلسْطيني، ما كفّاهُم سِرقِة الأرْض، حتّى التُّراث الفلسْطيني حاوَلوا إنّهُم يُسْرقوه.	10 Even Palestinian heritage—they weren't content with stealing the land; they also tried to steal Palestinian heritage.
النِّساء الفلسْطينيّات، مِن زمن النّكْبة في سنةْ ١٩٤٨، خرجوا معْهُم مُفْتاحْهُم، وخرجوا معْهُم الثَّوب اللي هُمّ لابْسينو.	11 Since the Nakba in 1948, Palestinian women left with their keys and the dresses they were wearing.
الثَّوب اللي... حتّى الثَّوب هدا اللي هُمّ نِساءْنا كانوا لابْسينو، ما سِلِم مِن إنّو الاِحْتلال يْحاوِل يِنْسِبو إلو.	12 Even those dresses that our women were wearing did not escape the occupation's attempts to claim them as their own.

زيّ باقي كْتير شَغَلات إلْها عِلاقة بِتُراثْنا الفَلَسْطيني، زيّ الفَلافِل والمَقْلوبة والحُمّص المْسَخّن، كْتير أكْلات حاوَلوا إنّهُم يِسرِقوهُم وينْسِبوهِن إلْهُم كمان هذا الثّوْب والتّطْريز حاوَلوا يِسرِقوا وينْسِبوا إلْهُم.	Like many other things tied to our Palestinian heritage, such as falafel, maqluba, hummus, and musakhan, many foods they tried to steal and claim as their own, they also tried to steal and claim our traditional dress and embroidery.
فا مثلاً، أعْتقِد في السِّتّينِيّات، وَزير الدِّفاع الإسْرائيلي جاب اللي هيّ زَوجتو ولابْسة الثّوْب الفَلَسْطيني عشان يْعَمِّم للْعالم إنّو هذا الثّوْب هُوّ لإلْهُم، وهذا التُّراث هُوّ لإلْهُم.	For example, I think in the 1960s, the Israeli Minister of Defense brought his wife wearing a Palestinian dress to present to the world as if this dress and heritage belonged to them.
هان بْيِجي دوْرْنا إنّو كيف نْعرِّف العالم إنّو هذا الإشي غيْر كْتير في عِنّا.	This is where our role comes in—how do we educate the world that this is something completely ours?
والأمْثلة، إنّو ظهروا عارْضات أزْياء إسْرائيلِيّات بإنّو هذا الثّوْب... لابْسين الثّوْب الفَلَسْطيني على إنّو بِيدِلّ على إنّو هُوّ تُراث إسْرائيلي، وإنّو الفِلَسْطينِيّين ما إلْهُم علاقة فيه.	The examples include Israeli fashion models appearing wearing the Palestinian dress, claiming it represents Israeli heritage and that Palestinians have no connection to it.
كيف إحْنا نْحاوِل نْعرِّف كُلّ العالم إنّو هذا الثّوْب إلْنا، وهذا مَوْروث فلسطيني؟	How can we try to show the world that this dress is ours and that it's part of Palestinian heritage?
مِن الأشْياء الكْوَيّسة، اللي يَعْني مُمْكِن نِعْتبِرْها إيجابية، إنّو اليونِسْكو إعْترفت في الثّوْب الفَلَسْطيني، كرمز لـ... الفِلَسْطينية أعْتقِد بـ٢٠٢١.	One positive thing we can consider is that UNESCO recognized the Palestinian dress in 2021.
إنّو فنّ التّطْريز هذا فن فلسطيني وأدْرجتو على لائِحِتْها للتُّراث الثّقافي غيْر المادّي.	They acknowledged the art of Palestinian embroidery as Palestinian and included it on their list of intangible cultural heritage.
هان إحْنا بِنْكون حقّقْنا نصِر ثقافي لـ... للْقَضِيّة الفِلَسْطينية، ودعمْنا عدم... وحمّيْناها مِن السِّرقِةْ، مُحاولات السِّرقة اليَهودية أوْ الإسْرائيلية، للثّقافة الفِلَسْطينية.	This is how we achieved a cultural victory for the Palestinian cause and protected it from theft—the Jewish or Israeli attempts to steal Palestinian culture.
إذا الدّوْر الكْبير بْيِجي على كاهِل الأُمّهات والأجْداد، بِحَيْث إنّهُم يِنْقلوا هذا التُّراث في ما يتعلّق بالتّطْريز ويْعلْموه لأوْلادهُم، ويْحاوْلوا يْنْشُروا قْدِر الإمْكان في العالم الخارجي.	The larger role falls on mothers and grandparents to pass down this heritage related to embroidery, to teach it to their children, and to try to spread it as much as possible to the outside world.

إنّو التُّراث الفِلِسْطيني مُرْتبِط بِالتّطْريز، وإنّو
التّطْريز هُوَّ جُزْءٌ مِن تُراثُنا الفلسْطيني.

22

Palestinian heritage is tied to embroidery, and embroidery is a part of our Palestinian heritage.

Answers

Main Idea: a **True-False:** 1. T[6] 2. F[7] 3. T[8] 4. F[18] 5. F[4-5, 21] **Multiple Choice:** 1. d[14] 2. a[18-20] 3. c[4-5, 21]

Matching: بحَيْث such that, in a way that / حسب according to, depending on / حَوالي approximately, about / إنّو on the basis that / على كاهِل upon / غيْر other than, not / في ما يتعلّق بِـ regarding, about / إنّو on the basis that / على كاهِل upon / غيْر other than, not / في ما يتعلّق بِـ regarding, concerning / قْدِر الإمْكان as much as possible / ما زال still ما كفّاهُم not enough for them / مثلاً for example / مِن زمان for a long time / مِن حَيْث in terms of / مِن حدّ ما from (the time) when / مِن أيّام since the days of / example / واجِب علَيْها must, obligated to

22 Bader: Culture

رابِطة bond   وِرْثة inheritance   مُصادَرة confiscation   مُزارِعين farmers

Main Idea

a. The economic value of land in Palestine.
b. The practical uses of land in Palestinian farming and agriculture.
c. The challenges Palestinian farmers face in making a living.
d. The bond Palestinians have with their land and the effort to protect it from confiscation.

True or False

1. Bader believes that the land's primary value is its financial worth.
2. Few Palestinians these days are landowners.
3. The phrase "Your land is your honor" is a government slogan to encourage land ownership.
4. Every Palestinian, even those living in cities, tries to take care of their land by visiting and maintaining it.
5. Bader mentions that Palestinian farmers receive a lot of support from the government to maintain their land.

Multiple Choice

1. Why does Bader say the bond between Palestinians and their land is unique?

   a. Because the bond is passed down through generations and is deeply emotional.

   b. Because the land has a very high material value.

   c. Because Palestinians rely solely on farming for their livelihood.

   d. Because the government provides strong support to Palestinian farmers.

2. What do Palestinians often do to maintain and protect their land?

   a. Build factories and commercial spaces on it.

   b. Hire workers to manage the land while they live in the city.

   c. Develop, tend to, and build terraces or gates to show ownership.

   d. Sell the land to prevent it from being confiscated.

3. Why do Palestinians feel the need to be constantly present on their land?

   a. To prevent it from being confiscated by showing that it has an active owner.

   b. To increase the value of the land for future sales.

   c. To build large farming businesses.

   d. To comply with government regulations.

Matching

أمّا	at any time
بالتّالي	like a motivation
بِدْهُم	from their own pocket
بَسّ لأنّهُم	present
خَلّينا نِحْكي	so consequently
دايِر بالو عليها	taking care of it
زيّ دافع	as for
صَعْب إنّو	let's say
فا بالتّالي	from generation to generation
في أيّ وَقْت	just because they
مِتْواجِد	they want
مِش ضروري	despite that
مع ذلِك	not necessary
مِن جيبِتْهُم	consequently
مِن جيل لجيل	it's difficult that

Text

أمّا بالنِّسْبة للرّابِطة أوْ الصِّلة المَوْجودة بيْن الفلسْطيني وأرْضو، فا هيّ رابِطة جِدّاً قَوية وجِدّاً مُميّزة، لأنّو هاي الرّابِطة عِبارة عن رابِطة مُتَوارِثة مِن جيل لجيل.

1

As for the bond or connection that exists between the Palestinian and their land, it is a very strong and very special bond because this bond is one that is passed down from generation to generation.

يَعْني كُلّ جيل بيسلِّم جيل الوِرْثة والأراضي لِمِّن جيل لجيل.	That is, every generation hands down the inheritance and the land from generation to generation.
كُلّ فلسْطيني في فلسْطين تَقْريباً يَعْني بوخِذ وِرْثة وعِنْدو أَمْلاك أراضي.	Almost every Palestinian in Palestine inherits land or has property.
هاي القيمة يَعْني الأراضي هاي بتِتْعدّى قيمِتْها المادّية.	This value, I mean, the land, its value exceeds its material value.
مِش عِبارة عن بسّ أرْض والْها قيمة مادّية وتْبيعْها وتوخِذ مصاري.	It's not just about land that has a material value and that you sell and take money for.
لا، لا، هيَّ أكْتر مِن هيْك، هيَّ عِبارة عن أرْض، زيّ ما بْيِحْكوها: "أرْضك عِرْضك".	No, no, it is more than that. It is about land, as they say: "Your land is your honor."
عِنّا في فلسْطين، في مِثال شعْبي بيحْكي إنّو : "أرْضك عِرْضك".	For us in Palestine, there is a popular saying that says: "Your land is your honor."
فا بالتّالي، الأرْض اللي عِنّا بتِتْعدّى قيمِتْها المادّية، وبْتوخِذ قيمة عاطِفية وقيمة جَوْهرية.	So, therefore, the land we have exceeds its material value and takes on an emotional value and an intrinsic value.
لأنّو في فلسْطين عِنّا، الوَضِع مِخْتِلِف شْوَيّ.	Because in Palestine, our situation is a little different.
لمّا حدا يْكون في عِنْدو أرْض، بيحاوِل دايماً هاي الأرْض يْدير بالو عليها، يْعمِّرْها، يْزبِّطْها، يِزرَعْها.	When someone owns land, they always try to take care of it, cultivate it, improve it, and plant it.
حتّى لَوْ ما إنّو فلّاح يَعْني مِش ضروري شخْص يَعْني مُزارِع شخْص إلو علاقة بالأرْض، لا لا هُوَّ أيّ حدا شخْص وعِنْدو قِطْعة أرْض، دائماً بيدير بالو عليها.	Even if they are not a farmer, it's not necessary that a person is a farmer or someone connected to the land—no, no. Anyone who has a piece of land always takes care of it.
بيعمِّرْها، بيشيِّكْها، بِبْني سناسِل، بِزرَعْها، وبوكِل مِن خَيْراتْها.	They improve it, check on it, build terraces, plant it, and eat from its produce.
هاي كُلّها أيّ فلسْطيني بيْعمِل هيْك حتّى إنّو عايِش بالْمدينة وعِنْدو قِطْعة أرْض، بيْطلع مِن المدينة يوْم جُمْعة سبْت يَعْني عَ أيّام العُطل، وبيروح بيزبِّط أرْضو.	All of this, every Palestinian does this, even if they live in the city and have a piece of land. They leave the city on Fridays or Saturdays, that is, on weekends, and go and tend to their land.
لأنّو خلص... لأنّو إحْنا بفلسْطين، عِنّا دائماً هاجِس إنّو هاي الأرْض مُمْكِن تْروح في أيّ وَقْت، هاي الأرْض مُمْكِن يْتِمّ مُصادرِتْها.	Because... because for us in Palestine, we always have the worry that this land could be lost at any time, that this land could be confiscated.

فا بِالتّالي، إنّك إنْتَ لمّا تْدير بالك عَ أرْضك، وتْكون دائماً مِتْواجِد فيها، وداير بالك عليْها ومْشيِّكْها، وكمان عامِل هيْك زيّ بوّابة مْزبِّطْها، دايْماً يَعْني بيكون في يَعْني بيكون زيّ دافِع إنّو مثلاً إنّو هاي الأرْض إلْها صْحاب.

| | So, therefore, when you take care of your land, are always present in it, tend to it, check on it, and even set up something like a gate or improve it, this always gives... I mean, it gives the impression that this land has owners. |
|15| |

وصعْب إنّو يْتِم مُصادرتْها.

| | And it becomes difficult for it to be confiscated. |
|16| |

فا كُلّ فلسْطيني، حتّى المُزارِعين، يَعْني المُزارِعين حتّى عنّا بْفلسْطين مع إنّهُم مِش مدْعومين كْتير ويَعْني مِن السُّلْطة خلّينا نحْكي مِن الحُكومة، مِش مدْعومين مع ذلِك هُمّ بيزْرعوا هُم بيدْفعوا مصاري مِن جيبتْهُم وبيتْحمّلوا الخسائِر.

| | So, every Palestinian, even the farmers—I mean, the farmers, even here in Palestine, although they are not greatly supported, meaning by the authority, let's say by the government—they are not supported. Despite this, they plant, they pay money out of their own pockets, and they bear the losses. |
|17| |

مع ذلِك، المُزارِعين بيزْرعوا وبْيزبْطوا أُمورْهُم بسّ لأنّهُم بدْهُم يْثبْتوا الأرْض، بدّهُم يْثبّتوا هاي الأرْض إنّها تْكون أرْض فلسْطينية.

| | Despite this, the farmers plant and manage their affairs only because they want to hold onto the land. They want to affirm that this land remains Palestinian land. |
|18| |

فا هاي الرّابِطة المَوْجودة بيْن الفلسْطيني وأرْضو رابِطة جِدّاً قَوية، ومَوْجودة في بيْت كُلّ فلسْطيني.

| | So, this bond that exists between the Palestinian and their land is a very strong bond and exists in every Palestinian household. |
|19| |

---

23 Nihad: Culture

Keywords

أَدَوات تُراثِية traditional tools   مُتْحَف museum   الأَصالة authenticity

Main Idea

a. The establishment of a heritage museum in Al-Kom and the community's involvement in the project.
b. The difficulties Nihad faced in constructing the museum becaus of bureaucracy and discrimination.
c. A detailed guide on how to organize events for museums.
d. The theft of artifacts from historical sites in Al-Kom and how they have been recovered.

True or False

1. The Ministry of Tourism successfully protected all the historical artifacts in Al-Kom from theft.
2. The heritage museum in Al-Kom was established in an area with ancient ruins.
3. Nihad and her team prepared traditional foods and served them to guests during the museum event.
4. The museum event was documented by local television stations and included interviews with guests and locals.
5. Nihad says they hosted guests from Ireland, Greece, and Austria during the event.

Multiple Choice

1. What kind of items did Nihad and her team collect for the heritage museum in Al-Kom?

   a. Mainly clothing and jewelry
   b. Modern art pieces
   c. Photographs and paintings
   d. Traditional agricultural tools, crafts, and old clothing

2. What did Nihad and her team do to ensure a large turnout for the event?

   a. They went door to door in the village to invite every resident.
   b. They made sure the event was free.
   c. They invited celebrities to the event.
   d. They created brochures, advertisements, and announcements.

3. Why does Nihad say they need to be careful during events like the museum opening?

    a. Because the artifacts are extremely fragile

    b. Because they had limited time to organize the event

    c. To avoid losing any of the guests' personal belongings

    d. To document every step and ensure the event holds weight and value

Matching

إشي طبيعي	therefore
بْإيدينا	at the same time
بِدّك	how much
بسّ	than what
زيّ هيْك	for every
طبْعاً	it's natural that
عَ كُلّ	by our hands
فا	from outside
قدّيْش	when
لِسّا	but
لمّا	you want
لهيك	so, therefore
مع إنّو	no matter how
مِن برّا	like this
مِن فتْرة	still
مِن ما	some time ago
مِن نفْس الوَقِت	although
مِهْما	of course

مِن فترْة تقْريباً أكْتر مِن خمِس شُهور بدأْنا في تأْسيس متْحف تُراثي في عنّا في قرْية الْكوم.	**1** About five months ago, we started establishing a heritage museum in our village, Al-Kom.
جمعْنا الأدوات التُّراثية الزِّراعية، الأشْياء اللي كانوا بِسْتخْدِموها في الحِراثة، الملْبوسات القديمةِ، والصِّناعات اليدوية البسيطة.	**2** We collected traditional farming tools, items used in plowing, old clothing, and simple handmade crafts.
وجمعْنا كُلّ هاي الشّغْلات.	**3** We gathered all these things together.
طبْعاً، إحْنا مرخّصين ومُوثّقين كُلّ شي، بسّ لِسّا الإنْشاء يَعْني رح ياخُذ وَقْت، وتجْميع الأدوات كمان.	**4** Of course, everything is licensed and documented, but the establishment process will take time, as will collecting all the items.
بالْمُناسبِة، إحْنا بلدْنا، الكوْم بالذّات، هيِّ تاريخية جمْعت عِدِّة عُصور مِن الكنْعانيِّين، الآشوريِّين، الرّومانيِّين.	**5** By the way, our village, Al-Kom specifically, is historic and has witnessed several civilizations: the Canaanites, the Assyrians, and the Romans.
كُلّو يَعْني كُلّ هاي الحضارات مرّت فيها، وإلْها آثار اسْتخْرجوها.	**6** All these civilizations passed through here and left behind artifacts that were unearthed.
طبْعاً باعوها، كان في سرْقات للْآثار.	**7** Unfortunately, many of these artifacts were sold, and some were even stolen.
مِهْما حاوَلِت وِزارةِ السِّياحة والآثار إنّها تْحافِظ، كان لأ... كان في ناس يجي يِسرقْها ويْبيعْها.	**8** No matter how much the Ministry of Tourism and Antiquities tried to protect them, people would come and steal and sell them.
طبْعاً إحْنا عْمِلْنا في منْطِقة هيِّ فيها آثار قديمةِ، لهيْك هيِّ بْتُعْتبر إنّو متْحف تُراثي مع منْطِقة تاريخية للْآثار.	**9** We worked in an area that has ancient ruins, which is why it is considered both a heritage museum and a historic archaeological site.
فا كانِت عْمِلْنا هيْك زْيارة يوْم لَوِزارةِ السِّياحة، والنّاس شخْصيّات مِن البلد ومِن برّا البلد.	**10** We organized a day of visits for the Ministry of Tourism, local figures, and people from outside the village.
عْمِلْنا أكْلات شعْبية، سِتّات اللي لِسّا مْحافْظين على لِبسْهُم التُّراثي، على الثّوْب الفلسْطيني، والشّاشية هاي اللي مِنْحْكيلْها غطا الرّأْس، مِنْحْكيلْها شاشية، الحْزام.	**11** We prepared traditional dishes, and women who still maintain their traditional attire wore Palestinian thobes, headscarves (which we call shashiya), and belts.
كُلّ هاي الأُمور حاوَلْنا إنّو نطْلع اليوْم بْأجْمل ما يِمْكِن.	**12** We tried to present everything in the most beautiful way possible.
عْمِلْنا أكْلات شعْبية، طبخْناها إحْنا بْأيدينا، قدّمْناها للضُّيوف.	**13** We cooked traditional food ourselves and served it to the guests.

طبْعاً، في أيّا مُناسبة زيّ هيْك لازِم نْوتِّق، وْوثّقْنا مع تلِفِزْيونات محلّية.	14	In any event like this, documentation is essential, so we documented everything with local TV channels.
عْملْنا بْروشورات، عْملْنا دعايات وإعْلانات في كُلّ مكان، عَ أساس إنّو يْكون الحُضور كْبير.	15	We made brochures, advertisements, and promotions everywhere to ensure a large turnout.
وسجّلْنا الحلقات، عْملْنا لقاءات مع النّاس، مع الضّيوف اللي إحْنا مِسْتضيفينْهُم، مع أهِل البلد كمان.	16	We recorded the events, conducted interviews with guests, and spoke with locals as well.
فا كان يَعْني الفعالية نفْسها تعْطيك شُعور بالأّصالةِ أكْتر مِن ما إنّو إنْتَ تِسْعى كُلّ الوَقِت أنّك إنْتَ تْكون حريص على الثّقافة والتّراث.	17	The event itself gave a sense of authenticity, more than just working hard to preserve the culture and heritage.
بسّ لمّا تْجمّعوا النّاس وشُفْتُهُم، شُفِت بعْيونْهُم قدّيش هُمِّ مُمْتنّين، عنْدْهُم شُعور باحْترام لهالمجْهود الكِبير اللي إحْنا مِنعْمْلو.	18	When you see people gathered and the gratitude in their eyes, you can feel their respect for the great effort we've put into this.
فا حكيْت إنّو لازِم كُلّ سنة نعْمل هيْك أيّام.	19	I decided we should make this an annual tradition.
طبْعاً، أجونا ضيوف مِن إيرلنْدا، ومِن اليونان، ومِن النّمْسا.	20	We even had guests from Ireland, Greece, and Austria.
كان إشي حِلو، ومِن نفْس الوَقِت مُتْعِب.	21	It was a wonderful experience but also exhausting.
لأنّو إنْتَ بدّك تْكون حريص على كُلّ خُطْوةٍ بْتِخْطيها، عَ كُلّ تفْصيلة بدّك تعْمِلْها، تْوَثِّقْها، تْكون فعْلاً إلْها وَزِنْها والْها قيمِتْها.	22	Because you need to be careful with every step you take, with every detail you want to carry out. You need to document it and make sure it truly has its weight and its value.
لمّا الآخر يِجي ويْشوف التّرْتيب، إشي طبيعي إنّك إنْتَ تْكون محطّ اهْتِمام يَعْني.	23	When others come and see the organization, it's only natural that you become a center of attention.

---

24   Khaled: Culture

Keywords

فُرْن الطّين clay oven   الزّعْتر za'atar (a traditional herb mix often eaten with bread)

Main Idea

a. A detailed explanation of Palestinian breadmaking as part of their cultural heritage.
b. The disappearance of all Palestinian traditions due to modern technology.
c. How Palestinian embroidery has become popular in modern fashion.
d. A focus on the introduction of new Palestinian dishes and cooking methods.

True or False

1. Khaled explains that some traditional customs, like breadmaking, have begun to disappear due to modern advancements like automated bakeries.
2. The entire breadmaking process is typically done by women, with no involvement from the men.
3. Palestinian bread can be turned into manaqeesh before it is fully baked.
4. Khaled describes Palestinian bread as carrying the scent of the homeland.
5. The bread is normally only eaten at breakfast and is often served with honey and olives.

Multiple Choice

1. According to Khaled, what has caused the resurgence of traditional breadmaking in Palestine?

    a. People prefer homemade bread for health reasons.

    b. The increasing cost of bread from bakeries

    c. War, lack of electricity, and the destruction of bakeries

    d. *None of the above*

2. What is one characteristic of traditional Palestinian bread that Khaled mentions?

    a. It's large, delicious, and has a wonderful smell.

    b. It's small and crunchy.

    c. It's baked quickly in a microwave.

    d. It's made using store-bought dough.

3. Which of the following statements about Palestinian bread is correct?

    a. It is made only during special occasions.

    b. It can be eaten with various toppings and fillings, like za'atar and cheese.

    c. It cannot be baked in a clay oven.

    d. *None of the above*

Matching

إلْها	now
بعْد ما	inside it
جُوّاه	maybe, possibly
حَواليْه	before
زيّ ما	after, behind
عفْواً	together
في عنّا	won't
في كُلّ حين	once again
قبِل ما	around it
كُلّ واحْدة	has
كمان مرّة	we have
مِش حَ	like what, as
مع بعْض	each one
مُمْكِن	one of its conditions
مِن شُروطو	excuse me (correction)
مهْما	after
هالأيّت	at any time
وَرا	no matter what

مسا الخيْر.	1	Good evening.
في عِنّا بِفِلسْطين كْتير عادات وتقاليد وتُراث شَعْبي، مِنْها الفُلْكْلور الفِلسْطيني، الدَّبْكة، والدَّحّية، والتَّطْريز الفلسْطيني.	2	In Palestine, we have many traditions, customs, and popular heritage, including Palestinian folklore, dabke, dihiyya, and Palestinian embroidery.
وفي أكْلات مشْهورة فيها فِلسْطين، زيّ المقْلوبة الفِلسْطينية وخبُز الخُبُز وغيرْها.	3	There are also famous dishes in Palestine, like Palestinian maqluba, taboon bread, and others.
كْتير أشْياء وُجود التِّكْنولوجْيا والتَّطَوُّر أدّى لاخْتِفاء أوْ بِدايةْ اخْتِفاء بعْض هدي العادات، زيّ الخُبُز، واسْتِبْدالْها بالمخابِز الآلية، اللي رَيَّحت كْتير مِن سِتّات البُيوت.	4	Many things—the presence of technology and development—have led to the disappearance or the beginning of the disappearance of some of these traditions, like breadmaking, which has been replaced by automated bakeries that made things much easier for housewives.
لكِن مع الحاجة والحرْب وانْعِدام الكهْرباء وانْعِدام وتدْمير المخابِز، ظهرت الحاجة كمان مرّة لهدي العادات الأصيلة، اللي هيّ أصْلاً جُزْء مِن الذّاكِرة، واللي مهْما مرّ الوَقِت مِش حَ نِنْساها.	5	But with the needs created by war, the lack of electricity, and the destruction of bakeries, the need for these authentic traditions has reappeared—traditions that are a part of our memory and that, no matter how much time passes, we will never forget.
حَ أتْكلّم هالّيْت عن كيف بْنِخْبِز الخُبُز وكمان عن فُرْن الطّين.	6	Today, I'm going to talk about how we bake bread and also about the clay oven.
اللي العيْلة بْتِتْجمّع حَوالَيه بعْد ما الشّباب يْحضّروا كُلّ أغْراض الخبْيز مِن طْحين وخميرة وغيرْها.	7	The family gathers around it after the men prepare all the breadmaking supplies, like flour, yeast, and other ingredients.
بْتيجي السِّتّات بْيِتْجمّعوا مع بعْض الإمّ والجدّة، والبنات الصّغار، كُلّ واحْدة إلْها دوْرْها.	8	Then, the women gather together—the mother, the grandmother, and the young girls—and everyone has their role.
بيحُطّوا المكوّنات على بعْض، وبْيِعْملوا العجين وبيقطّعوها لقطع صْغيرة هيْك. بعْد هيْك، بْيِفْردوها لخُبُز.	9	They mix the ingredients together, knead the dough, and cut it into small pieces. Then, they roll it out into flatbreads.
مِن مُواصفات الرّغيف الفِلسْطيني إنّو حجْمو كْبير وطعْمو كْتير زاكي، وريحْتو كْتير كْتير حِلْوة.	10	One of the characteristics of Palestinian bread is that it's large in size, has a very delicious taste, and smells absolutely amazing.
مِن شُروطو إنّو بينِخْبِز على خُبِز الطّين عفْواً على فُرْن الطّين.	11	One of its conditions is that it's baked in a clay oven.
اللي الشّباب بيولّعوه وبْيِجهْزوه، بيحُطّوا فيه الرِّغيف وَرا التّاني وَرا التّالِت.	12	The men light the oven and prepare it, placing the loaves one after another inside.

13	هدا الرِّغيف بيكون فيه ريحِةْ البْلاد، وريحِةْ الوَطن، وتْراب الوَطن.	This bread carries the scent of the homeland, the aroma of the soil, and the essence of the nation.
14	بعْد هيْك بْتِتْجمّع الأُسْرة ليتْعشّوا الدُّقّة والزّعْتر الفِلِسْطيني الجِبْنة وغيرْها.	After that, the family gathers to have dinner, with dukkah, Palestinian za'atar, cheese, and other foods.
15	هدا الخُبُزْ مُمْكِن يِتْحوّل قبل ما يِسْتْوي قبل ما يُدْخُل فُرْن الطِّين لمناقيش.	This bread can also be transformed before it's baked in the clay oven into manaqeesh.
16	هدي المناقيش هيّ وَجْبة كامِلة مُتكامِلة، مُمْكِن تِنْفع فْطور، مُمْكِن غدا، مُمْكِن عشا.	These manaqeesh are a complete, balanced meal. They can be eaten for breakfast, lunch, or dinner.
17	مُمْكِن بين الوجبات هدي بْيِفردوا الرِّغيف ويحُطّوا على وِجْهو الدُّقّة الفِلِسْطينية أَوْ الزّعْتر الفلسطيني، أَوْ مُمْكِن يحْشوا جُوّاه الجِبْنة البيْضا أَوْ الجِبْنة الصّفْرا أَوْ غيرْها.	Between meals, the flatbread is rolled out, and on top, Palestinian dukkah or za'atar is placed, or it can be stuffed with white cheese, yellow cheese, or other fillings.
18	بعْد ما تُدْخُل الفُرْن وتِسْتْوي، بِتْصير جاهْزة للأكْل.	Once it's placed in the oven and baked, it's ready to eat.
19	بْنِقطّع معْها البنْدوْرة والخْيار، وهيْك بْتاكُل أزْكى وَجْبة وأطْيَبْ وَجْبة، اللي هيّ أَصْلا أصيلة فينا واللي بْتِنْفع زيّ ما قُلِت في كُلّ وَقِت وفي كُلّ حين.	It's served with tomatoes and cucumbers, and you eat the most delicious and tastiest meal—a meal that is deeply rooted in us and can be enjoyed at any time and on any occasion.
20	وصحّة وهنا إن شاء الله.	Bon appétit, God willing.

Social Issues

25   Alaa on the Palestinian Experience

Keywords

| مطار airport   معْبر border crossing   حصار siege   تكاليف costs |

Main Idea

  a.   The development of Gaza's airport and its impact on the local economy.
  b.   The high costs associated with leaving Gaza.
  c.   The role of Egypt in facilitating travel for Gazans.
  d.   The personal experiences of Gazans in obtaining travel documents.

True or False

1. Gaza had an operational airport for twenty years before it was bombed and closed permanently.
2. Gaza residents have multiple ways to travel outside of Gaza besides going through Egypt.
3. Before the war, the unemployment rate in Gaza was around 25%.
4. Alaa and her family had to pay 20,000 dollars to leave Gaza during the war.
5. Alaa believes that the people of Gaza are to blame for paying such high amounts to leave.

Multiple Choice

1. Which service(s) does the Egyptian company Hala provide for travelers from Gaza?

   a. VIP assistance for crossing the border from Palestine into Egypt

   b. Flights from Cairo to the destination of choice

   c. Assistance with finding accommodation in Egypt

   d. *All of the above*

2. What was the daily wage in Gaza before the war, according to Alaa?

   a. 3 dollars   b. 13 dollars   c. 30 dollars   d. 33 dollars

3. How much does it currently cost for an adult to leave Gaza through Egypt after the war, according to Alaa?

   a. 500 dollars   b. 1,500 dollars   c. 2,500 dollars   d. 5,000 dollars

أساساً	for the better
إن شا الله	the same as
بدل ما	until, by (time)
خِلال	not more than
طَيِّب	until
عبيْن	during
على إنّهُم	basically
على خيْر	from it
علينْا	supposed to
فقط لا غيْر	upon us
لعِنْد	nothing more, other than
مِش أكْتر	God willing
مفْروض	that they
مِن نفْس	Oh Lord
مِنّو	instead of; rather than
يا ربْنا	well (discourse marker)

مرحبا، حابّة أَحْكي عن إشي يِمْكِن مُخْتِلِف أَوْ غير عن باقي كُلّ يَعْني دُوَل العالم.	**1** Hello, I want to talk about something that might be different or unique compared to the rest of the world.
ما أَعْتِقِد في دَوْلة في العالم دَوْلة بِتْعاني مِن نفْس المُعاناة اللي بيعاني مِنْها أهل غزّة.	**2** I don't think there's a country in the world that suffers the same as the people of Gaza.
في أيّ دَوْلة في العالم، عشان تْسافِر، إنْتَ بْتِحْجِز تذْكِرِة طَيارانك وبِتْروح على المطار وبِتْسافِر، بسّ الوَضِع بْغزّة مُخْتِلِف جِدّاً.	**3** In any other country in the world, to travel, you book your plane ticket, go to the airport, and travel. But the situation in Gaza is very different.
إحْنا كان مفْروض إنّو يْكون في مطار طبْعاً.	**4** We were supposed to have an airport, of course.
غزّة مُحاصرة مِن كُلّ الاتِّجاهات.	**5** Gaza is besieged from all directions.
وفي سنِة ١٩٩٨، بذْكُر كُنْت بالصَّفّ السّادِس تقْريباً، يَعْني كان عُمْري يِمْكِن ١١ سنة، سْمِعْنا عن إنّهُم رح يِفْتِحوا مطار، وكُنّا كْتير مبْسوطين.	**6** In 1998, I remember I was in sixth grade—so I was about 11 years old—we heard that they were going to open an airport, and we were very excited.
حتّى كانوا في رِحلات المدْرسية، ياخْدونا رِحْلة عَ المطار، إنّو إشي واو وإنّو نَعْمل بْغزّة، هدا الإشي صَعْب في دَوْلة أساساً هيَّ مُحْتلّة.	**7** They even used to take us on school trips to the airport. It was like a "wow" thing to have something like this in Gaza, which is, after all, an occupied land.
المطار في غزّة بَعْد هيْك اشْتغل سنتيْن، وبعْد ما اشْتغل سنتيْن، اتْوَقَّف عن العمل لأنّو انْقصف بذْكُر بالـ٢٠٠١ و٢٠٠٢.	**8** The airport in Gaza operated for two years, and after those two years, it stopped functioning because it was bombed—I remember it was in 2001 and 2002.
عبيْن بالـ٢٠٠٦، انْقصف كُلِّيّاً وبطّل مَوْجود اللي هُوَّ المطار نِهائِيّاً.	**9** By 2006, the airport was completely bombed and no longer existed.
فا صِرْنا عشان بِدّك تْسافِر مِن غزّة، ما إلك إلّا تْمُرّ عن طريق مصِر.	**10** So, for us to travel from Gaza, there's no option except to go through Egypt.
في فترة صَعْب كْتير، أساساً هُوَّ وَضِع المعْبر والمُعاملة كانت فيه سيِّئة جِدّاً.	**11** This has always been very difficult, and the situation at the border crossing was extremely bad.
سَواء يِمْكِن الجانِب الفلسطيني وهُناك، المُعاملة مْنيحة، بسّ لمّا كُنّا نوصل للْجانِب المصْري كانت المُعاملة كْتير سيِّئة.	**12** On the Palestinian side, the treatment might be okay, but once we reached the Egyptian side, the treatment was very bad.
وكان لازِم تِدْفع فْلوس، يَعْني مِن ٣٥٠ دوْلار، ٦٠٠ دوْلار.	**13** And you had to pay money—from $350 to $600.

لعِنْد الـ٢٠١٦ كُنّا طَبْعاً مِتْقَبْلين شْوَيّة المَوْضوع إنّو هدا تِدْفع بْهدا المَبْلغ، لعِنْد ٢٠١٩ ظهرت شِرْكة إسْمْها شِرْكِةْ هلا، عمِلَت خِدْمة شِرْكة مصْرِية عمِلَت خِدْمة إسمْها خِدْمةْ الـVIP.

إنْتَ بْتِدْفع فْلوس وبْتِطْلَع، يَعْني إنْتَ عشان تِطْلع مِن غْزّة لازِم تِدْفع ١٢٠٠ دوْلار بسّ عشان تْمُرّ. هدا غيْر تذْكِرة...

يَعْني إنْتَ بسّ بِتْمُرّ، إنّو تِقْدر الـ١٢٠٠ دوْلار بسّ بيخلّوك تِصل لمطار القاهرة.

لا بْيِدْفعوا لك تذْكِرةْ طَيَران للدّوْلة التّانْيِة اللي إنْتَ رايِحِلها.

ولا بْيِعْمَلولك أيّا إشي طَبْعاً مُعَدَّل البطالة بْغزّة كان كْتير عالي وصعْب كْتير تْجمِّع الـ١٢٠٠ دوْلار.

يِمْكِن مُعَدَّل البطالة قبل الحرْب وِصِل لخمْسين في المِيّة إذا ما كانِش أكْتر.

المتُوَسِّط اليَوْمي كان للأجْر تقْريباً بْغزّة، يَعْني اليوْم الواحد إذا بِدّك تِشْتِغِل بْغزّة كُنْت تاخُد ١٣ دوْلار، مِش أكْتر.

طَبْعاً إنْتَ مع الحرْب زاد المَبْلغ، والـ١٢٠٠ دوْلار بطّل يَعْني هالسِّعِر.

مِش مْنيح بالنِّسْبة لشِرْكِةْ هلا فا رفعوا السِّعِر للْشّخْص الكْبير، اللي هُوَّ فوق ١٨ سنة، لـ٥٠٠٠ دوْلار، وللْشّخْص الصّغير ٢٥٠٠ دوْلار إذا كان اقل مِن ١٢ سنة.

يَعْني إذا إنْتَ ١٨... هيَّ ١٨ سنة سوْري... إذا كان إنْتَ عُمْرك ١٨ سنة ويوْمْ، بِدّك تِدْفع ٥٠٠٠ دوْلار.

طَبْعاً أوْ إذا كان عُمْرك كُنْتي والدة والد طِفْل صغير عُمْرو بسّ يوْمْ، بِدّك تِدْفعي عليْه ٢٥٠٠ دوْلار.

وهدا الإشي اللي أنا عانيْت مِنّو خِلال الحرْب.

يَعْني أنا عِنْدي ٤ أطْفال وزوْجي، وأنا دفعْنا ٢٠٠٠٠ دوْلار.

Up until 2016, we sort of accepted this situation, paying these amounts. But in 2019, a company called Hala emerged, an Egyptian company that introduced a service called VIP Service.

14

You had to pay money, and just to leave Gaza, you had to pay $1,200, just to pass through. That's excluding the ticket...

15

This means that just to pass, you pay $1,200, and that only gets you to Cairo Airport.

16

They don't pay for your plane ticket to the other country you're traveling to.

17

Nor do they do anything else for you. Of course, with the unemployment rate in Gaza being so high, it was very hard to save $1,200.

18

Before the war, the unemployment rate in Gaza reached 50%, if not more.

19

The average daily wage in Gaza was about $13 per day—not more.

20

With the war, the amount has increased, and $1,200 is no longer the price.

21

And this price is not suitable for Hala, so they raised it—to $5,000 for adults over 18 years old and $2,500 for children under 12 years old

22

Meaning that if you're 18 years old and one day old, you have to pay $5,000.

23

Even if you've just given birth to a baby that's only one day old, you still have to pay $2,500 for them.

24

This is what I experienced during the war.

25

I have four children and a husband, and we paid $20,000.

26

هدا الـ٢٠٠٠٠ دولار ما بْتِعْمِلّك أيّ إشي، بسّ بْتِسْمح لك إنّك تِطْلَع مِن غزّة وتُدْخُل الأراضي المصرية فقط لا غيْر.	27	This $20,000 doesn't get you anything—it only allows you to leave Gaza and enter Egyptian territory, nothing more.
كْتير ناس بِتْلوم على أهِل غزّة، إنّو ليْش طِلْعوا؟ طيّب وليْش يِدْفعوا هيْك مبالغ؟ وليْش هادي المبالغ تِنْدفع؟ إحْنا إنّو إحْنا هيْك بِنشجّعْهُم على إنّهُم يِسْتغِلّونا.	28	Many people criticize the people of Gaza, asking why they left, why they paid such amounts, and why these sums were paid—saying we're encouraging exploitation.
أعْتقِد إنّو الأفضل بدل ما يْلوموا على أهِل غزّة ليْش دفعوا هيْك مبالغ، في ناس أنا بعْرِفْها دفعت 100000 دولار لتِقْدر تِطْلَع هيّ وعائِلاتْها ووْلادْها وأحْفادْها.	29	I think instead of blaming the people of Gaza for paying these amounts—some people I know paid $100,000 to leave with their families, children, and grandchildren—they should hold the responsible parties accountable and look into who made the situation worse for us.
بدل ما يْلوموا علينا، أنا بتْمنّى مِنْهُم إنّهُم يْحاسبوا ويْشوفوا الجِهّة المسْؤولة واللي زادت الوَضِع علينا.	30	Rather than placing blame on us, I hope they focus their attention on the entities truly responsible—those who have exacerbated our situation.
يَعْني يْسوء يا ربْنا يِفْرِجْها إن شا الله ويتْغَيّر الحال وتخَلِّص هالْحَرْب على خيْر.	31	May God grant us relief, and may the situation change, and this war end peacefully.

Answers

Main Idea: b **True-False:** 1. F[8-9] 2. F[10] 3. F[19] 4. T[26] 5. F[28-30] **Multiple Choice:** 1. a[15-17] 2. b[20] 3. d[22-23]

Matching: طيّب well / خِلال during / بدل ما instead of; rather than / إن شا الله God willing / أساساً basically (discourse marker) / على إنّهُم that they / على خيْر for the better / علينا upon us / مفْروض supposed to / مِش أكْتر not more than / لعِنْد until / فقط لا غيْر nothing more, other than / عبيْن until, by (time) / يا ربْنا Oh Lord / مِنّو from it / مِن نفْس the same as /

26 Bader on the Palestinian Experience

Keywords

أمان safety   طمأنينة reassurance   صَواريخ missiles

Main Idea

a. The challenges of finding employment in Palestine.
b. The role of international organizations in helping Palestinians.
c. The economic situation in Palestine and how it affects daily life.
d. The daily struggles Palestinians face due to the ongoing occupation and war.

True or False

1. Bader feels a strong sense of security and peace in Palestine despite the occupation.
2. According to Bader, Palestinians feel in full control of their future despite the occupation.
3. Bader mentions that every ten years or so, there is a war or incursion in Palestine.
4. Bader mentions that missiles frequently explode in the sky, and their fragments can fall on innocent people.
5. Bader mentions that his own family's home was destroyed by missiles.

Multiple Choice

1. How does Bader describe the effect of the current war on the already difficult situation in Palestine?

   a. It has led to a new sense of pride and unity.

   b. It has remained the same.

   c. It has improved slightly due to international aid.

   d. It has gotten much worse, with more fear and destruction.

2. What example does Bader give to illustrate the unpredictability of life in Palestine?

   a. Frequent changes in government policies   c. The availability of job opportunities

   b. The destruction of houses due to missiles   d. The lack of access to education

3. What does Bader say about the global community's ability to solve the Palestinian issue?

   a. The issue is too complex for the global community to solve easily.

   b. The international community has completely ignored the issue.

   c. The global community has solved many of the problems.

   d. The issue is actually simple, and solutions are being implemented.

Matching

أضْعاف أضْعاف	around us
الله يْعين	still
بِحْتاج	every period
حَوالينا	many times more
زيّ ما مْنِحْكي	(progressive marker)
عِدّةْ عَوامِل	needs
عم	may God help
في لحْظة	have nothing to do with
كُلّ فتْرة	must happen
لازِم تْصير	several factors
لدرجِةْ إنّو	in a moment
لِسّا	as we say
ما إلْهُمِ دخل بـ	to the degree that

Text

أمّا بالنِّسْبة لِلْوَضِع القائِم في فلسْطين، فا هُوَّ وَضِع يَعْني هُوَّ الوَضِع الحالي بِفلسْطين كُلّو عِبارة عَن وَضِع مُعقّد لِدرجة كْبيرة، ومُعقّد بِشكِل كْبير.

1 As for the current situation in Palestine, it is a situation... that is, the current situation in all of Palestine is a highly complex situation, and it is extremely complicated.

لِيش؟ لأنّو إنْتَ كمُواطِن فلسْطيني عايِش في فلسْطين، يَعْني صعْب جدّاً إنّو تْحِسّ بِأيّ نَوْع مِن أنْواع الأمان.

2 Why? Because as a Palestinian citizen living in Palestine, it is very difficult for you to feel any kind of safety.

صعْب إنّك إنْتَ تْحِسّ بِالطّمْأنينة، صعْب إنّو يْكون يَعْني بيظلّ عِنْدك شُعور بِالقلق شُعور بِالخَوْف شُعور مِن عدم ضَمان المُسْتَقْبل.

3 It is difficult for you to feel reassured; it is difficult because you always have a feeling of anxiety, a feeling of fear, a feeling of uncertainty about the future.

لأنّ إنْتَ في فلسْطين ما تِقْدر تِتْحكّم في مُسْتَقْبلك، عَ الأقلّ حتّى المُسْتَقْبل القْريب، ما تِقْدر تِتْحكّم فيه، ما بْتِقْدر تْخطّط لُه حتّى.

4 Because in Palestine, you cannot control your future, at least not even the near future. You cannot control it, and you cannot even plan for it.

لأنّو إنْتَ مثلاً يَعْني تخيّل واحد حالو، كُلّ سنْتيْن بيصير في حرْب كُلّ سنْتيْن كُلّ فترة بيصير في اِقْتِحام.

5 For example, imagine someone living here, every two years there is a war, every two years there is an incursion.

يَعْني إحْنا عايْشين، لمّا إنْتَ كمُواطِن فلسْطيني عايِش تحْت اِحْتِلال، هاي الأمور كُلّها بِتْخلّي المُواطِن الفلسْطيني دائماً عايِش حَياة عدم الأمان، عدم هيْك الرّاحة، دائماً في وَضِع الخوْف والتّوتّر.

6 So, we are living... as a Palestinian citizen living under occupation, all these things make the Palestinian citizen always live in a state of insecurity, a lack of comfort, always in a state of fear and tension.

هاي الأمور كُلّها يَعْني مُشْكِلة كْبيرة بِتْواجِه كُلّ بيْت فلسْطيني.

7 All these things are a major problem that every Palestinian household faces.

وحاليّاً، في الحرْب الحالية لِسّا، الوَضِع جدّاً أكْبر.

8 And currently, with the ongoing war, the situation is even greater.

اِضْرب اللي بيصير الوَضِع السّابِق أُضْرْبو، يَعْني الوَضِع صار أضْعاف أضْعاف في الحرْب الحالية اللي بِتْصير اللي صارت في غزّة، واللي حاليّاً امْتدّت للشمال في لِبْنان.

9 Multiply the previous situation, multiply it, well, the situation has become many times worse in the current war that is happening, the one that happened in Gaza, and that has now extended to the north in Lebanon.

إحْنا عم كُلّ يوم تقْريباً مِنْشوف طَيّارات حرْبية في السّماء، كُلّ يوم مِنْشوف تقْريباً صَواريخ في السّماء.

10 We are, almost every day, seeing warplanes in the sky, almost every day seeing missiles in the sky.

هاي الصَّواريخ في مِنْها شَظايا بْتِفْقع في السَّما بْتِتْفجَّر قي السَّما وتِنْزِل على البْيوت، وتِنْزِل على النَّاس اللي إلْهُم ما دخل بْأَيّ إشي.	11	These missiles have shrapnel that explodes in the sky, detonates in the sky, and falls on houses and on people who have nothing to do with anything.
يَعْني، إنْتَ كمُواطِن فلسْطيني مُمْكِن تْكون في بيْتك، ومُمْكِن في لحْظة ثانْيَة تْلاقي بيْتك مُكسَّر مْدمَّر، بسّ لأنّو في حدا كان بِدّو يعْمل هيْك.	12	So, as a Palestinian citizen, you could be in your home, and in a second, you could find your house broken, destroyed, just because someone wanted to do that.
بسّ لأنّو إنْتَ ما بْتِقْدر تتْحكّم في حَياتك فا هاي الأُمور.	13	Just because you cannot control your life—this is how things are.
الوَضِع الحالي في فلسْطين عِبارة عن وَضِع مُعقّد.	14	The current situation in Palestine is a complicated situation.
وَضِع بِحْتاج يَعْني مُعقّد جدّاً لدرجِةْ إنّو ما حدا في... حتّى في... يَعْني في السّاحّة العالمية الدُّوَل العالمية... الدُّوَل اللي حَوالِيْنا، يَعْني مِش قادْرين حدا يْحِلّوا مُشْكِلةْ فلسْطين، لأنّو في اِحْتِلال مَوْجود، وفي يَعْني أطْماع لازِم تْصير.	15	A situation so complicated that even... even on the global stage, the international community, the countries around us, no one is able to solve Palestine's problem because there is an ongoing occupation and ambitions that must be achieved.
فا الله يْعين زيّ ما مِنْحْكي، المَوْضوع جدّاً جدّاً مُعقّد، وبِحْتاج عِدّةْ عَوامِل لحتّى يَعْني يْحِسّ المُواطِن الفلسْطيني إنّو مُواطِن وإنّو إنْسان.	16	So, as we say, may God help us. The issue is extremely complicated and requires many factors before the Palestinian citizen can feel that they are a citizen and that they are a human being.

27 Khaled on the Palestinian Experience

Keywords

حِصار blockade   اِحْتِلال occupation   حُدود مُغْلقة closed borders

Main Idea

a. How medical services have been disrupted by the recent war.
b. Khaled's personal travel experiences and how they were impacted by the siege.
c. The development of advanced infrastructure in Gaza despite the difficulties.
d. The restrictions on supplies, movement, and everyday life in Gaza, and how people adapted with creative solutions.

True or False

1. The siege on Gaza started in 2006 when Khaled was around 11 years old.
2. The only border that remains open to Gaza is the one with Egypt.
3. People in Gaza had to wait months to travel because of the restricted movement.
4. Electricity in Gaza is available 24 hours a day, although it is unstable in winter.
5. People in Gaza came up with alternative solutions, like using cooking oil for cars, due to shortages caused by the siege.

Multiple Choice

1. What did the siege make difficult for people in Gaza, according to Khaled?

   a. Traveling, building homes, and accessing medical supplies

   b. Traveling freely and buying luxury items

   c. Visiting neighboring countries for work

   d. *None of the above*

2. How did the people of Gaza adapt to the fuel shortages caused by the siege?

   a. They started using cooking oil for cars and firewood for cooking.

   b. They used solar power for cooking.

   c. They built electric cars.

   d. *None of the above*

3. What impact did the siege have on the younger generation in Gaza, according to Khaled?

    a. It encouraged them to travel more frequently.

    b. It created a generation that dreams of travel but finds it difficult to leave Gaza.

    c. It motivated the younger generation to develop Gaza's tourism industry.

    d. It helped them gain more freedom in travel.

Matching

بِالْمُناسبة	by way/means of
بِتْمنّى إنّو	I hope that
بِحاجة	by the way
بدل عن	wasn't
زيّ باقي	as a result of
شْوَيّة	a bit
على الأقلّ	like the rest
عن طريق	never (in one's life)
فا	at least
لأنّو	since when
ما عُمْرو	because
ما كان	so, therefore
مِن لمّا	instead of
نتيجة لـ	in need of

1

سنة الـ٢٠٠٦، أيّ لمّا كان عُمْري حَوالي ١١ سنة، انْفرض حِصار شديد على قِطاع غزّة.

In 2006, when I was around 11 years old, a severe blockade was imposed on the Gaza Strip.

2

قِطاع غزّة يْحِدّو مِن الغرْب البحر الأبْيض المُتَوَسِّط، ومِن الجنوب جُمْهوريةْ مصِر العربية، ومِن الشّمال والشرْق دوْلةْ الاِحْتِلال.

The Gaza Strip is bordered to the west by the Mediterranean Sea, to the south by the Arab Republic of Egypt, and to the north and east by the occupying state.

3

وبِالتّالي، مِن لمّا انْفرض الحِصار، هدي الحُدود الأرْبعة صارت مُغْلقة تماماً.

Consequently, since the blockade was imposed, these four borders became completely closed.

4

صِرْنا مُقيّدين في سِجِن كْبير، الجِهة الوَحيدة اللي مفْتوحة مِنّو هِيّ السّما، والجِهات الأرْبعة كانت مُغْلقة تماماً.

We became confined in a large prison, with the only open direction being the sky, while the four borders were entirely closed.

5

فا بِالتّالي كان في تقْيِيد لحركةْ الأفْراد.

As a result, there was a restriction on people's movement.

6

كُنّا نحْلم إنّا نْسافِر، واللي حابب يْسافِر كان يِسْتنّى دوْرو على المعْبر بِالأشْهُر.

We used to dream of traveling, and anyone who wanted to travel had to wait their turn at the crossing for months.

7

كُنّا بحاجة دايْماً لكْتير أدَوات، وكان دايْماً هدي الأدَوات تُدْخُل بِشُروط الاِحْتِلال.

We were always in need of many tools, and these tools were always subject to the conditions of the occupation.

8

اللي كان يِسْمح بِدخولو كان يُدْخُل واللي كان يُرْفُضو ما كان يُدْخُل.

Whatever was allowed to enter would enter, and whatever was denied would not.

9

فا بِالتّالي كُنّا دائِماً بحاجةْ كْتير مِن الأدَوات اللي هِيّ مفْقودة مِن السّوق.

As a result, we were always in need of many tools that were missing from the market.

10

كانت أكْتر الأدَوات المفْقودة هِيّ أدَواتْ البِناء كان الواحد كْتير يِتْغلّب لمّا بِدّو يِبْني بيْت أوْ يْجدِّد بيْتو.

The most commonly missing tools were construction materials. It was very difficult for anyone who wanted to build a house or renovate their home.

11

وكانت الأسْعار دايْماً كْتير غالْية وكْتير عالْية.

Prices were always very high and extremely expensive.

12

برْضو، كان في دايْماً نقْص في الأمور المُسْتلْزمات الطِّبّيّة، مِن أدْوية مِن أدَوات صحّية وغيْرْها.

There was also always a shortage of medical supplies, including medicines, health tools, and other necessities.

13

هدي الأدَوات كانت لمّا بِدّها تُدْخُل على قِطاع غزّة كانت تُدْخُل عن طريق تنْسيق مِن الوُفود الخارِجية مع الاِحْتِلال لهيْك كانت تُدْخُل.

These supplies, when they were allowed into Gaza, would enter through coordination between external delegations and the occupation—that's how they would enter.

14

كان دايْماً لمّا الاِحْتِلال بِدّو يْضَيِّق الحِصار بِيْقْدر يْضَيِّقوا لمّا بِدّو يِفْتحو شْوَيّة بِيْقْدر يْخفِّفو شْوَيّة.

Whenever the occupation wanted to tighten the blockade, they could; and whenever they wanted to ease it a little, they could.

كان الواحد حاسِس حالو دايماً مُقيّد، ودائماً مَرْبوط بِقَرارات مِن الاحْتِلال.	15	People always felt restricted and tied to the decisions of the occupation.
الواحد كان حاسِس حالو أسير في بلدو.	16	People felt like prisoners in their own land.
هدا الحِصار اللي بدأ مِن ٢٠ سنة تقْريباً، خلق جيل عُمْرو ما شاف السّفر، وكان يِحْلم في السّفر، وصعِب كْتير إنّو يِقْدر يْسافِر أَوْ يِقْدر يْوَسِّع أُفْقو لأشْياء برّا غزّة.	17	This blockade, which began about 20 years ago, created a generation that has never seen travel, a generation that dreams of traveling, and for whom it is incredibly difficult to travel or expand their horizons beyond Gaza.
كان دايماً الو خَيارات محْدودة مِن الأكل والشُّرْب والمُسْتلْزمات الصّحّية والجوّالات والتِّكْنولوجْيا والتّطوُّر.	18	Their options for food, drink, medical supplies, phones, technology, and development were always limited.
ونتيجة لقِلّة الأدَوات في السّوق وصُعوبةْ إدْخال الأشْياء الجْديدة، فا هدا الحِصار أجْبر النّاس إنّها تِخْلِق حاجات يِمْكِن ما كانت مَوْجودة قبل هيْك.	19	As a result of the lack of supplies in the market and the difficulty of bringing in new items, this blockade forced people to create things that may not have existed before.
ولأنّو: "الحاجة أُمّ الاخْتِراع".	20	Because, as they say: "Necessity is the mother of invention."
أَوْجدت النّاس بدايِل لكْتير أشْياء.	21	People invented alternatives for many things.
فا لمّا كان ينقطع الوُقود، ينقطع السّولار ينقطع البنْزين ينقطع الغاز، كانوا النّاس يِسْتخْدِموا زيْت القلي للسّيّارات.	22	So, when fuel, diesel, gasoline, and gas were unavailable, people used cooking oil for cars.
وكانوا يِسْتخْدِموا الخشب والحطب والفحِم لأغْراض الطّبْخ بدل عن الغاز.	23	They used wood, timber, and coal for cooking purposes instead of gas.
صاروا يِسْتخْدِموا الحَيوانات كبدايِل للمُواصلات.	24	They started using animals as alternatives for transportation.
وصاروا يْحاولوا يْولّْدوا الكهْرباء عن طريق الشّمْس.	25	They tried generating electricity through solar energy.
بالمُناسبة، الكهْربا كانت تِقْطع ٨ ساعات في اليوْم وتيجي ٨ ساعات.	26	By the way, electricity used to cut off for 8 hours a day and come back for 8 hours.
وتِرْجع تِقْطع ٨ ساعات وتيجي ٨ ساعات كان جدْوَل الكهْربا ما كان مُسْتقِر.	27	Then it would cut off again for 8 hours and come back for 8 hours—the electricity schedule was unstable.
في الشّتا كانت تِقْطع الكهْربا مُعْظم الوَقْت، وكانت النّاس تْتجمّد مِن البرودة.	28	In winter, electricity was cut off most of the time, and people would freeze from the cold.
وفي الصّيْف، كانت الكهْربا تِقْطع مُعْظم الوَقْت، وكانت النّاس تْموت مِن الحرّ.	29	In summer, electricity was cut off most of the time, and people would die from the heat.

لكِن، برْضو، اتْعايَشْنا شْوَيّة.	30	But, still, we adapted a little.
صِرْنا نِسْتخْدِم الهَوّايات اليَدَوية في الصّيْف، ونِسْتخْدِم نْزوّد حْرامات والبطّانِيّات في الشِّتا.	31	We started using hand fans in the summer and added blankets and covers in the winter.
بِتْمنّى إنّو الحِصار هدا يِنْفك، ونِرْجع نْعيش زيّْنا زيّ باقي البْلاد وزيّْنا زيّ باقي النّاس.	32	I hope that this blockade will be lifted and that we can go back to living like the rest of the countries and like the rest of the people.

Answers

Main Idea: d **True-False:** 1. T[1] 2. F[4] 3. T[6] 4. F[26-27] 5. T[22] 6. T[13] 7. T[24] **Multiple Choice:** 1. a[5-12] 2. a[22-23] 3. b[17]
Matching: زيّ باقي like / بدل عن instead of / بِحاجة عن in need of / بِتْمنّى إنّو I hope that / بالْمُناسبة by the way / لأنّو because / فا so, therefore / عن طريق by way/means of / على الأقلّ at least / شْوَيّة a bit / باقي the rest / نتيجة لـ as a result of / مِن لمّا since when / ما كان wasn't / ما عُمْرو never (in life) /

Keywords

القضية الفِلسْطينية the Palestinian cause   صمود resilience

Main Idea

a. The ongoing suffering of Palestinians due to land loss, war, and the blockade, and the importance of the Palestinian cause as a matter of right and wrong.
b. The technical difficulties she faces in her work as a voiceover artist and civil engineer as a result of the Gaza war.
c. A detailed explanation of the Gaza war and its impact on her family.
d. A historical overview of Palestinian governance changes from 2000 to the present.

True or False

1. Najd describes the Palestinian cause as one of right and wrong, not just a disagreement between two sides.
2. Najd describes the Gaza blockade as making travel and access to basic materials, including music, very difficult.
3. Najd was able to easily access materials for her work in civil engineering despite the blockade.
4. Najd believes the Palestinian cause is important only for Palestinians and no one else.
5. Najd mentions that she hopes that people around the world will recognize the importance of the Palestinian cause.

Multiple Choice

1. What does Najd describe as the root cause of the ongoing suffering of Palestinians?

    a. A disagreement between Palestine and neighboring countries

    b. A natural disaster that displaced people

    c. An internal conflict among Palestinian political groups

    d. A land theft, where others claimed Palestine as their ancestral land

2. What does Najd emphasize about the importance of the Palestinian cause?

    a. It is a conflict between two equal sides.

    b. It is an issue of human rights and justice that everyone should care about.

    c. It is mainly a political issue that should be resolved diplomatically.

    d. It is primarily a matter for historians and scholars to study.

3. What does Najd say about her father and brother?

   a. They both left Gaza before the war started.

   b. They were involved in civil engineering like her.

   c. They were martyred in the Gaza war.

   d. They are still missing after the war.

Matching

بِالْحقيقة	absolutely
بِالذّات	oh Lord
بِالنِّهاية	because of
بِسبب	until now
على أيّ أَساس	honestly
لغايةْ هلّأ	although
لِلأْسف	in the end
لِلأْمانة	especially, specifically
محدِّش	for the sake of
مع إنّو	after that
معْلِشّ	sorry
مِن أَجِل	on what basis
مِن بعْدْها	no one
نِهائيّاً	unfortunately
هيْك بْساطة	in reality
يا ربّ	just like that

مرْحَباً، اليوْم رح نِحْكي عن قضية فِلِسْطينية،
القضية الفِلِسْطينية اللي حرّكت العالم كُلّه.

إحْنا الفلسطينيّين، يَعْني للأسف، من ١٩٤٨ بدت
المُعاناة الكبيرة للكُلّ، بدت المُعاناة اللي ضيعت
كْتير ناس وغيّرت وغرّبت كْتير ناس.

المُعاناة بدت مِن لمّا اليَهود قرّروا إنّو أرْضْهُم
وأرْض أجدادْهُم هيّ أرْض فلسطين.

إحْنا كُلّنا عارفين إنّو في صراع عم بيدور بْفِلِسْطين
وبين فِلِسْطين والدّوْلة المُجاوِرة، ولكِن هُوّ
بالْحقيقة مِش صراع، هُوّ بالْحقيقة مُمكِن نْقول
سرقة أرْض.

إحْنا أرْضنا وأرْض أجدادْنا، والأرْض اللي أجْداد
أجْدادْنا عاشوا فيها، هيّ فِلِسْطين.

للأسف، بسبب فِكْرة ما بعْرف مين تْبَنّاها ما بعْرف
على أيّ أساس انْحطّت، مُسْتقْبلْنا ومُسْتقْبل
الفلسطينيين دايماً مُبْهم، ويالذّات اللي مِن أهل
غزّة مِتِلْنا إحْنا.

غزّة كانت كُلّ سنة تْكون في حرْب.

مِن سنة الـ٢٠٠٠ بدأت الانْتِفاضة، سنة الـ٢٠٠٤ بدا
الحُكْم انْتقل مِن حُكْم فتح لحُكْم حماس، ومِن
بعْدَها اتْغيّرت الدّنْيا كُلّها.

بدا يصير في حرْب كُلّ سنة، كُلّ سنة كُنّا نفْقِد ناس
عزيزة، كُلّ سنة كان الحِصار يْضيّق عليْنا أكْتر.

للأسف، كان في كْتير أشياء كُلّ العالم بْتِقْدر
تِعْملها بْسهولة إلّا إحْنا، مِتل السّفر.

ما مِنْقدر نْسافِر، ومِتل حاجات كْتيرة تانْية في مَوادّ
كْتيرة، حتّى الموسيقى.

حتّى أنا، كشُغْلي في التّعْليق الصّوْتي أوْ في
الهنْدسة المدني، كُنْت للأسف يَعْني مِتْصعْبة بسبب
الحِصار الخانِق على غزّة.

---

1. Hello, today we'll talk about a Palestinian issue—the Palestinian cause that moved the whole world.

2. We Palestinians, unfortunately, have faced great suffering since 1948. It's suffering that displaced many people, changed lives, and scattered families.

3. The suffering began when the Jews decided that their land and the land of their ancestors was Palestine.

4. We all know there's a conflict going on in Palestine, between Palestine and the neighboring state, but in truth, it's not a conflict—it's a land theft.

5. This is our land, the land of our ancestors, the land where the ancestors of our ancestors lived—it is Palestine.

6. Unfortunately, because of an idea that someone adopted on some unclear basis, our future and the future of Palestinians has always been uncertain, especially for those of us in Gaza.

7. Gaza has experienced war almost every year.

8. In 2000, the Intifada began, and in 2004, the governance shifted from Fatah to Hamas, and after that, everything changed.*

9. Every year, there was war; every year, we lost loved ones; every year, the siege tightened its grip on us more.

10. Unfortunately, there were many things that the rest of the world could do easily, but we couldn't—like traveling.

11. We couldn't travel, and the same went for many other things, like access to certain materials, even music.

12. Even for me, with my work in voiceover or civil engineering, it was unfortunately difficult because of the suffocating siege on Gaza.

الحِصار يَعْني كان يمْنع دُخول أشْياء كْتيرة، مَوادّ لِلْهنْدسة المدَني، وحتّى المَوادّ اللي بِسمح فيها كان لِلْأسف يطوّل كْتير وَقِت لتُدْخُل.	13	The siege restricted the entry of many materials, including those needed for civil engineering. Even when materials were allowed in, it took a very long time for them to arrive.
وبالتّالي، المباني أوّ العُمْران في البلد كان، لِلْأمانة، رتِم بطيء.	14	As a result, construction and infrastructure development in the country were, honestly, very slow.
يَعْني في شحّ بالمَوادّ، في شحّ في كُلّ إشي.	15	There was a shortage of materials, a shortage of everything.
بسّ الحمْدُ لله يَعْني، إحْنا بالنّهاية شعْب بيدّو يْقاوِم بيدّو يُصْمُد.	16	But thank God, in the end, we are a people who want to resist and persevere.
أيْ نعْم، لا زال المُسْتقْبل مجْهول وقْلوبْنا مَوْجوعة كْتير لأنّو لغايةْ هلّأ محدِّش عارِف أيْش اللي عم بيصير.	17	Yes, the future is still unknown, and our hearts are deeply pained because even now, no one knows what's happening.
بسّ قضيةْ فلِسْطين قضية مُهِمّة جدّاً، لازِم الكُلّ يعْرف عنْها.	18	But the Palestinian cause is very important; everyone needs to know about it.
قضّيةْ فلِسْطين قضّية كُلّ إنْسان عنْدو إنْسانية وكرامة - قضية كُلّ إنْسان.	19	The Palestinian cause is the cause of every person with humanity and dignity—it's everyone's cause.
يَعْني، بيكفّي إنّك تْكون إنْسان حتّى تِحْكي عن فلِسْطين.	20	You just need to be human to talk about Palestine.
ويمْكِن مِعلِّش هُوَّ الإشي موجِع لِلْأمانة، بالذّات إنّو يَعْني الكُلّ عارِف أكيد عن حرْب غزّة.	21	And it's painful, honestly, especially since everyone knows about the Gaza war.
غزّة هلّأ في حرْب وأنا فقدِت بابا وفقدِت أخويا.	22	Gaza is at war now, and I've lost my father and my brother.
الحمْدُ لله، استِشْهدوا، وينْحاوِل نُصْمُد.	23	Thank God, they became martyrs, and we're trying to endure.
وفقدْنا كْتير ناس والله عزيزة على قلْبْنا.	24	We've lost many dear to us.
فقدِت صاحِبةْ عُمْري لُجَين، لُجَين الصّفدي، بسّ الحمْدُ لله، يَعْني برْضو صامِدين، وينْحاوِل وينْعافِر إنّو نْكمِّل طريقْنا.	25	I lost my lifelong friend, Lujain Al-Safadi. But thank God, we remain steadfast and keep striving to continue our path.
وبتْمنّى مِن الكُلّ إنّو يِسْمع قضيتْنا ويحْكي عنْها، ويعْرف إنّو قضيتْنا قضيةْ حقّ وباطِل، مِش قضية تْنين اختلفوا في وِجْهات النّظر.	26	I hope everyone listens to our cause, talks about it, and understands that it's a matter of right and wrong, not just a disagreement in perspectives.
نِهائيّاً، هُوَّ الحقّ والباطِل.	27	It's ultimately about justice and injustice.

الأرْض مَعْروفة لِمين، ولكِن غيرْهُم بدُّهُم ياخْدوها هيْك بْبَساطة، مع إنّو بْلاد الله واسْعة	28	The land's rightful ownership is clear, but others want to take it just like that, even though God's earth is vast and there are plenty of places they could go.
يَعْني وفي كْتير بْلاد ومَناطِق بْيِقْدروا يْروحوا عليْها، بسّ سُبْحان الله، الأرْض هاي أرْض مُقدّسة وأرْض الأنْبِياء، فا الكُلّ عم بيصارِع عليْها.	29	But this land is sacred; it's the land of the prophets, and that's why everyone is fighting over it.
ويا ربّ يَعْني يْحسّن هالأوْضاع شُكْراً لإسْتِماعْكو.	30	May God improve this situation. Thank you for listening.

---

* Najd's statement contains a factual inaccuracy: Hamas won the legislative elections in 2006. However, disputes over transferring power led to Hamas taking military control of Gaza in 2007.

Answers

Main Idea: a[1-37] **True-False:** 1. T[1-2] 2. F[4-5] 3. T[11, 15] 4. F[20] 5. F[24-25] **Multiple Choice:** 1. d[18-20] 2. d[26-27] 3. c[35-36]

Matching: بِالْحقيقة in reality / بِالذّات especially, specifically / بِالنِّهاية in the end / بِسبب because of / محدّش no / للْأمانة honestly / للْأسف unfortunately / لغايةِ هلّأ until now / على أيّ أساس on what basis / one / مع إنّو although / مَعْلِشّ sorry / مِن أجِل for the sake of / مِن بعْدْها after that / نِهائيّاً absolutely / يا ربّ oh Lord / هيْك بْبَساطة just like that

Keywords

طبَقات اِجْتِماعْية social classes	الفُقَراء the poor
عُمّال workers	راتِب salary

Main Idea

a. The effects of poverty and restricted movement on Palestinians.
b. The history of social classes in Palestine and how they have changed in recent decades.
c. The relationship between the governments of Palestine and Israel.
d. Nihad's personal experiences working as a government employee in Palestine.

True or False

1. Nihad explains that the wealthy class in Palestine is largely unaffected by war and difficult circumstances.
2. According to Nihad, there is a significant middle class in Palestine that balances between the rich and the poor.
3. Workers who used to enter Israel to work are now severely restricted and face punishment if caught entering illegally.
4. According to Nihad, government employees typically receive between $800 and $1,000 as a salary.
5. Nihad mentions that schoolchildren in Palestine who struggle to pay for school fees can apply for scholarships.

Multiple Choice

1. What has been the financial situation of government employees in Palestine, as described by Nihad?

    a. Government employees are paid regularly and in full.

    b. Government employees are paid extra during times of crisis.

    c. Government employees are only affected by salary issues during war.

    d. Government employees have not received full salaries for a long time.

2. What does Nihad say about the mental and social effects of financial stress?

    a. Financial affects mental health.
    b. Financial stress affects social relationships.
    c. Financial stress affects daily life.
    d. *All of the above*

3. What does Nihad say about her family's attempts to cope with the difficult situation?

    a. She always tells her family the truth about the difficulties they face.

    b. She does not speak to her family about the situation.

    c. She tries to reassure her family by saying things will improve, but she feels it is a lie.

    d. She avoids talking about the future.

Matching

إمّا... أَوْ	in the end
بِالْآخِر	either... or
بْعاد عن	so you can tell
بْيومو	there isn't anything
حالِيّاً	there's no way
شو بِدّك	equally
على سَواء	what do you want
لتِحْكي	either... or
لشو لأَيْش	far from
ما في ما	nor, not even
ما في مجال	currently, now
وَلا	day by day
يا... يا	for what reason

1	عِنّا بْفَلَسْطين طَبَقتينْ مَعْروفات في المُجْتَمَع: طَبَقةْ الأغْنِياء، واللي هُمّ أصْحاب رُؤوس الأمْوال، رِجال الأعْمال والمَناصِب العالْية في السُّلْطة.	In Palestine, we have two well-known social classes: the wealthy, who are the owners of capital, businesspeople, and high-ranking officials in power.
2	هدوْل الفِئة توْب يَعْني ما في... ما... وَلا حَرْب وَلا إشي بْيِقْدر يْغيِّر مِن ظُروفْهُم حَياتْهُم.	This group is untouchable—neither war nor any circumstance affects their lives.
3	والطَّبْقِة الثّانْية، اللي هُمّ البُسَطاء الفُقَراء، المُوظّفين الحُكوميّين.	The second class is the simple, poor people, including government employees.
4	ما في عِنّا طبقة مُتَوسِّطة إنّو تاخُد مِن هدوْل وهدوْل.	We don't have a middle class that bridges these two groups.
5	ما في عِنّا ناس مِرْتاحين مادِيّاً أوْ عِنْدْهُم أمْلاك ووَضْعْهُم مُتَوَسِّط. إمّا فُقَراء أوْ أغْنِياء.	There are no moderately well-off people with properties and financial stability. It's either poverty or wealth.
6	فا هِيَّ الفِئة الأكْثر اتْضَرّرت، أكْثر إشي فِئة العُمّال، المُزارِعين، والمُوَظّفين الحُكوميّين.	The group most affected is the workers, farmers, and government employees.
7	العُمّال طبْعاً بِتْحِسّْهُم هُمّ أكْثر فِئة عاشت فقر، عايْشِة حالِيّاً عاشت وبِتْعيش هاي الأيّام أسْوأ أيّام حَياتْها، لأنّو هِيَّ مِش قادْرة تْوَفِّر أبْسط احْتِياجات البيْت، أبْسط احْتِياجات الإبن.	Workers, in particular, have lived in poverty and are currently enduring the worst days of their lives. They can't even provide the basic needs of their families.
8	لمّا بِدّو يْروح المَدْرَسة، ما مَعو مَصْروف يْروح.	When a child goes to school, they don't have money for lunch.
9	لمّا بِدّو يِشْتري أيّا شَغْلِة نِفْسو فيها، ما في.	When they want to buy something they desire, there's no money.
10	لَوْ شيكِل واحد ما في.	Sometimes, they don't even have a single shekel.
11	فا صاروا العُمّال طبْعاً، العُمّال بْيِشْتِغْلوا بْمَناطِق الدّاخِل الفلَسْطيني أوْ المُسْتَوْطنات.	Many workers used to find jobs in the Palestinian interior or settlements.
12	وفي عُمّال في الضّفّة، بَسّ ما في حَرَكِة في الضّفّة.	Others worked in the West Bank, but movement within the West Bank is very restricted now.
13	يَعْني اللي إلو بَسْطة في الخَليل، إلو بَسْطة في محَلّ هيْك، باب محَلّ في دورا في مَناطِق الشّمال، المُزارِعين، هاي مُمْكِن إنّْهُم يِتْرزّقوا مِنْها.	Some might have stalls in Hebron, a shop in Doura, shops in the northern areas, or are farmers—these are among the few who can still earn a living.
14	بَسّ العُمّال اللي بيفوتوا على إسْرائيل يِشْتِغْلوا، حالِيّاً ما في إلْهُم أيّا مَجال يْفوتوا.	But those who worked in Israel currently have no way to enter.

بِيعاقْبوهُم إذا لِقوهُم دخلوا بْطريقة غيْر شرْعية، إمّا بيسجّنوهُم، بْضُرْبوهُم، بِعذّبوهُم، أوْ بيرجّعوهُم مع غرامة إنّو يِرْجع على بيْتو، وممْنوع يِرْجع يْفوت على البلد اللي كان يِشْتِغِل فيها، مناطِق إسْرائيلية طبْعاً.	If they're caught entering illegally, they're punished—either imprisoned, beaten, tortured, or fined and sent back home. They're also banned from returning to the areas where they used to work, especially in Israel.
فا بْتُشْعُر إنّو في كُلّ العالم ضِدّو.	You feel like the whole world is against them.
المُوظّفين نفْس الإشي.	The same applies to government employees.
المُوظّف ما بوخِذ راتِب كامِل مِن زمان، مِن قبِل الحرب.	Government employees haven't received full salaries for a long time, even before the war.
وحالِيّاً الاقْتِطاعات اللي بِتصير بِتْأثِّر على الرّاتِب.	Currently, the deductions from their paychecks significantly affect their income.
طبْعاً المُوظّف بوخِذ تقْريباً ١٨٠٠ شيكِل ما يُقارِب الـ٥٠٠ دوْلار أوْ أقلّ.	A government employee earns about 1,800 shekels, approximately $500 or less.
يَعْني فا لشو لأيْش وأيْش يَعْني بِدّها تْسَوّي هاي المصاري بِتْروح مِنْها فواتير، بيروح مِنْها كُلّ إشي، يَعْني المصْروف اليَوْمي، المسْؤولِيّات البَيْتية على سَواء على ربّ الأُسْرة أوْ سِتّ البيْت.	How far can this money go? It's spent on bills, daily expenses, and household responsibilities, whether for the head of the household or the homemaker.
يَعْني نفْس الإشي يَعْني.	It's basically the same thing.
ما في الشّيكِل اللي بيطْلع ما في إشي يِرْجع مكانو.	Nothing remains—it's just not enough.
مثلاً الطُّلاب المدارِس، ما معْهُم مصاريف، ما معْهُم يِدْفعوا الرُّسوم للْمدْرسة.	For example, school students don't have money for expenses or to pay school fees.
طبْعاً الحُكومية، بسّ بِدْفعوا هاي اللي بيسمّوها تبرُّعات، حتّى صارت المدارِس تُطْرُدْهُم لأنّو ما معْهُم يِدْفعوا هاي التّبرُّعات.	Even at public schools, they're asked for "donations," and some schools have started expelling students who can't pay.
فا الوَضِع المادّي بيأثِّر أكيد على النّفْسية، بيأثِّر على العلاقات الاجْتِماعية، بيأثِّر على كُلّ إشي.	The financial situation undoubtedly affects mental health, social relationships, and everything else.
إذا إنْتَ ما معاك، طبْعاً مِش رح تْروح وَلا أيّا مِشْوار، مِش رح تِقْدر تِتْواصل مع حدا.	If you don't have money, you can't go anywhere or connect with anyone.
ما في تِدْفع فَواتير الكهْربا وَلا مَيّ، وَلا تْجيب إنْترْنِت وَلا إشي يَعْني.	You can't pay for electricity, water, internet, or anything else.
إلّا النّاس اللي يَعْني بيكون إلْهُم حدا يْدير بالو عليْهُم، هيْك إشي.	Only those with someone supporting them can get by.

The numbers 15–29 appear in the central column between the Arabic and English text:

15, 16, 17, 18, 19, 20, 21, 22, 23, 24, 25, 26, 27, 28, 29

يَعْني الوَضِع بْشكِل عام ما في ناس مِرْتاحين، حتّى الأمان.	30	Generally, no one is truly comfortable—not even safe.
مُسْتَوى الأمان يَعْني مِش كْتير عِنّا بالضّفّة.	31	The level of safety in the West Bank is not very high.
مع إنّو إحْنا يَعْني شْوَيّة بْعاد مِنْطِقة قَرَوِيّة، بْعاد عن وِسْط المدينة، بسّ إلّا ما يْصير يَعْني في نِقاط التّماس، الإغْلاقات، التّسْكيرات، كُلّ هاي بِيتْأثِّر.	32	Even though we live in a rural area far from the city center, there are still clashes, closures, and checkpoints that impact everything.
بْتِعمل ضغِط عَ البْني آدم، بْتِعمل حتّى على العلاقات في داخِل الأُسْرة نفْسْها.	33	This creates pressure on individuals and even affects relationships within families.
يَعْني بِتْحِسّ إنّو في... إنْتَ بْتِبْذِل مجْهود أكْبر مِن طاقْتك.	34	You feel like you're exerting more effort than you can handle.
لتِحْكي لوْلادك، لأُسْرْتك، لأنّو لا إن شاء الله رح تُفْرِج، والوَضِع كْوَيِّس، إنْتَ بْتِكْذِب عَ حالك، وبْتِكْذِب عليْهُم.	35	You tell your children or family, "Inshallah, things will get better; life will improve," but you're lying to yourself and to them.
يَعْني بالآخِر هُمَّ عارْفين وعايْشين كُلّ يوْم بْيومو، وإنْتا بْتحاوِل تْهوِّن المَواضيع على النّاس المُحيطين فيك، بسّ ما في مجال.	36	Deep down, they know the reality—they live it every day—and you try to ease the burden on those around you, but there's no way to escape it.
يَعْني شو بِدّك تعْمل؟ إن شاء الله إنْها الحرْب تِخْلص، والنّاس تِرْجع لحَياتْها الطّبيعية.	37	What can you do? InshaAllah, this war will end, and people will return to their normal lives.

Keywords

المُجْتَمَع الإِسْرائيلي Israeli society   التّعْبير عن الرأي freedom of expression   علم flag

Main Idea

a. The cultural differences between Palestinians and Israelis.
b. A discussion on the economic situation of Palestinians in the 1948-Territories.
c. The difficulties Palestinians face in expressing their identity and opinions, social tensions, and the need for unity among Palestinians.
d. The political divisions among Palestinians in the 1948-Territories.

True or False

1. Suheil mentions that Palestinians in the 1948-Territories can easily express their opinions and display the Palestinian flag.
2. Suheil mentions that some Palestinians in the 1948-Territories have been fired from their jobs for posting in solidarity with Gaza on social media.
3. Suheil mentions that some Palestinians in the 1948-Territories support Israel and Zionism.
4. Suheil says that there is no support for a two-state solution among Palestinians in the 1948-Territories.
5. Suheil emphasizes that Palestinians in the 1948-Territories, Gaza, the West Bank, and the diaspora are divided and have different cultures.

Multiple Choice

1. What could happen to Palestinians in the 1948-Territories if they speak out in support of Palestine, according to Suheil?

    a. They could be praised by their neighbors.

    b. They could be invited to participate in political debates.

    c. They would receive financial compensation.

    d. They could face imprisonment, travel restrictions, or confiscation of their belongings.

2. What is the approximate percentage of Palestinians in the 1948-Territories that Suheil says are in solidarity with the Palestinian cause?

    a. 50%   b. 75%   c. 90%   d. 100%

3. What does Suheil say about the Druze community in the 1948-Territories?

    a. The entire Druze community is in solidarity with the Palestinian cause.

    b. The Druze community doesn't face any issues with Palestinians or Israelis.

    c. Some Druze support Zionism, which causes social tension.

    d. The Druze community is completely neutral in the conflict.

Matching

أمّا	not the best
إيد واحْدِة	besides that
بْشكِل عامّ	all meaning
بِيْنْفِعِش	what else
حدّي	in general
شو كمان	normally
عادي	really, truly
عالْآخِر	united (lit. one hand)
عنْجدّ	completely
غيرْ عن هيْك	so that's how
فا هيْك	cannot
كُلّ يَعْني	everything
كُلْشي	needs
لازِمْها	for example
متلاً	next to me
مِش أحْسن	while, whereas

Text

مِن المشاكِل اللي عِنّا هون، إحْنا أهْل فلسْطين بالدّاخِل، بالـ٤٨، بالأراضي اللي مِتْحكّمة فيها إسْرائيل مِيّة بالمِيّة عسْكريّاً وإداريّاً وسياسيّاً وكُلّ شي، هيِّ إنّو إحْنا مِش عنْجدّ بْنِفع نْعبِّر عن رأينا.

1

One of the problems we face here, we Palestinians in the interior, in the '48 territories under complete Israeli military, administrative, and political control, is that we can't really express our opinions freely.

138 | Palestinian Arabic Voices

لإنّو أيّ شغْلِة صْغيرِة بْتِعْجِبِش الدّوْلِة، مُمْكِن نِنْحْبِس عليْها.	2	Because even the smallest thing that the state doesn't like can get us imprisoned.
علم فلسْطين كْتير صعْب نِرْفعو، بسّ بْمُظاهرات قليلِة يَعْني مُمْكِن نْشوفو.	3	It's very difficult to raise the Palestinian flag—only in rare demonstrations might we see it.
بينْفعِش أَعلّق علم فلسْطين على باب بيْتي، أمّا اليَهودي اللي حدّي عادي، يْعلّق علم إسْرائيل عادي، وبِفْخِر.	4	I can't hang the Palestinian flag at my house, while the Jewish neighbor next door can easily hang the Israeli flag and take pride in it.
بسّ إحْنا لا، يَعْني ممْنوع.	5	But for us, no—it's prohibited.
فا ملان شغْلات بينْفعِش شيلي نْعبّر عن رأْينا بْملان مَواضيع.	6	So, there are many things we can't express our opinions about.
ومِش بسّ مْنِنْحْبِس و بيعذّبونا، مُمْكِن يِمْنعوك متلاً، إنّك متلاً أنا بسافِر.	7	And it's not just imprisonment and mistreatment; they might, for example, ban you from traveling.
إذا شافوا إنّي كْتير بحْكي عن فلسْطين، مُمْكِن يِمْنعوني مِن السّفر متلاً، أَو يْحِبْسوني يْعذّبوني.	8	If they see that I talk a lot about Palestine, they might ban me from traveling or imprison me and mistreat me.
مُمْكِن يْصادْروا لك اشْيئاء، لأنّو هِنّ عِنْدِهِن قوّة عالآخِر عليْك.	9	They could confiscate your belongings because they have immense power over you.
فا هاي شغْلِة.	10	That's one issue.
تاني شغْلِة مُمْكِن، مِن ناحْيَةْ المُجْتمع إحْنا حَوالينا، مُجْتمع إسْرائيلي كُلّو.	11	Another issue is that socially, we are surrounded by an entirely Israeli society.
مُمْكِن إذا شافوك حطّيْت بوسْت متلاً تضامُن مع غزّة على الإنْستاجْرام، مُمْكِن عادي يْطلّعوك مِن الشُّغُل، مُمْكِن ما يِقْبلوكاش بْملان محلّات.	12	If they see that you posted something in solidarity with Gaza on Instagram, they might fire you from your job, or many places might refuse to hire you.
مُمْكِن ملان شغْلات تْصير، مُمْكِن مُسْتوطْنين يهِجْموا عليْك.	13	A lot could happen—even settlers might attack you.
فا اِجْتماعِيّاً كْتير صعِب.	14	So socially, it's very difficult.
وغيْر عن هيْك، في ملان، مِش ملان بسّ، في قِسِم قْليل مِن هون بالـ٤٨، فلسْطينيّين اللي مِتْضامْنين مع إسْرائيل، وهِنّي صهاينِة يَعْني.	15	Beyond that, there's a minority here in the '48 territories—Palestinians who are supportive of Israel, and they're Zionists.
فا كمان بيْنّا وبيْنْهِن مِش أحْسن أَوْضاع،	16	So, the relationship between us and them isn't great either.

فا هِنّي كْتير مع إسْرائيل ضِدّ الفِلَسْطينية بالضّفة وغزّة وهِنّي فصلوا حالْهِن عن أهْلْنا بالضّفة وغزّة،	17	They're very pro-Israel and against Palestinians in the West Bank and Gaza, and they've disconnected themselves from our people in the West Bank and Gaza.
فا شْوَيّ صِعِب يَعْني نِتْقبّلْهِن ويِتْقبّلونا،	18	So, it's a bit difficult for us to accept them, and for them to accept us.
هِنّي أكْتر مِخْتِلْطين بالْمُجْتمع الإسْرائيلي وهيْك.	19	They're more integrated into Israeli society and so on.
في ناس مع حلّ الدّوْلتين، وفي ناس مع حلّ دَوْلةٍ واحْدة للْجميع.	20	Some people support the two-state solution, and some support a one-state solution for everyone.
في آراء مُخْتِلفة عنّا.	21	There are differing opinions among us.
كمان، هون بالـ٤٨، في مسيحية وفي مُسْلِمين، وفي كمان دْروز.	22	Also, here in the '48 territories, there are Christians, Muslims, and Druze.
الدّروز في قِسِم مِنْهِن مَوْقِفْهِن داعِم لِلصّهْيونية، وعنّا في شْوَيّ مشاكِل اِجْتِماعية.	23	Among the Druze, some of them have a position that supports Zionism, and we have some social issues because of that.
ولكِن بْشِكِل عامّ، إحْنا أغْلبْنا يَعْني بْتِقْدر تْقول تِسْعين بالْمِيّة هِنّي مُتضامنين.	24	But generally speaking, the majority—about 90%—are in solidarity with us.
هِنّي مِش مُتضامنين. هِنّي قضيّتْهِن يَعْني القِضية الفِلَسْطينيّة فا هيْك.	25	Those who are not in solidarity don't see the Palestinian cause as their cause. That's how it is.
وشو كمان وفي كمان مشاكِل في شْوَيّ عائِلات إجْرام عنّا بالـ٤٨، وهاي كمان لازِمْها حلّ.	26	Also, there are issues with some criminal families here in the '48 territories, and this also needs a solution.
بسّ بْشِكِل عامّ، كُلّنا شعب واحد إحْنا.	27	But overall, we are all one people.
إحْنا بالـ٤٨، بغزّة، بالضّفة، وبالْقُدْس، وبالشّتات، كُلّنا شعب واحد، لُغة واحْدة، كُلّ يَعْني... كُلّشي ثقافة واحْدة، أكِل كُلّشي حضارة وتاريخ.	28	We in the '48 territories, Gaza, the West Bank, Jerusalem, and the diaspora—we're all one people, one language, one… everything—one culture, one food, one civilization, and one history.
فا كُلّنا لازِم نْكون إيد واحْدة، وهيْك.	29	So, we all need to be united, and that's it.

Answers

Main Idea: c **True-False:** 1. F[1-5] 2. T[12-13] 3. T[15-16] 4. F[20] 5. F[28-29] **Multiple Choice:** 1. d[2, 7-9] 2. c[24] 3. c[22-23]

Matching: أمّا while, whereas / إيد واحْدة united / بْشِكِل عامّ in general / بِيْنفعِش cannot / حدّي next to / غير عن هيْك besides / عنْجدّ really, truly / عالآخِر completely / عادي normally / شو كمان what else / me / لازِمْها needs / متلاً for example / كُلّشي everything / كُلّ يَعْني all meaning / فا هيْك so that's how / that / مِش أحْسن not the best

Free Topics

31 Khaled: My Work as a Doctor

Keywords

مُسْتشْفى hospital   الطَّواقِمِ الطِّبّية medical staff   كافْتيرْيا cafeteria

Main Idea

a. The variety of specialties and services offered by Al-Shifa Hospital.
b. The cafeteria's role in providing food and drinks to the hospital staff.
c. The hospital's recovery from a financial crisis and how it improved its services.
d. Khaled's experiences working at Al-Shifa Hospital and how the hospital has endured despite the war.

True or False

1. Al-Shifa Hospital is a referral hospital for complicated surgeries and advanced health services.
2. The hospital staff at Al-Shifa Hospital spends more time at work than at home.
3. The hospital cafeteria was a place where only doctors would meet and discuss their cases.
4. Despite being raided during the war, Al-Shifa Hospital began to recover and resume its normal operations.
5. Al-Shifa Hospital will remain closed after the war, according to Khaled.

Multiple Choice

1. Why does Khaled describe Al-Shifa Hospital as the largest hospital in Gaza?

   a. Because it has the most advanced medical equipment

   b. Because it has the largest number of buildings

   c. Because of the large number of staff and the variety of services it offers

   d. Because it is the most profitable hospital in Gaza

2. What role did the hospital cafeteria play for the staff at Al-Shifa Hospital?

   a. It was a place to eat alone and quietly rest.

   b. It was a gathering place for staff to share stories and discuss work.

   c. It was only for doctors and not open to other hospital staff.

   d. It was a place for hospital staff to plan new projects.

3. What happened to Al-Shifa Hospital during the war?

   a. It remained open and was never affected.

   b. It was raided, and the staff and patients were forced to leave.

   c. It expanded its services during the war to accommodate the many injured.

   d. It closed temporarily but reopened without any issues.

Matching

إسّا	so, therefore
بْأَيْدي	by the hands of
بالقُوّة	after a while
برْضو	by force
بعِد فترْة	let me
حرْفيّاً	also
خلّوني	all the time
زيّ ما	not because
طول الوَقِت	literally
فا	just as
كإنّهُم	from when first
كمان	than before
مِش لأنّو	for the sake of
مِش مُتَوَفِّرة	not available
مِن أجِل	also, as well
مِن أوّل	as if they
مِن أوّل ما	now

Text

مساء الخيْر.	1	Good evening.
خلّوني أحْكيلْكوا عن مكان عملي.	2	Let me tell you about my workplace.
زيّ ما إنْتو عارْفين، أنا دُكْتوْر، بشْتِغِل في أكْبر مُسْتشْفى في قِطاع غزّة، وهُوَّ مُسْتشْفى الشِّفا.	3	As you know, I'm a doctor. I work at the largest hospital in the Gaza Strip, which is Al-Shifa Hospital.
هالمُسْتشْفى هاد هُوَّ المُسْتشْفى الرّئيسي اللي بيقدِّم خدماتو طول الوَقِت ٢٤ ساعة في اليوْم، ٧ تيّام في الأُسْبوع، كُلّ يوْم.	4	This hospital is the main hospital that provides its services 24 hours a day, 7 days a week, every day.

المُسْتشْفى اللي يُعْتبر أكْبر مُسْتشْفى، مِش لأنّو عدد المباني كْتيرة، حَوالي ١٠ مباني: مبْنى للْجراحة، مبْنى للْباطنة، مبْنين للنِّسا والولادة، مبْنى للْأشّعّة، و مبْنى لِغسيل الكِلى، مبْنى لصَيْدلية، مبْنى للْحُروق، وغيْرْها مِن المباني،

It is considered the largest hospital, not because of the number of buildings—it has around ten buildings: a surgery building, an internal medicine building, two buildings for obstetrics and gynecology, a radiology building, a dialysis building, a pharmacy building, a burns building, and other buildings—

5

وَلا لأنّو بيقدِّم كْتير من الخدمات الصِّحّية، لكُلّ التّخصّصات تقْريباً، من باطنة وجراحة وكُلّ التّخصّصات الجِراحة الفرْعية، وخِدْمةْ الباطْنجة الفرْعية.

nor because it provides many health services for almost all specialties, from internal medicine to surgery and all subspecialties of surgery and internal medicine.

6

كُلّ التّخصّصات اللي كانت مُعْظم المُسْتشْفَيات الأُخْرى تْحوِّل لهدا المُستشْفى الرّئيسي مِن أجل عمليّات مُعقّدة أوْ حالات صعب علاجْها، أوْ مِحْتاجين صُوَر إشّعّة مُتقدّمة أوْ غيرْها من الخدْمات الصِّحّية مِش مُتَوَفّرة في أيّ مكان تاني.

All the specialties for which most other hospitals would refer patients to this main hospital—for complex surgeries, cases that were difficult to treat, or those requiring advanced imaging or other medical services not available anywhere else.

7

هيّ اكْبر مُسْتشْفى بِسبب كُبر عدد مُوَظّفيها اللي هُمّ بِيْتعامَلوا مع بعْض كإنّهُم أُسْرة واحْدة.

It is the largest hospital because of the large number of employees who work there and who treat each other as if they are one family.

8

كُلّ واحد فيهم بْيِعْتبر هدي المُسْتشْفى هُوّ بيْتو التّاني حرْفِيّاً، لأنّو بْيِقْضي فيها وَقت أكْتر ما بْيِقْضي في بيْتو الأوّل مع أُسْرتو الأولى.

Each of them literally considers this hospital their second home because they spend more time there than in their first home with their primary family.

9

أنا وزُملائي، كُنّا تقْريباً نْداوِم حَوالي ٦٠ ساعة في الأُسْبوع.

My colleagues and I used to work approximately 60 hours a week.

10

هدوْل الـ٦٠ ساعة، كُنّا نْشوف بعْض الصُّبْح الظُّهُر المسا.

During those 60 hours, we would see each other in the morning, at noon, and in the evening.

11

كُنّا نْنام مع بعِض في السّكن، وكُنّا نقْضي وَقِت كْتير طيِّب مع بعْض في هدا المكان.

We used to sleep together in the staff housing and spend a lot of good times together in this place.

12

برْضو كان في منْطقة كْتير لطيفة وكْتير جميلة، وهيّ كافتيرْيا المُسْتشْفى.

There was also a very pleasant and beautiful area, which is the hospital cafeteria.

13

هدا المكان كان يْوَفِّر أطْيَب أكِل وألذّ مشْروبات كُنّا دايْماً مِحْتاجينْها.

This place provided the tastiest food and the most delicious drinks, which we always needed.

14

كان هُوَّ يْشكّل مُلْتقى لكُلّ مُوَظّفين المُسْتشْفى، مِن أطبّاء وتمْريض وصَيادلة وفنّيّين أشعّة ومُخْتبرات وكُلّ التّخصُّصات.	15	It served as a gathering place for all hospital staff, from doctors to nurses to pharmacists, radiology technicians, lab technicians, and all specialties.
فا كانت الكافْتيرْيا هيَّ مكان الكُلّ يُقْعُد فيه، يِحْكي فيه كُلّ واحد عن مشاكْلو عن الحالات اللي بيشوفْها، عن القِصص اللي صارت معو.	16	So the cafeteria was the place where everyone sat, talked about their problems, about the cases they had seen, and about the stories that had happened to them.
وهدا الإشي قوّى العلاقات بين مُوَظّفين المُسْتشْفى وبين الأطبّاء، وخلّاهُم فعْلاً يْصيروا إيد واحْدة، ويْصيروا أُسْرة واحْدة، هْمومْهُم واحْدة وأفْراحْهُم واحْدة وأحْزانْهُم واحْدة.	17	This strengthened the relationships among the hospital staff and doctors, making them truly one hand, one family, sharing the same worries, joys, and sorrows.
ظلّو هدا الإشي مُسْتمرّ مِن أوّل ما فتحت مُسْتشْفى الشّفا مِن سْنين طَويلة، حتّى هدي الحرْب، حتّى اقْتِحام المُسْتشْفى وإجْبار الطَّواقِم الطّبّيّة والمرْضى والنّاس اللي فيها إنّهُم يِتْرْكوها بالْقُوّة.	18	This continued from the time Al-Shifa Hospital opened many years ago until this war, until the hospital was stormed, and the medical staff, patients, and everyone in it were forcibly evacuated.
هدي هيَّ قِصّة بْمكان عملي، لكِن بعْد فتْرة رجْعت النّاس، ورجْعت الدّكاترة، ورجْعت الطَّواقِم تِشْتغل.	19	This is now my workplace story, but after some time, people returned, the doctors returned, and the staff went back to work.
المُسْتشْفى هدي بدأت تِتْعافى وتسْترِدّ جُزْء مِن حَياتْها العادية.	20	This hospital has started to recover and regain some of its normal life.
بْأيْدي هدوْل الاطبّاء والنّاس الفِلسْطينيّين إن شاء الله ربّ العالمين، بعْد الحرْب، حَ تِرْجع أحْسن وأفْضل مِن أوّل، إن شاء الله.	21	With the hands of these doctors and the Palestinian people, God willing, after the war, it will return to being even better and greater than before, God willing.

Answers

Main Idea: d **True-False:** 1. T[7] 2. T[9-10] 3. F[13-16] 4. T[18-20] 5. F[19-21] **Multiple Choice:** 1. c[5-8] 2. b[13-17] 3. b[18]

Matching: إسّا now / بْأيْدي by the hands of / بالْقُوّة by force / برْضو also, as well / بعِد فتْرة after a while / كإنّهُم as if they / فا so, therefore / طول الوَقِت all the time / زيّ ما just as / خلّوني let me / حرْفيّاً literally / مِن أجِل for the sake of / مِن أوّل than before / مِش مُتَوَفّرة not available / مِش لأنّو not because / كمان also / مِن أوّل ما from when first /

Najd: Marketing Yourself

| تسْويق marketing | مهارة skill | منصّات platforms |

a. The essential role of marketing in achieving success.
b. The importance of learning new skills and constantly improving them.
c. A step-by-step guide to writing a CV.
d. The history of marketing and how it has evolved in recent years.

1. According to Najd, you only need strong skills to reach your career goals; marketing is not essential.
2. Writing a good CV is a form of marketing.
3. People with strong skills always succeed regardless of their marketing abilities.
4. Najd considers LinkedIn and Twitter as two of the most important platforms for marketing yourself.
5. Najd believes that studying marketing is not essential as long as you're skilled in your field.

1. What is one of the key strategies Najd suggests for marketing yourself effectively?

   a. Focusing only on social media platforms like Instagram

   b. Asking your friends to share your content

   c. Writing an appealing CV and using key phrases that address the client's needs

   d. Ignoring social media and focusing only on in-person networking

2. What advice does Najd give about targeting companies with your CV?

   a. Research companies related to your field and focus on the platforms they follow.

   b. Send your CV to as many companies as possible, regardless of their relevance to your field.

   c. Only apply to small businesses to increase your chances of being noticed.

   d. Avoid social media and send physical copies of your CV directly to companies.

3. What does Najd emphasize about promoting your content?

    a. Promoting your content only helps in certain fields, like marketing and design.

    b. Promoting your work is only necessary if you have less experience.

    c. The more you promote your work, the more it will be seen and talked about and reach a wider audience.

    d. Promoting your work doesn't make much difference to your career.

Matching

يْإنّو	to, on
بِدّك تعْرف	but, just
بسّ	must, have to
بْنفْسك	currently, now
حالِيّاً	without
سَواء... أوْ	whether... or
عَ	you need to know
علشان	the more
قدّيْش كان	even if
كُلّ ما	by (that)
لازِم	yourself
لَوْ إنّو	no matter how much
مِش رح	despite that
مع هيْك	in order to
مِن غيْر	won't

Text

مرْحبا، اليوْم رح نِحْكي عن مَوْضوع مُهِمّ جِدّاً جِدّاً جِدّاً في عالمْنا، وبِالذّات في هدا الوَقْت، ألا وهُوَّ الماركِتينْج (التّسْويق).	1	Hello, today we're going to talk about a very, very, very important topic in our world, especially at this time, which is marketing.

قدّيش كان عِنْدك مهارة كْتير قَوِية وعِنْدك ثِقة عالْيَة في نفْسك، إن ما كُنْت بْتِعْرف تْسوّق لنفْسك، مِش رح تِشْتِغِل.	No matter how strong your skills are or how confident you are in yourself, if you don't know how to market yourself, you won't find work.
لازِم يْكون عِنْدك مهارة التّسْويق، مهارة جِدّاً عالْيَة.	You must have marketing skills—very strong skills.
لازِم تْكون عارِف إنّو أيّ مهارة تانْيَة مِن غيْر التّسْويق ما رح تْوِصل فيها لأيّ مكان، سَواء كُنْت شاطِر في الأوْنلايْن أوْ حتّى في تخصّصك.	You need to understand that any other skill, without marketing, won't get you anywhere, whether you're skilled online or even in your field of expertise.
حتّى في تخصّصك، مِحْتاج التّسْويق.	Even in your field, you need marketing.
لازِم تعْرف كيْف تُكْتُب السّي في (CV).	You have to know how to write a CV.
طريقَةِ كِتابِة السّي في لمّا إنْتا تُكْتُب السّي في تبعك بْطريقة مُلْفتة هدا تسْويق.	The way you write your CV, when you write it in an appealing way—that's marketing.
التّسْويق يُكُلّ إشي بْيِدْخُل.	Marketing applies to everything.
لمّا إنْتَ تِحْكي عن حالك، بدّك تعْرف كيْف تِحْكي عن حالك، وبْكيْف تِبْدأ، وويْن تْروح والمكان اللي لازِم تْحُطّ فيه السّي في تبعك أوْ تْحُطّ فيه حالك لأنّك تِحْكي عنْها.	When you talk about yourself, you need to know how to talk about yourself, where to start, where to go, and where to put your CV or present yourself.
أنا بعْرف كْتير ناس، ما شاء الله، كان عِنْدها المهارة وكان عِنْدها مهارة جِدّاً قَوِية كمان، ولكِن لم تُوفّق.	I know many people who, masha'Allah, had great skills and strong abilities but didn't succeed.
وبعْرِف كمان كْتير ناس كان عِنْدها برْضو مهارة ولكِن مِش بْقوّة النّاس التّانْيَة اللي أنا بعْرِفْها، مع هيْك، وُفّقت ووصْلت لمناطِق عالْيَة كْتير وبْتِشْتِغِل أحْسن شُغُل. السّبب الأساسي هُوّ التّسْويق.	And I also know others who had skills but not as strong as those first ones, yet they succeeded and reached high positions and better jobs. The main reason is marketing.
كُلّ ما إنْتَ بِتْسوّق لحالك عَ السّوْشال ميدْيا، عَ المنصّات، في السّي في الخاصّ فيك، كُلّ ما إنْتَ تِبْدِع أكْتر وبْتوصل لمناطِق أحْسن، وأكيد كُلّ ما رح توصل لمناطِق أحْسن ومناطِق إنْتَ بدّك إيّاها وإنْتَ بتِرْغبْها.	The more you market yourself on social media, on platforms, and in your CV, the more creative you'll be, and the better opportunities you'll reach—the ones you want and desire.
أكيد رح تْزيد ثِقتك بفي نفْسك، وكُلّ ما زادت ثِقتك بفي نفْسك، حَ يْزيد تطوّرك في مجالك.	This will definitely boost your confidence, and as your confidence grows, so will your development in your field.
وبالتّالي، رح تعْرِف حاجات وحَ تُدْخُل في حاجات يمْكِن إنْتَ بْنفْسك ما كانت تُخْطُر لك.	You'll learn more and get into things you might never have imagined.

فا علشان إنْتَ تْحسِّن مِن التَّسْويق، لازِم تْروح وتْشوف النّاس اللي وِصْلت لهدي المراحِل العالْيَة كيْف وِصْلت كيْف سوّقت لحالْها كيْف دخلت المجال.	15	To improve your marketing, you need to look at how others who've reached high levels marketed themselves and got into the field.
في كْتير طُرُق طبْعاً، السّوْشال ميدْيا مِتِل لينْكِد إن تْويتر، هدول المنصّتيْن بالذّات، والفيْسبوك كمان، طبْعاً.	16	There are many ways, of course. Social media platforms like LinkedIn and Twitter—especially these two—and also Facebook, of course.
بسّ تْويتر ولينْكِد إن كانوا مِن أكْتر المنصّات اللي النّاس بْتِشْتِغِل عليْها أكْتر في الماركتينْج. والفيْسبوك برْضو الفيْسبوك مْنيح.	17	But Twitter and LinkedIn are among the most used platforms for marketing. Facebook is good, too.
وفي طبْعاً عِنْدك البْلاتْفورْمْز اللي هُوَّ منصّات المَوْجودة على... عَ النّت برْضو مِتِل مُسْتقِلّ خمْسات أب وُرْك، هدي المنصّات برْضو منصّات جِدّاً مُهِمّة لأنّها توصِّل مهارتك.	18	And there are also platforms like Mostaql, Khamsat, and Upwork. These platforms are very important because they showcase your skills.
بسّ بِدّك تعْرف إنْتَ كيْف تِلْفِت الزّبون أوْ "الكْلايِنْت"، بِدّك تعْرف كيْف تِلْفِتو بالتّقْديم لإلو.	19	You need to know how to attract clients or customers and how to present yourself to them.
يعْني، لازِم يْكون عِنْدك كِلِمات مُفْتاحِية.	20	You need to use keywords.
لازِم تِحْكي أوّل إشي عن إشي اللي هُوَّ الزّبون مِحْتاجُه إنّو إنْتَ لَوْ مِحْتاج كذا كذا كذا.	21	You must start by addressing the client's needs, like saying, "If you need such and such."
بِدّك تْبَيِّن لَوْ إنّو إنْتَ كمان فاهِم وقريْت عَ أيْش هُوَّ عم يِحْكي.	22	You should show that you understand and have read what they're talking about.
فا في كْتير تفاصيل صْغيرة، لَوْ إنْتَ ركّزِت عليْها، رح تْفرِّق معك بْخُطْوات كْتير كْبيرة.	23	There are many small details that, if you focus on them, will make a big difference in your progress.
فا التّسْويق، ركِّز عَ التّسْويق.	24	So, focus on marketing.
قدّ ما كانت مهارتك قَوية، قدّ ما كُنْت شاطِر فيها، لازِم تِدْرس التّسْويق وتْركِّز عليْه.	25	No matter how strong your skills are or how good you are at them, you need to study marketing and focus on it.
لأنّو التّسْويق حالِيّاً هُوَّ المِجْتاح عالمْنا، هُوَّ لُغَة العصِر.	26	Because marketing now dominates our world—it's the language of the era.
أيّا مكان بِتْروح عليْه بِدّك تعْرف كيْف تْسوِّق بْحالك.	27	Wherever you go, you need to know how to market yourself.
ومِن الأشياء برْضو المُهِمّة في التّسْويق، طبْعاً إنّو تعْرف الشّرِكات اللي بِتْخُصّ مجالك.	28	Another important thing in marketing is knowing the companies in your field.

يَعْني، إنْتَ لمّا بدّك تِبْعت السّي في تبعك، بدّك تِعْرف إنّو مين هيّ الشّرِكات اللي إنْتَ بدّك تِبْعتِلْها.	29	When you send out your CV, you need to know which companies you're targeting.
شرِكات تْكون معْروفة، أَوْ تْروح على الصّفْحات اللي الشّرِكات بْتِقْرا مِنْها أَوْ بْتِتْواصل معْها أَوْ إلْهُم علاقات.	30	Target well-known companies or go to the pages these companies read or engage with.
يَعْني في كْتير ناس أنا بعْرِفها وِصْلت لقناةْ الجّزيرة كيْف بْإنّو كانت تْنزِّل مثلاً عَ اللّينْكِد إن.	31	I know many people who got to Al Jazeera by posting on LinkedIn.
بْتابعوا كْتير اللّينْكِد إن في التّعْليق الصّوْتي طبْعاً هدا الكلام.	32	LinkedIn is closely followed, especially for voiceover work.
مُمْكِن في التّصْميم وفي الأشْياء التّانْية أكيد.	33	And the same applies to design and other fields.
كُلّ شِرْكة إلْها مِنصّة خاصّة فيها، بِتْتابِع عليْها أكْتر.	34	Every company has its own platform that it focuses on the most.
وكُلّ ما إنْتَ بْتِشْهِر أكْتر اعْمالك سَواء في التّسْويق، سَواء في التّصْميم، أَوْ في التّعْليق الصّوْتي، أَوْ في كِتابِةْ المُحْتَوى، أَوْ في أيّ شُغْل تاني هنْدِسةْ تصْميم، كُلّ ما إنْتَ بْتِشْهِر مُحْتَواك، كُلّ ما ناس أكْتر حَ تْشوفُه، كُلّ ما ناس أكْتر رح تِحْكي عنّو، وكُلّ ما حَ يوصل لناس أكْتر.	35	The more you showcase your work, whether in marketing, design, voiceover, content writing, or any other field—engineering, design—the more you publicize your content, the more people will see it, talk about it, and share it.
وبِالتّالي، رح توصل لمناطِق وشرِكات إنْتَ ما كُنْت تِحْلم فيها. وبسّ!	36	And this way, you'll reach places and companies you never dreamed of. That's all!

Keywords

كشْمير Kashmir   الضِّيافة hospitality   الطّبيعة nature

Main Idea

a. Suheil's experiences exploring India, discovering cultural similarities with Kashmir, and the hospitality he received as a Palestinian traveler.
b. A detailed guide on how to travel around India and do interviews with locals for social media.
c. A focus on the history of the conflict in Kashmir and its similarities with the Palestinian conflict.
d. Suheil's opinions on the food and accommodations in India.

True or False

1. Suheil describes his trip to India as a very spontaneous and unplanned adventure.
2. Suheil visited the Dalai Lama and hiked in the Himalayas during his trip to India.
3. Suheil found that the people of Kashmir have a similar conflict with India to the one Palestinians have with Israel.
4. Suheil found that the food in Kashmir was very different from the rest of India.
5. Suheil met and traveled with a girl during his trip to India.

Multiple Choice

1. How did the people of Kashmir react when they saw Suheil with the Palestinian flag?

   a. They were indifferent and uninterested.

   c. They asked him to take it down.

   b. They didn't recognize the flag.

   d. They were very excited and supportive.

2. What regions did Suheil visit during his trip to India?

   a. Only New Delhi and Kashmir

   c. Rajasthan, Gujarat, Punjab, and more

   b. Only cities near the coast

   d. Primarily religious sites

3. What kind of hospitality did Suheil experience during his travels in India?

   a. He was usually ignored by locals.

   b. He was frequently invited to people's homes and even attended weddings.

   c. He stayed only in hotels and guesthouses.

   d. He didn't interact much with the local people.

بِدّيش	and so
بِشْبهوا	then, after that
بعْدين	backward
بينْ	since then
طبْعاً	together
طيِّب	how much
عَ الآخِر	okay, well
قدّيْش	resemble
لَوَرا	when
مع بعِض	completely
مِن بعْدْها	after that
مِن وَقْتْها	this much
هالْقدّ	I don't want
وَقْت ما	between, among
وهيْك	of course

	طَيِّب، إسّا بِدّي احْكيلْكو قُصّة.
1	Okay, now I want to tell you a story.
	واحْدِة مِن أَحْلى الأَوْقات اللي عِشْتْها بْحَياتي هِيَّ وَقْت ما طْلِعت مِشْوار على الهِنْد.
2	One of the best times I've experienced in my life was when I went on a trip to India.
	كان صَدْمة ثَقافية وحَضارية كْتير كْبيرِة.
3	It was a huge cultural and civilizational shock.
	الهِنْد كْتير مُخْتلِفة عنّا مِن ناحْيِة كُلّ شي.
4	India is very different from us in every way.
	فا كان مِشْوار عَفَوي جِدّاً جِدّاً جِدّاً.
5	So, it was a completely spontaneous trip.
	أوّل إشي، نْزِلْت بمَدينِة نْيودِلْهي، والمَدينة فيها حَوالي ٣٠ مَلْيون شَخْص.
6	First, I arrived in New Delhi, a city with about 30 million people.
	فا كْتير كْبيرِة وكتير غير كْتير عن كيف عايْشين.
7	It's very big and very, very different from how we live.
	المَدينِة مِش هالْقدّ نْظيفة الصَّراحة، والأَكِل كْتير حار كْتير، وبَرْضو مِش كْتير نْظيف أَكْل الشَّوارِع.
8	The city isn't very clean, honestly, and the food is very spicy, and street food isn't very clean either.
	فا بَعِد يومين تْشوفوا قدّي المِشْوار كان عَفَوي.
9	After two days, you'll see how spontaneous the trip was.
	حَكى معي شَخْص مِن ناحْيَة تَطْبيق سَفر، اللي بدّو يِطْلع مِشْوار عَ الهيمالايا، يِلْتْقي بالدَّلاي لاما ويِعْمل مسار تَسَلُّق يَعْني بالْهيمالايا.
10	Someone contacted me through a travel app, wanting to go on a trip to the Himalayas, meet the Dalai Lama, and do a hiking trail in the Himalayas.
	فا بَعِد يومين حْمِلْت حالي ورُحْت عِنْدو.
11	So, after two days, I packed my things and went to meet him.
	قَعِدْت أُسْبوع هُناك، ومِن بَعْدْها قَرّرِت بِدّي أروح على مِنْطِقة أُسْمْها كَشْمير.
12	I stayed there for a week, and afterward, I decided to go to a place called Kashmir.
	هاي مِنْطِقة الهِنْد مِتْحكّمة بِقِسِم مِنْها، باكِسْتان مِتْحكّمة بِقِسِم مِنْها.
13	Kashmir is a region partly controlled by India, partly by Pakistan.
	ولكِنَّ أَهِل الشَّعِب أَغْلَبْهِن بِدُّهِن اِسْتِقلال بْدولة إلْهِن لحال.
14	However, most of the people there want independence and their own state.
	كمان الصّين مِتْحكّمة بْجُزْء مِنْها.
15	China also controls a part of it.
	فا كْتير لقيت عِلاقة بين أَهِل كَشْمير وأَهِل فلسْطين.
16	I found a strong connection between the people of Kashmir and the people of Palestine.
	هِنّي كمان شايْفين هاي العِلاقة، وهِنّي كمان كْتير مُتْضامِنين مع القضية الفِلسْطينية.
17	They also see this connection, and they are very supportive of the Palestinian cause.
	ثقافِتْنا وحَضارتْنا شُوَيّ بِشْبهوا بعِض.
18	Our cultures and civilizations are somewhat similar.

هِنِّي أَغْلَبُهِن مُسْلِمِين، في مِنْهِن سُنَّة في مِنْهِن شيعة.	19	Most of them are Muslim—some are Sunni, and some are Shia.
ولكِن هِنِّي كمان عِنْدُهِن أنا كُنْت بالْجُزْء اللي الهِنْد مِتْحَكَّمة فيو، كان عِنْدُهِن كمان مُقاوْمة ضِدّ الهِنْد، وكتير مِتْضامْنِين مع المُقاوْمة الفلسْطينية طبْعاً.	20	But in the part of Kashmir controlled by India where I was, they also resist Indian control and are, of course, very supportive of Palestinian resistance.
فا هِنِّي فاهْمين على أهل فلسْطين عَ الآخِر، كُلّ إشي مارْقِين فيّو، وعِنْدِهِن تَقْرِيباً نفس الحرب مع الهِنْد.	21	They fully understand what Palestinians are going through and have almost the same struggle with India.
وهيْك كْتير حبّوني كفلسْطيني.	22	So, they really loved me as a Palestinian.
كْتير كانوا يْحِبّوا لمّا يْشوفوا العلم الفلسْطيني.	23	They loved seeing the Palestinian flag.
يكيّفوا كُلُّهِن، يجوا يِتْصَوّروا معو ويْعبْطوا فيِّ.	24	Everyone was excited, taking pictures with it and hugging me.
الكُلّ كان يِعْزِمْني عِنْدو، الضّيافة عِنْدُهِن حُبّهِن لأرْضُهِن.	25	Everyone invited me to their homes—they were so hospitable and proud of their land.
والطّبيعة هُناك كْتير حِلْوة، فا كْتير حبيْتْها لكشْمير والأكِل عِنْدُهِن كْتير زاكي كمان.	26	The nature there is very beautiful, and I really loved Kashmir, and their food is also very tasty.
كمان بِتْحِسّ حالك رُجِعِت بالزّمن لَوَرا لمّا تْروح على كشْمير.	27	You feel like you've gone back in time when you visit Kashmir.
فا حِلْوة الحَياة هُناك.	28	Life there is beautiful.
ومِن بعْدْها رُجِعْت على مناطِق تانْية بالْهِنْد،	29	After that, I went to other areas in India.
فُتت على راجسْتان وجوجارات كمان، التّاج محلّ،	30	I visited Rajasthan, Gujarat, and the Taj Mahal.
رُحْت عليه وكان مِشْوار حِلو وانْضمّتْلي صبية، وكْتير انْبسطْنا مع بعِض.	31	I went there, and it was a wonderful trip. A girl joined me, and we had a great time together.
انْعزمْنا على كْتير أَعْراس بْمناطِق مِخْتِلْفة بالْهِنْد.	32	We were invited to many weddings in different parts of India.
بْنْجاب كمان كُنْت، عِنْدْهِن ثقافِة حضارة تانْية عَ الآخِر.	33	I also went to Punjab—they have a completely different culture and civilization.
دِيانة جْديدة عِنْدْهِن أُسْمها السّيك، وعِنْدْهِن كمان عادات وتقاليد كْتير غريبة.	34	They have a new religion called Sikhism, and their traditions are very unique.
بيحِمْلوا معْهِن سِكّينة دايماً الزّلام بيحِلْقوش شعِرْهِن.	35	The men always carry a knife and don't cut their hair.
وبْراجسْتان كان كْتير حِلو كمان.	36	Rajasthan was also very beautiful.

برْضو أغْلَب وَقِتْنا كُنّا نِنْعْزِمِ عِنْد ناس، نْنام عِنْدْهِن، وكان كْتير حِلو.	37	Most of the time, we were invited to people's homes, where we stayed, and it was very nice.
عنْجدّ كان كْتير حِلو.	38	It was truly wonderful.
مِن وَقِتْها بعْدِيْن كمّلِت على جنوب شرْق آسْيا: تايلانْد وفِيِتْنام وكمْبودْيا ولاوُس.	39	After that, I continued to Southeast Asia: Thailand, Vietnam, Cambodia, and Laos.
كمان كانت كْتير حِلو.	40	That was also very beautiful.
وطبْعاً، أكْتر بلد بحِبّها بيْن كُلّ المحلّات اللي رُحْتْها هِيَّ فلسطين، هِيَّ مِن أحْلى البْلاد بالْعالم، وهيْك.	41	And of course, my favorite country among all the places I visited is Palestine. It's one of the most beautiful countries in the world. That's it.

Answers

Main Idea: a **True-False:** 1. T[4-5] 2. T[10-11] 3. T[20-21] 4. F[26] 5. T[31] **Multiple Choice:** 1. d[22-24] 2. c[29-33] 3. b[25, 32, 37]

Matching: بدّيش I don't want / بِشْبهوا resemble / بعْدِيْن then, after that / بيْن between, among / طبْعاً of / مِن together / مع بعِض backward / لَوَرا how much / قدّيش completely / عَ الآخِر okay, well / طيِّب course / وهيْك and so / وَقِت ما when / هالْقدّ this much / مِن وَقِتْها since then / بعْدْها after that

حَواجِز عسْكرية military checkpoints   تحدّي challenge

Main Idea

a. How Palestinians have found ways to overcome the occupation and live in peace
b. Bader's experiences working in Ramallah under military occupation
c. The economic impact of occupation on Palestinian farmers
d. The personal and daily challenges faced by Palestinians due to military occupation

True or False

1. Bader mentions that there are military checkpoints on every road.
2. Bader mentions that nearly every Palestinian household has had someone who was a prisoner or detained by the occupation.
3. Bader mentions that he feels lucky that there are rarely military checkpoints between his village and Ramallah.
4. Bader mentions that traveling between cities or villages in Palestine involves being cautious of military checkpoints and settlers.
5. Bader mentions that military checkpoints have increased in recent years.

Multiple Choice

1. How does Bader describe the experience of occupation for Palestinians?

   a. It is something they experience and witness daily, both directly and indirectly.

   b. It is a distant issue that rarely affects daily life.

   c. It only affects certain areas and not the entire country.

   d. It has mostly been resolved, and people live peacefully.

2. What does Bader say about the feeling of safety for Palestinians?

   a. It is something they experience when traveling between villages.

   b. It is restored when they return home from work.

   c. It does not exist for Palestinians living under occupation.

   d. It only applies to those who live in certain areas.

3. According to Bader, how do many Palestinians react to the daily challenges of living under occupation?

   a. They stay at home and avoid going to work in order to avoid hardships and harassment.

   b. They continue to work, face the challenges, and try to succeed despite the occupation.

   c. They protest regularly against the occupation.

   d. They try to leave the country to escape the occupation.

Matching

بْشكِل شخْصي	we live it
بْشْكِل مُباشِر	by (passive)
بِغضّ النّظر	regardless
بْيِضْطرّوا	what can you do
تبعك	they are forced to
شو بدّك تِعْمل	your (possessive)
في الآخِر	or not
لِمِّن	reached to
ماخِذ	in the end
مِن قِبِل	taking (active participle)
منْعيشْها	personally
وِصْلِت لـ	when
ولّا	directly
يا... يا	either... or

Text

بالنِّسْبة مع تجْرِبْتي مع الاحْتِلال العسْكري، أوْ يَعْني مع الاحْتِلال بْشكِل عامر، طبْعاً هاي تجْرُبة نقْدر نِحْكي إنّها تجْرُبة يَوْمية، تجْرُبة منْعيشْها كُلّ يوْم، أوْ أنا بعيشْها بْشكِل شخْصي كُلّ يوْم.	As for my experience with military occupation, or, let's say, with occupation in general, of course, this is an experience we can say is a daily experience, one we live every day, or I personally live every day.

1

2	Of course, most Palestinians live it every day, and they are not only forced to live it, but they are forced to see it every day.

طَبْعاً أَغْلَب الفِلَسْطِينِيّين بِيْعِيشُوها كُلّ يَوْم، وبْيِضْطَرّوا إنّهُم يَعْني مِش بَسّ يْعِيشُوها، لا، بْيِضْطَرّوا يْشُوفُوها كُلّ يَوْم.

3	And it is very direct for them, I mean, it is not indirect—no, every Palestinian has to see the occupation with their own eyes every day.

وبتْكُون بْشَكِل مُباشِر جِدّاً إلْهُم، يَعْني ما بِتْكُون بْشَكِل غَيْر مُباشِر، لا، كُلّ فلسطيني لازِم يْشُوف الاحْتِلال بْعِيْنو كُلّ يَوْم.

4	Either through the news or through going out to work, where there are military checkpoints on the roads, of course, on every road.

بتْكُون يا عن طريق الأخْبار، يا عن طريق إنّو بِيكُون بْطْلَع على الشُّغُل، وفي بِيكُون في حَواجِز عَسْكَرِية على الطُّرُقات طَبْعاً في كُلّ طريق.

5	Or there are incursions into villages and towns every day. So, therefore, they will see the incursions, the confrontations, and, beyond that, the news of killings and the news of prisoners—they take prisoners and detainees.

يا إنّو بِيكُون في اقْتِحام للقُرى والمُدُن كُلّ يَوْم، فا بِالتّالي إنّو رح يْشُوف الاقْتِحامات والمُواجَهات، وغير الأخْبار القَتِل وأخْبار الأسْرى، إنّهُم يَعْني بوخْذوا أسْرى، وبوخْذوا مُعْتَقلين.

6	All of this reaches, you know, every Palestinian household, where it is almost certain that there is someone who is a prisoner or someone who has been detained by the occupation.

كُلّ هاي وصْلِت ل يَعْني كُلّ بيْت فلسطيني إلّا ما يكُون في عِنْدو شَخِص أسير أوْ شَخِص تمّ أسْرو مِن قِبل الاحْتِلال.

7	These things, you know, we as Palestinians live them in a very daily manner.

هاي الأُمُور يَعْني إحْنا كفلسْطِينية مِنْعِيشْها بْشَكِل يَوْمي جِدّاً جِدّاً.

8	So, I, as a person living the daily experience of occupation, can say it is a very bad experience.

يَعْني أنا كشَخِص بيعيش تَجْرُبَةُ الاحْتِلال اليَوْمية، بقَدِر أقُول إنّها تَجْرُبة جِدّاً سيِّئة.

9	For example, any ordinary person, when they leave work or need to move from one place to another, they are supposed to feel some kind of safety when, for instance, going from the city of Ramallah to the village where they live, or from one place to another.

كمِثال، أيّ شَخِص عادي لمّا يطْلَع مِن الشُّغُل أوْ بدّو يْرُوح على... أوْ بدّو يِتْنقّل مِن مكان لمكان، يَعْني مفْرُوض إنّو يْحِسّ بْنوع مِن الأمان لمّا يْرُوح مثلاً مِن مدينة رام الله للقَرْية اللي هُوّ عايش فيها، أوْ مثلاً مِن مكان لمكان.

10	But for us, for example, when we move, I personally, when I need to move from the village where I live to the city of Ramallah, I first have to be cautious of the occupation and the military checkpoints.

لكِن إحْنا لمّا مثلاً مِنْتنقّل، أنا شخْصِيّاً لمّا بدّي أتْنقّل مِن القَرْية اللي أنا عايش فيها لمدينة رام الله، بضْطَرّ إنّو أوّل إشي أكُون داير بالي مِن الاحْتِلال والحَواجِز العسْكَرية.

اللي بِتْكون عَ الطَّريق دائماً ويكون دايماً داير بالي مِن المُسْتَوْطِنين، اللي بيكونوا تابْعين لِلاحْتِلال على الطَّريق.	11	These checkpoints are always on the road, and I always have to be cautious of the settlers who are affiliated with the occupation and are present on the road.
فا بِالتّالي الواحد لازِم يْكون داير بالو، ولازِم يْكون هيْك ماخِذ احْتِياطات أمان لمّا يِطْلع عَ الطَّريق، لأنّو دائماً هيْك بيكون يَعْني بيكون دايْماً يْفكّر بِالأَسْوأ.	12	So, therefore, a person has to be cautious and must take safety precautions when going out on the road because they are always thinking of the worst.
فا بِالتّالي شُعور الأمان مِش مَوْجود عِنْد أيّ شخص فلسطيني أوْ أيّ شخص بْتِنقّل في الطُّرُقات مِن مكان لمكان.	13	Therefore, the feeling of safety is not present for any Palestinian or for anyone moving on the roads from one place to another.
لأنّو هاض يَعْني الأمان نفْسو مِش مَوْجود لمّا يْكون الشّخْص عايِش تحْت احْتِلال.	14	Because this safety itself is not present when a person is living under occupation.
فا بِالتّالي إحْنا مِنْضطرّ إنّو نِتْعامل مع هدا الـ... مع هاي حقيقة بْشكِل يَوْمي ونِضطّر إنّو يَعْني نِتْعايش معْها، والعكْس كمان إنّو نِشْتغِل ونْروح ونيجي مع هاي الصُّعوبات.	15	So, therefore, we are forced to deal with this reality on a daily basis, and we are forced to live with it, and, at the same time, to work, to go out and come back, and to deal with these difficulties.
وفي الآخِر، زيّ ما مُنحْكي، إحْنا الفلسْطينية يَعْني بِالآخِر إنْتَ عايِش تحْت احْتِلال، شو بدّك تعْمل؟	16	And in the end, as we say, we Palestinians—at the end of the day, you are living under occupation. What can you do?
يا إنّك تِرْمي كُلّ الأسْباب وكُلّ الهُموم عَ الاحْتِلال وتُقْعُد في البيْت وتْضلّ قاعِد وما تِشْتغِل، يا إنّك تْروح تِشْتغِل وتِتْحدّى الصِّعاب، وتِتْحدّى الاحْتِلال، وتِشْتغِل وتْجيب الرِّزق تبعك وتمشّي أُمورك وتِنْجح، بغضّ النّظر في احْتِلال ولّا ما في احْتِلال.	17	Either you blame all the reasons and all the hardships on the occupation and stay home, doing nothing, or you go out, work, challenge the hardships, challenge the occupation, work, earn your living, manage your life, and succeed, regardless of whether there is occupation or not.

Answers

Main Idea: d **True-False:** 1. T⁴ 2. T⁶ 3. F 4. T¹⁰⁻¹² 5. F **Multiple Choice:** 1. a¹⁻⁵ 2. c¹³⁻¹⁴ 3. b¹⁶⁻¹⁷
Matching: بْيِضْطرّوا they are / regardless بغضّ النّظر / directly بْشكِل مُباشِر / personally بْشكِل شخْصي /
forced to / تبعك your (possessive) / شو بدّك تعْمل what can you do / في الآخِر in the end / لِمّن when /
or not ولّا / reached to وصِّلت / لـ we live it مِنْعيشها / by (passive) / مِن قِبل / taking (active participle) ماخِذ
either... or يا... يا /

35 Alaa: Me, Myself, and Math

Keywords

الرِّياضِيّات mathematics	الطّريق الأدبي humanities track
علامات (school) grades	مُسابقات competitions

Main Idea

a. Alaa's academic achievements in all subjects except math.
b. Alaa's journey from struggling with math to helping her daughter enjoy and excel in the subject.
c. The difficulties of working as a math teacher with limited resources in Gaza.
d. Alaa's experience with various math tutors for herself and for her daughter.

True or False

1. Alaa struggled with math starting in the first grade.
2. Alaa chose the humanities track in high school was influenced by her dislike of math.
3. Alaa's experience with a great math teacher in eleventh grade helped her realize that the problem had been with her previous teachers, not her ability.
4. Alaa hired multiple math tutors to help her daughter enjoy and succeed in the subject.
5. Alaa assumed her daughter would struggle with math just like she did.

Multiple Choice

1. Why did Alaa struggle with math in school?

   a. She wasn't interested in any academic subjects.

   b. She preferred artistic subjects like painting and music.

   c. She didn't understand the material, and her teachers didn't explain it well.

   d. She didn't spend enough time studying.

2. How did Alaa's daughter feel about learning math from her mother?

   a. She enjoyed it and found it easy to learn.

   b. She preferred to learn math on her own.

   c. She refused to learn math altogether.

   d. She said it would lead to fights and frustration.

3. How did Alaa feel about her daughter's success in math competitions?

    a. Indifferent because she fully expected her daughter to excel

    b. Disappointed because she thought her daughter could do better

    c. Surprised and happy because she thought her daughter wouldn't like math

    d. Concerned about the pressure of competitions

Matching

إلّا	really, truly
إلو علاقة بـ	when
إمّا... أَوْ	includes
الصّراحة	except
بالرّغِم مِن	from the beginning
بِالْفِعِل	must turn out
بِشْمل	indeed
طول النّهار	somewhat
عبيْن ما	either... or
عنْجدّ	until now
عنْدْما	despite
لازِم تِطْلع	related to
لحتّى الآن	honestly
لدرجِةْ إنّو	I wasn't
ما كُنْتِش	to the extent that
مِن الأصِل	until
نَوْعاً ما	all day

1	اخترْت أحْكي عن مادةِ الرِّياضيّات أوْ مُعاناتي مع مادةِ الرِّياضيّات لأنّها مأْثّرة على حَياتي،
2	يَعْني تقْريباً مِش بْشكْلٍ كْبير، بسّ كانت لعْبِت كْتير يَعْني دوْر كْبير في تغْيّرُ إخْتياراتي، ولحتّى الآن هيّ نوْعاً ما مأْثّرة على أشْياء بْحَياتي.
3	مُعاناتي مع الرِّياضيّات بدأت بْصفّ أعْتقد الرّابع.
4	كان علَيْنا نحْفظ جدْوَل الضّرْب، وأنا ما كُنْتش حافْظاه، بالرّغمِ من إنّي أنا كُنْت بنْت شاطْرة في جميع المَوادّ، وكُنْت يَعْني أجيب علامات عالْيَة فوْق الـ٩٥ من ميّة.
5	يَعْني تْلاقي علامْتي آخِر الفصْل إلّا مادةِ الرِّياضيّات. تْكون حرْفيّاً بْزُقّ فيها زقّ.
6	يَعْني مُمْكن تْلاقيني جايْبة فيها ٩٠، ٨٩، ٨٨ من ميّة فا كانت هيّ المادّة اللي بتْخلّي علاماتي، بتْخلّي وَضْعي بالصّفّ مِش بْصفّ المدْرسة مِش كْتير كْوَيّس.
7	بْصفّ خامس... بالصّفّ الخامس، إجت مُعلّمةِ الرِّياضيّات ما كانت تِشْرح يَعْني، أوْ ما أعْرف ما كُنْت بفْهم علَيْها، يمْكن أسْلوبْها أوْ طريقتْها كانت مُخْتلفة.
8	في صفّ سادس، في صفّ سابع، لا عِنْدما وْصِلت للصّفّ العاشِر، بْصفّ العاشِر كانت برْضو المُعلّمةِ كْتير سَيّئة، لدرجةِ إنّي أنا جيت مثلاً بالتّمانينات في بدايةِ الـ٩٠... ٨٩، ٩٠ هيْك كانت علامْتي طبْعاً العلامة مِن ميّة.

I've chosen to talk about the subject of mathematics or my struggles with mathematics because it has impacted my life.

Not in a major way, but it did play a significant role in changing my choices, and to this day, it still somewhat affects certain aspects of my life.

My struggles with mathematics began in, I believe, the fourth grade.

We had to memorize the multiplication table, and I hadn't memorized it, even though I was a top student in all subjects and used to score high marks, above 95 out of 100.

You'd find that my grades at the end of the semester were excellent—except in mathematics. It was literally the subject I had to scrape through.

For example, you'd find me getting 90, 89, or 88 out of 100 in it. This was the subject that dragged my grades down and made my position in the class, or in school, not very good.

In the fifth grade... in the fifth grade, the mathematics teacher didn't explain well, or I didn't understand her. Maybe it was her style or approach—it was different.

In sixth grade, in seventh grade, and even when I reached tenth grade, the math teacher was also terrible, to the point that I'd score, for instance, in the 80s—89, 90—those were my grades, and the mark was out of 100.

<table>
<tr><td>

بْصفّ العاشِر، لازِم تِخْتار إمّا بْجانِب... أوْ طريق اللي هُوَّ مِنْحْكي عنّو بْفلسطين الطّريق العِلْمي، اللي هُوَّ بيكون فيه الفيزْيا والكيمْيا والرِّياضِيّات، بْتاخُد كْتابيْن رياضِيّات: كْتاب فيزْيا، كْتاب كيما، كْتاب ضخِم،

</td><td>

9

</td><td>

In tenth grade, you have to choose between two paths: the science track, which includes physics and chemistry, and two mathematics textbooks—a physics book, a chemistry book, and a massive math book.

</td></tr>
<tr><td>

أوْ بْتِخْتار الطّريق الأدبي، اللي هُوَّ فيه التّاريخ والجُغْرافْيا، والرِّياضِيّات، فيه بسّ بيكون الكِتاب صْغير يَعْني تقْريبا مِيّة وَرقة، برْضو بيكون فيه كْتاب عُلوم برْضو صْغير اللي هُوَّ العُلوم اللي هُوَّ بِشْمل الفيزْيا والكيمْيا والأحْياء.

</td><td>

10

</td><td>

Or you choose the humanities track, which includes history and geography, and the math textbook is small—about 100 pages. There's also a small science textbook covering physics, chemistry, and biology.

</td></tr>
<tr><td>

طبْعاً أنا، لأنّي أنا بكْرهَ الرِّياضِيّات، بالرّغِم من إنّي بحِبّ العُلوم وكُنْت شاطْرة فيه، اخْترْت الطّريق الأدبي.

</td><td>

11

</td><td>

Of course, because I hated mathematics, even though I loved science and was good at it, I chose the humanities track.

</td></tr>
<tr><td>

ونظْرِةْ النّاس بْغزّة للّي بْيُدْخُل الطّريق الأدبي إنّو غبي وما بْيِفْهم، فا دخل الأدبي لأنّو ما بْيِفْهم بالرِّياضِيّات مِش ذكي.

</td><td>

12

</td><td>

The perception in Gaza of those who choose the humanities track is that they're stupid and don't understand, and they chose humanities because they can't grasp mathematics or aren't smart.

</td></tr>
<tr><td>

بْصفّ حْدعْش، درّسْني أُسْتاذ كان رائِع، لدرْجِةْ إنّو أنا جِبْت في الرِّياضِيّات ١٠٠.

</td><td>

13

</td><td>

In the eleventh grade, I was taught by a teacher who was excellent, to the point that I scored 100 in mathematics.

</td></tr>
<tr><td>

فا يِمْكِن بْهادي السّنة اسْتَوْعبْت إنّو كان العيْب في المْعلّمات وفي الأسْاتْذة اللي درّسوني، ما كانِش العيْب فِيّا أوْ في مُخّي.

</td><td>

14

</td><td>

That year, I realized that the problem was with the teachers who taught me, not with me or my mind.

</td></tr>
<tr><td>

أوْ يِمْكِن لَوْ درّسْني حدا مِن الأصْل أوْ يِمْكِن لَوْ درّسْني بسّ هذا الأُسْتاذ بْصفّ عاشِر لكُنْت اخْترْت الطّريق العِلْمي يَعْني وما اخترْتِش الأدبي.

</td><td>

15

</td><td>

If I had been taught by someone like that teacher in tenth grade, I might have chosen the science track instead of humanities.

</td></tr>
<tr><td>

الإشي اللي أثّر على حَياتي حالِيّاً إنّو تدْريس الرِّياضِيّات لِبِنْتي.

</td><td>

16

</td><td>

What affects my life now is teaching mathematics to my daughter.

</td></tr>
<tr><td>

أكْتر شغْلة يَعْني بِتْوتّر العلاقة فيها.

</td><td>

17

</td><td>

It's the biggest thing that strains our relationship.

</td></tr>
<tr><td>

فا كان تدْريس الرِّياضِيّات لحدّ الأن مُعاناة، السّنة اللي فادت اللي هِيَّ قبِل الحرْب، لقيْت حلّ وبديْت أجيب لَها معلّمة صرْت إخْتار المْعلّمة بْعِنايَة.

</td><td>

18

</td><td>

Teaching her mathematics was still a struggle until last year, before the war, when I found a solution and started hiring a tutor for her. I carefully selected the tutor.

</td></tr>
</table>

ما كانش الهدف بسّ إنّها تْجيب في الرِّياضيّات ١٠٠ أوْ إنّها تْعلّي عَلامِتْها، الهدف الكْبير كانت إنّها تْحِبّ المادّة.

ضلّيْتني أختار في المْعلّمات وأغيّرْلها مْعلّمة لمْعلّمة، عبين ما لقيت معلّمة تيجيلها تْدرّسْها بْشكِل يَعْني خاصّ الهدف قُلْتِلها إنّو البِنْت تْحِبّ الرِّياضيّات.

وبالفِعِل، البِنْت كْتير يَعْني بِنْتي كانت لمّا أنا أجي أدرّسْها رياضيّات تْقول لي إنّو: رح نِتْقاتل رح تعصّبي عليَّ.

الإشي الوَحيد اللي بيوَتّر عِلاقْتي كان فيها هُوَّ الرِّياضيّات يَعْني سبب العَلاقة السَّيّة كان بسّ الرِّياضيّات يَعْني ما كُنْت أعصّب عليها طول النّهار بسّ هيَّ الرِّياضيّات اللي بِتْخلّيني أعصّب أوْ وَقِت ما إنّي أدرّسْها رياضيّات.

فا كان هدفي إنّها تْحِبّ الرِّياضيّات، ونْجِحت في هدا الإشي.

لأنّو بعد... قبل الحرْب، كانت تُدْخُل في مُسابقات صارت تُدْخُل بْمسابقات رياضِيّات.

اكْتشفت إنّو بِنْتي ذكية بالرِّياضيّات، وإنّو يَعْني أنا كُنْت مِتْوقّعة إنّو تِطْلع لا، هيَّ بِتْحِبّ المَوادّ الأدبية مَوادّ الحِفِظ والتّاريخ والجُغْرافيا.

بسّ اكْتشفت إنّو هيَّ عنجدّ مُبْدعة في الرِّياضيّات، إشي غريب إنّو يْكون...

كُنْت أعْتقد إنّو إشي إلو عِلاقة بالوَراثة أوْ مُمْكِن تِطْلع إنّو لازِم تِطْلع زيّي وما تْحِبّش الرِّياضيّات تُدْرُس المَوادّ الأدبية،

بسّ طِلْعِت غلْطانة وصارت تْشارِك في المُسابقات رياضيّات وتِطْلع الأولى فيهُم.

تْسكّر تْجيب عَلامة كامْلة بالرِّياضيّات، وهدا شي ابْسطني كْتير.

19	The goal wasn't just for her to score 100 in mathematics or improve her grades. The bigger goal was for her to love the subject.
20	I kept changing tutors for her until I found one who could teach her in a personalized way. I emphasized to the tutor that the primary goal was for my daughter to develop a love for mathematics.
21	And indeed, my daughter used to tell me when I helped her with math that, we'd fight and that I'd get angry with her.
22	The only thing that strained our relationship was mathematics—the reason for the tension was always math. I never got angry with her all day except when teaching her math.
23	My goal was for her to love mathematics, and I succeeded in that.
24	Before the war, she started participating in math competitions.
25	I discovered that my daughter has a natural talent for mathematics. I had initially assumed she would prefer the humanities, like history, geography, and those requiring memorization.
26	But I discovered that she's genuinely gifted in mathematics, which was surprising.
27	I used to think it might be hereditary or that she'd turn out like me and dislike mathematics, focusing on the humanities.
28	But I was wrong, and she started participating in math competitions and coming in first place.
29	She excelled in her math exams, consistently achieving full marks, and this brought me immense joy.

Honestly, I wish the same had happened to me.

30   الصّراحة كُنْت بتْمنّى إنّو يْصير معي نفْس الإشي.

Answers

Main Idea: b **True-False:** 1. F[2] 2. T[11-12] 3. T[13-14] 4. T[18-20] 5. T[27] **Multiple Choice:** 1. c[7-8] 2. d[21-22] 3. c[28-29]

Matching: بالرّغِم مِن / despite / الصّراحة / honestly / إمّا... أوْ / either... or / إلو عِلاقة بـ / related to / إلّا / except / لازِم / when / عِنْدما / really, truly / عنْجدّ / until / عبيْن ما / all day / طول النّهار / includes / بِشْمل / indeed / بالْفِعل / from / مِن الأصِل / I wasn't / ما كُنْتِش / to the extent that / لدرجةْ إنّو / until now / لحتّى الآن / must turn out / تِطْلع / the beginning / نوْعاً ما / somewhat

Keywords

المنْظومة التّعْليمية education system   إضْراب المعْلّمين teachers' strike

أهالي parents   دافِعية motivation

Main Idea

a. The rise of online learning in Palestine during COVID and how this has saved a generation from missing out on their education.

b. How COVID-19 was managed in Palestine compared to other countries.

c. The challenges faced in Palestine due to COVID and the deterioration of the education system.

d. How recent teacher strikes in Palestine have led many to homeschool their children.

True or False

1. Nihad explains that Palestine had a teachers' strike in addition to the effects of COVID on education.

2. Nihad believes that parents played a critical role in their children's education during the pandemic.

3. Nihad mentions that the Tawjihi results were inflated despite the students not truly understanding the material.

4. Nihad is optimistic that the education system will quickly recover after the challenges of COVID, strikes, and war.

5. Nihad believes that the parents in Palestine are more motivated than ever to push their children to study and succeed.

Multiple Choice

1. What does Nihad say about the motivation of students during the ongoing challenges with education?

   a. Students are more motivated than ever to succeed.

   b. Students have lost motivation, and parents struggle to encourage them to care about their future.

   c. Students are indifferent, but teachers are working hard to motivate them.

   d. Students are unaffected by the strikes and war.

2. How does Nihad describe the situation for students in Gaza during the war?

    a. They are learning in tents, trying to maintain their education with the simplest means.

    b. They have no motivation to continue their education.

    c. They are receiving full support from the ministry to continue their lessons online.

    d. They have given up on education due to the war.

3. What did Nihad mention about the role of teachers during the ongoing education crisis?

    a. Teachers are fully committed to giving lessons despite the challenges.

    b. Teachers are unable to provide lessons due to lack of pay and transportation issues.

    c. Teachers have enough resources to give online lessons from home.

    d. Teachers have decided to leave the profession entirely.

بِالتّالي	especially, specifically
بِالذّات	after
بِدْناش	that's it/all
خلص	by himself
زيّ كإنّو	on the basis that
زيّ ما كان	as if
عَ	now
عَ أساس	there isn't
فيشِّ	we don't want
لحالو	like it was
لَوْلا	consequently
ما بعْد	to, on
مِش بسّ	from the perspective of
مِن ناحْية	from where
مِن وينْ	if not for
هسّا	not just

Text

أكْبر مُشْكِلة كانت فلسْطين تْعاني مِنْها اللي هِيّ كوْروْنا، مِش بسّ فلسْطين، كُلّ العالم.	1	One of the biggest problems Palestine faced was COVID-19—not just in Palestine but worldwide.
بسّ فلسْطين بِالذّات كان الوَضع سيِّئ لأنّو بعْد الكوْروْنا، مُمْكِن سنة ونُصّ كوْروْنا، ما بعْد الكوْروْنا صارت إضْراب مْعلْمين.	2	However, in Palestine specifically, the situation was dire because, after nearly a year and a half of COVID, there was a teachers' strike.
يمْكِن في باقي الدُّوَل ما كان في هيْك إشي. الحَياة اسْتمرّت وعاشوا وكمّلوا تعْليم كمّلو.	3	In other countries, life resumed, and they continued their education.
فا إحْنا عِنّا في فلسْطين، المْعلْمين بِالذّات ما كانوا ياخْذوا رَواتِب.	4	But in Palestine, teachers, in particular, weren't receiving their salaries.

هاي المُشْكِلِة قبِل الحرِب، يَعْني إحْنا مِن حَوالي خمْس سْنين، وهاي الـ... أكْتَر مِن خمْس سْنين، بسّ إنّو يَعْني كُلّ سنة صار المَوْضوع يعْمِل مُشْكِلِة للأهالي، للطُّلّاب، للمنْظومِة التّعْليمية كُلّها.	**5** This issue started even before the war, nearly five years ago—or actually more than five years.
	6 Each year, the situation worsened, affecting parents, students, and the entire education system.
فا أكْتَر مرْحلِة تأثّرِت اللي هِيّ المرْحلِة الأساسية، مِن صفّ الأوّل للصفّ الرّابِع.	**7** The most impacted were primary school students from first to fourth grade.
اتْخيّل معي الصّفّ الأوّل، يَعْني أوّل أساسي رايِح عَ المدْرسة.	**8** Imagine a first grader attending school for the first time.
بلّشت الكوْروْنا، ما أخذ وَلا إشي. الأهالي هُمّ اللي بِبْذُلوا مجْهود طبْعاً.	**9** Then COVID began, and they learned nothing. Parents had to make all the effort.
هُمّ بيحْكولِك على التّيمْز وإلِكْتُروْني، وهاي المنْظومِة اللي هُمّ أسّسولْنا إيّاها.	**10** They introduced online learning through Teams and similar systems.
إنّو إحْنا نْتابِع وْلادْنا على التّيمْز، طبْعاً مِش كُلّ النّاس عِنْدها نِتّ في فلسْطين، وإحْنا مُجْتمع قرْوي يَعْني، ما في عِنّا.	**11** But not everyone in Palestine has internet, especially in rural communities like ours.
كُلّنا وَسطْنا نفْس الوَسط كُلّنا يَعْني مُتساوْيين مِن ناحْيِة الأُمور المادّية، مُمْكِن تْلاقي خمْسِة سِتّة عِنْدهُم نِتّ والباقي لا.	**12** Most of us share similar financial conditions—only five or six families might have internet, while the rest do not.
مُمْكِن أنا أعْطي غيْري نِتّ يَعْني جيراني، يِمْكِن في نفْس الدّار أنا عِنْدي اثْنين وَلديْن بالْمدارِس نفْس الصّفّ أكيد لأنّهُم تَوْأم، بسّ غيْري عِنْدو أرْبع وْلاد خمْس وْلاد.	**13** I might share my internet with my neighbors, or in the same household, I might have two children in the same grade because they're twins, but someone else might have four or five kids.
طبْعاً إحْنا بيخلّفوا كْتير عِنّا في العائِلات، مُمْكِن سِتّة يْكونوا كُلّهُم بالْمدْرسة، كُلّ واحد في صفّ كُلّ واحد عِنْدو حِصّة.	**14** In our families, it's common to have six children, all in school, each with their own grade and schedule.
فا كم مِن جِهاز بِدّك؟ كم جِهاز iPad، كم جِهاز تيليفوْن، كم جِهاز computer؟	**15** How many devices would you need? How many iPads, phones, or computers?
مثلاً لنفْرِض إنّو كُلّهُم بِدّهُم يِفْتحوا في نفْس الوَقِت، فا كان ضغْط عليْنا أكْتر مِن ما إنّو راحة.	**16** If everyone needed to be online at the same time, it was more of a burden than a solution.

هيْك التّرْبية، والتّعْليم، ما بعْرِف كيف هيْك كانوا يْفكّروا.

مِن ويْن أجوا بهالْفِكْرة إنّو نعْمل نْحوّل التّعْليم لإلِكْترْوني تفادياً للْعدْوى تفادياً مِش عارِف أيْش ويِتْحجّجوا فيها سنِة وسنتيْن.

طبْعاً الوضْع كان لباقي العالم مشت أمورْهُم يعْني، بسّ إحْنا في فلسْطين لا.

خلّصْنا مِن الكورْونا، الأكْثر إشي اللي اتْضرّروا اللي هُمِّ دخلوا صفّ أوّل.

سنِة ونُصّ، يعْني احْسِب سنِة كامِلة صفّ أوّل، ونُصّ الصّفّ الثّاني.

النُّصّ الثّاني صار، يعْني بِدّك تحْسِب كمان سنِة إنّو فِش رَواتِب، والسّنِة اللي بعْدها طبْعاً فِش رَواتِب، في إضْراب مْعلّمين، ما في دَوام.

يعْني الطّالِب ما بيروح عَ المدْرسة وَلا في إلِكْترْوني كمان، يعْني اعْتبِر إنّو عُطْلة.

ما في لحْظة بْيِفْتح كْتاب لحالو، إحْنا لَوْ لا الأهالي، إحْنا يعْني حريصين على وْلادْنا.

إحْنا مِنْتابِع عَ المَواقِع عَ اليوتْيوب، كُتُب، كُلّ إشي مْنِقْدر عليه مِنْجيبهُم.

مُمْكِن أنا مُتمكِّنة شْوَيّ إنّي بقْدر أروح واجي وأجيب، بسّ غيْري لا.

مُمْكِن أنا وضْعي بيِخْتِلِف شْوَيّ، مُمْكِن أتابِع، مُمْكِن أنا مِتْعلِّمة شْوَيّ، يعْني معي شِهادة جامِعية.

في أمّهات أُمّيّات، في أهالي فُقراء جِدّاً.

فا المنْظومة التّعْليمية كُلّها تْدهْوَرت.

مِش بسّ إنّو المرْحلِة الأساسية، بسّ هُوّ ألأكْثر ضرراً.

للْيوْم هاي إلْها خمْس سْنين، يعْني بلّشْنا في السّابِع... حتّى مِش خمْسِة، سبْع سْنين، وإحْنا مِش كْتير.

17 This approach to education and learning—how did they even think of it?

18 Where did this idea of moving education online come from? To avoid infections or for whatever other reasons they claimed, it lasted one or two years.

19 Meanwhile, other countries moved on, but in Palestine, we didn't.

20 After COVID, the most affected were those starting first grade.

21 A full year of first grade was lost, plus half of second grade.

22 Then, the second half of the year came, and there were no salaries, no schooling, and no teaching.

23 Students didn't go to school, and there was no online learning—it was as if they were on an extended vacation.

24 Without parents' efforts, children wouldn't have opened a book. Parents were the ones trying to keep their kids on track.

25 We relied on YouTube, books, and any resources we could get our hands on.

26 I might have been able to manage this because I could afford to access resources, but others couldn't.

27 My situation might differ because I'm somewhat educated and have a university degree.

28 But there are mothers who are illiterate and families in extreme poverty.

29 The entire education system collapsed.

30 It wasn't just primary education that was affected, but it bore the greatest damage.

31 For five, even seven years now, things haven't been right.

يَعْني حتّى قبِل الكوروْنا كمان كان في إضرابات، مع الكوروْنا ورجِّعْنا للإضرابات، والسّنة هاي حرْب، فا ما في تعْليم، ما في دَوام، ما في نِتّ.

32 Even before COVID, there were strikes, then during COVID, and now with this war—no education, no school, no internet.

يْكمُّلوا إلِكْتروْني، ما في.

33 They tried to continue online learning, but it didn't work.

الأهالي ملّوا، والطُّلّاب ملّوا.

34 Parents are tired, and students are tired.

حتّى اللي كانوا توْجيهي، رفّعوهُم، ما بعْرف رعّوهُم في التّصليح الامْتِحانات الوِزارية، عَ أساس إنّو يْكون في نتائج عشان يطْلعوا ويْقدّموا للجامِعات.

35 Even high school seniors who graduated were barely prepared. Their final exam results were inflated so they could enter universities.

نتائج التّوْجيهي كُلّو تِسْعينات وثمانينات مِن مِيّة، بسّ في الواقع، روح أسْأل الطّالِب، بِفْهمْش إشي، بْيِعْرِفْش إشي، هُوَّ حافِظ مِش فاهِم.

36 Tawjihi (high school exam) scores came back in the 80s and 90s out of 100, but in reality, ask the students—they understand nothing, they know nothing. They've memorized, not learned.

فا في الآخِر، يَعْني أنا حتّى كمان وْلادي، لمّا بِدّي أجي أسْألُهُم إشي، لازِم أشْرح كذا مرّة عَ أساس يِسْتَوْعِبوا إنّو أنا شو بِدّي أوْ شو هدفي مِن السُّؤال.

37 Even with my own children, I have to explain something several times before they understand what I'm asking or trying to teach them.

فا هدا الإشي بيوجعْنا إحْنا يَعْني بوجع الأهِل أكْتر مِن الأوْلاد.

38 This hurts us as parents even more than it hurts the children.

مُمْكِن الأوْلاد يَعْني في هاي المرحِلة مِش حاسّين إنّو أنا لازِم إبْني مُسْتقْبلي لازِم إنّي أتْعلّم أتْعب على حالي، ما أغلّب أهلي، بسّ هُمَّ في واد وإحْنا في واد.

39 The kids might not realize at this stage that they need to build their future through learning and hard work. They're in one world, and we're in another.

هسّا شو اللي بيصير؟ إنّو هاي السّنة بالذّات، عشان الحرْب، الكُلّ تِعب، الكُلّ مِش قادْرين.

40 This year, especially with the war, everyone is exhausted and struggling.

يَعْني بسّ كيف مِنْطّلّع للأمُور؟ إنّو شوفوا أهِل غزّة لمّا نْشوفهُم في الخِيَم بِتْعلّموا وبِأبْسط الوَسائِل بيحاولوا إنّهُم يْحافْظوا على التّعْليم وعَ المُسْتقْبل.

41 But when we look at families in Gaza, we see them learning in tents with the simplest tools, trying to preserve education and their future.

بيصير عِنْدهُم دافِعية، بسّ لمّا يْروحوا عَ المدْرسة، بيحْكيلِك الأُسْتاذ: "أنا ما معايَ أُجْرِة المُواصلات أجي أعْطيك حِصّة، وَلا معايَ أدْفع فاتورِة النّت عشان أعْطيك إلِكْتروْني."

42 There's motivation, but when students go to school, the teacher might say, "I can't afford transportation to come and teach you or pay for internet to teach online."

فا بِالتّالي في فشل ذريع في المَنْظومة التّعْليمية، والجيل كامِل.	43	This has led to a catastrophic failure in the education system, affecting an entire generation.
يَعْني إنْتَ بْتِحْسِب سِتّ سْنين سبْع سْنين راحت مِن عُمْر الطُّلّاب. ما أخذوا المخْزون اللي لازِم يوخْذوه مِن المعْرِفة والتّعْليم.	44	Six or seven years of the students' lives have been wasted. They haven't gained the knowledge they should have.
فا هدا الإشي كْتير بِيأثِّر علَيْنا، كْتير على الطُّلّاب نفْسْهُم.	45	This deeply impacts us and the students themselves.
يَعْني مُمْكِن أنا بظلّ أعيد وأكرِّر نفْس الإشي، نفْس الحكي، لأنّو ما في عبارات تْصيغ المَأْساة اللي إحْنا فيها.	46	I might repeat myself because there are no words to describe the tragedy we're living through.
مع الوَضِع الحالي، يَعْني كُلّ الأهالي صار عِنْدْهُم زيّ كإنّو لا مُبالاة.	47	In the current situation, parents have developed a sense of indifference.
درسْتوا ما درسْتوا، رُحْتوا على المدْرسة ما رُحْتوش، خلص.	48	Whether the kids go to school or not, it doesn't matter anymore.
إحْنا هاليَوْم بِدّنا نْعدّيه بِدّنا بْأقلّ نِسْبة مِن العصبية، بِدّناش نْظلّ مْعصّبين، أُدْرْسوا أُدْرْسوا روحوا.	49	We just want to get through the day with the least amount of stress—study if you want, don't study, go if you want, don't go.
فيشّ عِنْدْهُم دافِعية لِوْلاد، يَعْني.	50	There's no motivation left, even for the children.
مِش عارْفين، إن شاء الله إنّو هالْأيّام تِنْتهي، ويِرْجع كُلّ شي زيّ ما كان.	51	We don't know—God willing, these days will end, and everything will return to how it was.
والله يِهْديهُم المْعلّمين والوِزارة كُلْها يَعْني.	52	May God guide the teachers and the Ministry of Education.

<hr>

Answers

Main Idea: c **True-False:** 1. T[2-3] 2. T[9, 24-25] 3. T[35-36] 4. F[33-46] 5. F[47-49] **Multiple Choice:** 1. b[39-40, 50] 2. a[41] 3. b[42]
Matching: بِالتّالي consequently / بِالذّات especially, specifically / بِدّناش we don't want / خلص that's it/all / لحالو by himself / فيشّ there isn't / عَ أساس on the basis that / زيّ ما كان like it was / عَ to, on / زيّ كإنّو as if / مِن ناحْية from the perspective of / مِش بسّ not just / ما بعْد after / لَوْ لا if not for / مِن وين from where / هسّا now

www.ingramcontent.com/pod-product-compliance
Lightning Source LLC
Chambersburg PA
CBHW081328120626

46546CB00011B/3259